Foundations of Social Theory

Foundations of Social Theory: A Critical Introduction accessibly introduces students to classical and contemporary social theory, exploring the foundational theories which shape the discipline while also engaging critically with their contribution and presenting the more progressive and contemporary theorists in dialogue with canonical figures.

Social theory is introduced as the construction and connection of concepts which make social inquiry possible while appreciating that the study of society is never truly objective. The relationship between positionality, politics, research, and knowledge production is discussed and ideas from critical theorists, feminist theorists, and decolonial, and critical race theorists are foregrounded. Travelling chronologically and thematically from the birth of the discipline and the work of Marx, Weber, and Durkheim through to intersectionality, queer theory, and decolonial and postcolonial theory, this book gives students a strong foundation in the broad field of social theory while also encouraging them to think critically about the theories and theorists presented.

Equipped with end-of-chapter questions and further reading, this book will be essential reading for any student studying social theory for the first time.

Neal Harris is a Senior Lecturer in Sociology at Oxford Brookes University, UK. His most recent books include *Critical Theory and Social Pathology: The Frankfurt School Beyond Recognition* (Manchester University Press, 2022) and *Capitalism and its Critics: Capitalism in Social and Political Theory* (co-authored with Gerard Delanty, Routledge, 2022). He has taught social and political theory at University of Sussex, University of Brighton, and Oxford Brookes University.

Foundations of Social Theory

A Critical Introduction

Neal Harris

Routledge
Taylor & Francis Group

LONDON AND NEW YORK

Designed cover image: © Getty Images

First published 2024
by Routledge
4 Park Square, Milton Park, Abingdon, Oxon OX14 4RN

and by Routledge
605 Third Avenue, New York, NY 10158

Routledge is an imprint of the Taylor & Francis Group, an informa business

British Library Cataloguing-in-Publication Data
A catalogue record for this book is available from the British Library

ISBN: 978-1-032-41749-3 (hbk)
ISBN: 978-1-032-41747-9 (pbk)
ISBN: 978-1-003-35955-5 (ebk)

DOI: 10.4324/9781003359555

Typeset in Sabon
by SPi Technologies India Pvt Ltd (Straive)

Contents

Acknowledgements

This book has developed out of countless discussions in seminar rooms, lecture theatres, and conferences. And far, far more pub sessions. There are too many people to thank so I shall be lazy and not attempt to. I had better acknowledge the following though, or else I'll get in trouble. They know where I live. As such, a special thanks goes to Maïa Pal, James Stockman, Onur Acaroglu, Irmak Karademir-Hazir, Audrey Reoch, Pedro Salgado, Ployjai Pintobtang, Priya Raghavan, Andy Kilmister, Ane Englestad, and Robin Jervis. Maïa Pal deserves special thanks for her extensive contribution to the chapter on Marx. I dedicate the book to my daughter, Rosa, in the hope it will put her off becoming an academic.

Introduction: Question Everything!

Contents

DOI: 10.4324/9781003359555-1

Back in 1865 Karl Marx was handed a quiz by his daughters. Among other questions the girls wanted to know their father's favourite food (*fish*), his favourite colour (*red*), and his idea of happiness (*to fight!*). Marx's answer to 'favourite motto?' came to my mind when I was thinking about how to introduce this book. His response was a Latin phrase, *de omnibus dubitandum*, which loosely translates as 'question everything!'. That is the spirit which runs throughout this text. I don't want you to be in awe of the famous names or perspectives discussed in these pages. I want you to read this book and go 'hang on: does that idea make sense?'. You should feel empowered to think for yourself when it comes to social theory, to question everything!

While the big thinkers introduced here shaped social theory (and world history), it doesn't mean they cracked it or that they found the best solutions. Every theorist needs to be challenged; all ideas need to be pushed. This is as much the case when it comes to studying Karl Marx as it is anyone else; indeed, it is what he would have wanted. Developing your own critical perspective is rewarding and valuable. It is where the marks are for undergraduate essays and where satisfaction comes from in developing your own thinking. Knowing about these thinkers is useful, but having a critical engagement with them is immeasurably more gratifying.

Throughout this book you will see that social theory is full of puzzles, that neutral 'objective' research may not be possible (or desirable), that power and knowledge are connected, and that the social world is immeasurably complex and contradictory. But out of this maze come possibilities for new forms of thinking, new ways of interrogating society, new possibilities for critique. That is the challenge and reward of turning these pages, of engaging with social theory.

Before we kick off, take a moment to consider the social world around you. Are you struck by:

- Conflict and exploitation?
- Harmony and stability?
- So many stories and meanings to be interpreted?
- Complexity and hybridity?
- Oncoming disastrous climate meltdown?
- Racism and the legacy of empire?
- Gender oppression?
- Intergenerational conflict: boomers versus snowflakes?
- Progress and the power of science?

Perhaps all of these topics jump out at you. Or just one. Or something entirely different.

These topics, and many more, echo throughout social theory, and throughout this text. Social theorists have tried to respond to these concerns, with varying degrees of success. Some theories we discuss may strike you as out of date and problematic, failing to live up to changing social norms and values. Equally, many contemporary theories will turn out to be imperfect, perhaps complicit in the very structures they seek to challenge. As such, as you read on, you will be presented with more questions than answers. Social theorising is an ongoing project and it is increasingly expanding to look at ever more areas of the social world. With a world on fire, gender inequalities increasingly acknowledged, and colonial legacies slowly reckoned with, now is the perfect time to come to social theory. There has never been a more important time to try to understand the social world in which we all struggle to survive and to thrive.

What is Social Theory?

But what actually is social theory? What unites the topics to come in this book?

Let's start with the question 'what is theory?'. 'Theory' refers to the intellectual tools developed to help us comprehend the world. You cannot touch a theory or throw it across a lecture hall, but you can use theories to help you understand something. There are several terms here which are worth clarifying: *concepts*, *theories*, and *perspectives*. Social theory deals with all three of these (and many more things besides). Let's discuss these three in turn.

Concepts

Concepts are the building blocks of all theory. They are mental tools which help us make sense of the world. Concepts thus refer to a special subset of ideas which help us make sense of the actions, practices, and systems within society. For example, the idea of 'employment' is an important concept. It is a mental tool which groups together various sorts of social behaviours. You cannot touch 'employment' but you can use the concept to help understand and categorise different forms of social action. 'Employment' helps us to understand social relationships, resource distributions, family set-ups. You can see people who are 'employed' or 'in the course of their employment' even if you cannot see the concept itself. While employment is a conceptual abstraction, it speaks to something very real and material. The concept 'employment' helps us to think about the particular exchange relationship between labour and (typically) financial remuneration: i.e. someone does a job and they get paid. It is a crucial aspect of the social world. Concepts can focus on real-world phenomena (like employment) or can focus on more abstract ideas (such as the concepts of 'homogeneity' or 'hegemony'). Concepts are the building blocks which we bring together to help make sense of the world. This book is largely about concepts. Without concepts, there can be no theory and no meaningful research.

Theories

Theories are typically made up of multiple concepts to try and help explain why or how something happens. Let's return to the concept of employment. Karl Marx famously produced a theory connecting employment with other key concepts to produce his 'theory of surplus value'. Now for Marx, this theory was all about how people were not paid enough for the work that they did. He connected concepts such as 'labour', 'commodity', and 'surplus value' to make this argument. What Marx did, and what all social theorists do, was to bring concepts together to try to produce a way of explaining how a particular part of society works. That is what social theorists do: they present explanations for different social phenomena by linking together multiple concepts.

Perspectives

Perspectives are made up of multiple theories. They refer to the way of viewing the social world as a whole. Perspectives speak to the big picture through which society as a whole can be explored. For example, 'Marxism' is a perspective for exploring society more broadly; it does not focus only on labour but also looks at ideology, social change, even family relationships. In this book you will encounter various different perspectives, for example: feminism, interpretivism, post-structuralism, functionalism. A perspective is thus a way of viewing the entirety of the social world which is an amalgam of various different theories. For example, Marxism combines multiple theories, including a theory of surplus value, a theory of ideology, and a theory of social change (historical materialism).

However, as we shall see in this book, concepts can also be used in other ways. For example, they can be used to inform particular methods for researching the social world. The key point to remember is that social theory all comes down to *concepts*. These are the abstract building blocks of thinking about society that help us make sense of our social order.

Introduction

What is Society?

Okay, so that's theory. But what is 'society'? Famously, Margaret Thatcher (UK Prime Minister 1979–1990) said, 'there is no such thing as society'. It is worth clarifying what it is we are studying if someone can say that it doesn't even exist. Society is a concept and like all concepts it is an abstraction. So, at one level Thatcher is entirely right: society does not exist materially; it cannot be touched; you cannot put your hand against a society, or eat one for breakfast. Yet, that isn't what Thatcher was getting at. Society is a particularly sensitive concept and it is *political*: it suggests that there are connections, institutions, values, obligations, and stories which bind people together. For neoliberals like Thatcher, who are invested in the primacy of the free individual, society can seem to be a limiting construct which functions to stop change and market dynamism. It was this understanding of society, as a network of cooperators, obligations, and mutual dependences, that Thatcher opposed.

In contrast, for most other thinkers and politicians, whether they are conservatives or Marxists, 'society' is seen as not merely existing but being something that is crucial to people's lives. For socialists (think 'society-ists') humans are social animals, they are natural cooperators who share values and who achieve most when they work together. Marxists and socialists believe that humans should strive to create a fairer society, and that our social bonds are not chains on our individualism but can be the source for progress and individual self-realisation. For conservatives and for functionalists, society is equally important. Such thinkers argue that we are shaped by our societies which are the amalgam of generations of experiences. As such, from their perspective, we should be very careful before making any big social changes. Edmund Burke (1729–97), a famous early social and political thinker, captured this view when he said that society was 'a partnership between those who are dead, those who are living, and those who are yet to be born'.

So the very topic of society and whether it exists is political. As a concept, society speaks to the institutions, bonds, norms, obligations, and identities which structure our lives. As such, it is a vast topic, and one that has changed considerably over the years.

So What is Social Theory?

Putting it all together, we can say that social theory is a subject which focuses on refining and building concepts, theories, and perspectives to help us understand the social world. The focus is typically on social institutions, norms, values, identities, and social transformations. The role of the social theorist is to provide clarity on concepts, to build theories out of them, and to build, refine, and clarify perspectives so we can best explore the social world.

Social theory is typically taught as part of sociology. This makes sense because social theorists have very similar objectives to sociologists, seeking to understand, and often to improve, society. Yet social theory is not only of interest to sociologists and should not be understood as a 'subset' or 'module' of sociology. Anyone whose work connects to 'society' needs to draw upon the concepts which social theorists produce. As such, social theory connects with economics (especially political economy), international relations, gender studies, critical race studies, literary theory, law, criminology, the list is endless. Some famous sociologists, like Theodor W. Adorno (1903–69), even brought their concepts from social theory into discussions on music theory and aesthetics. As such, social theory can be viewed as a subject which has many commonalities with sociology, but it remains a distinctive field of thought. Where sociologists seek to explore the social world empirically, by conducting fieldwork (through interviews, surveys, etc.), social theorists seek to understand the social world through the construction of concepts, theories, and perspectives. Typically, social theory and sociology get along reasonably well; however, there can be disagreements between the two over methodologies and political viewpoints. Historically, social theory is more politically radical and progressive, while sociology, especially American sociology, has tended to be more conservative in orientation. This book is pure social theory; it focuses solely on concepts, theories, and perspectives. As you will see, many of these thinkers and perspectives are progressively minded, seeking to understand the social world as part of an objective of trying to improve it, to help it become fairer and less irrational.

The Past, Present, and Future of Social Theory

Society is always changing and social theorists have to keep on their toes. With the notable exception of Karl Marx, typically it is a case of social theorists desperately playing catch-up, trying to explain what is *happening* or *has happened* after the events have occurred. Marx, however, is really unusual in that he was writing about capitalism while it was in its infancy, before it took over the world as the dominant mode of production. As a result of exactly the kinds of changes Marx predicted, the rise of capitalism and globalisation, social theory has changed dramatically over the years. As society transforms, social theories change and develop in response. Social theory also changes for another reason, on the basis of developments within 'theory'. The philosophies, concerns, and methodologies popular among theorists gain or lose popularity in keeping with broader intellectual and cultural changes. To help make sense of the massive shifts that have occurred, we tend to place social theory into two different categories: 'classical' and 'contemporary'. These two categories reflect different topics and different methods and philosophies.

Classical Social Theory

Classical social theory typically refers to the work of Karl Marx (1818–83), Émile Durkheim (1858–1917), and Max Weber (1864–1920). Despite their differences, the three have much in common. All were writing between 1830 and 1920 and had a commonality of focus, reflecting both the socio-historical conditions and intellectual currents in which they lived. This period was dominated by the rise of capitalism and by the massive migrations of people: both from the countryside to the city to work in the rapidly expanding factories, and from Europe to the colonies, especially to North America. Key themes for classical social theorists were industrialisation, the state, secularisation, urbanisation, and most of all *capitalism*. There was also a constant question of what keeps all these people working together living peacefully. For centuries, rural communities had existed with shared labour patterns, values, languages, cultures. Now, with rapid urbanisation, people from different communities were being forced together, often with little in common, slaving away in soul-destroying and dangerous jobs for little pay; often entirely unable to communicate with each other. Classical sociologists wanted to know how this society was holding together: what was preventing rioting, disorder, and revolution? Marx, Weber, and Durkheim all provided very different answers, but all sought to explore variations on this shared theme.

Despite their differing perspectives, the classical sociologists all shared a commitment to producing explanations for long-term societal changes. Marx famously made claims about the 'history of all hitherto existing society'; his scale of analysis was massive. Classical social theory was invested in what we call 'grand narratives', seeking to present big stories to explain titanic social changes. Despite their substantive differences, Durkheim, Weber, and Marx can all be seen to be producing grand theories seeking to explain multigenerational, society-wide transitions. These grand narratives all focused on social structures and social institutions. For instance, there was a shared focus among classical sociologists on class and social stratification. Despite the significant disagreements in their answers, the classical social theorists were interested in exploring how different social institutions connected with each other and produced social subjects facilitating smooth social reproduction.

Contemporary Social Theory

There is a notable gap between the end of 'classical social theory' (c.1920) and the start of 'contemporary social theory' (c.1960). As such, there is a period of approximately 40 years where social theorists such as the Frankfurt School emerged, who don't fit clearly into either category.

Contemporary social theorists, such as Michel Foucault (1926–84), Jürgen Habermas (1929–), Judith Butler (1956–), and Pierre Bourdieu (1930–2002), engage with a changed social world from that which presented itself to the classical social theorists. This new society was one where urbanisation and capitalism had become normalised, and where industrialisation was slowly giving way to a post-industrial, increasingly digital economy. The focus of these contemporary social theorists was changing to reflect these transitions across society. Increasingly new, complex identities and intersectional social inequities were coming to the fore. These shifts were not merely happening within the nation-state; society was becoming increasingly global in nature. Contemporary social theorists have to understand the role of new communication technologies, international mobility, and increasingly shared global risks (climate changes, terrorism, diseases, etc.) in shaping our social lives.

Contemporary social theory is also distinguished by its change in focus and scale of analysis. Where classical social theorists presented grand narratives, contemporary social theorists are more likely to offer smaller scale, context-dependent analyses. As discussed, Marx spoke of a 'history of all hitherto existing society'. Few contemporary social theorists would aspire to such grand claims; instead, contemporary social theory focuses carefully on experiences in clearly demarcated societies, in particular spaces and in particular times. There is no longer a widespread belief among social theorists that a singular perspective can be developed which can explain the entirety of the social world. Instead, contemporary social theorists embrace hybridity, complexity, and a plurality of interpretive frameworks. There is also a tendency to reject stable categories and concepts. While classical social theorists spoke of class and gender as abstract universal terms which could be deployed cross-culturally without complication, today's social theorists focus on the complexities of discourse and language, rejecting a belief in static social structures and universal modes of interpretation. There is also an increasing sensitivity to the forms of knowledge which are given precedence, with decolonial scholars speaking of a 'coloniality of knowledge' which reinforces forms of colonial domination.

Society is not going to stop changing any time soon. New challenges are always emerging which call out for new concepts. Concerns at the cutting edge of social theory today include the increasing fusion of human bodies and technology. When was the last time you had a whole day where you didn't touch your phone? As we use technology to shape our social lives, how is that shaping us as social and biological beings? Some scholars suggest that we are moving towards a cyborg society, where our reliance on technology reshapes what it is to be social agents. Our memories are expanded by our phones, our bodies reinforced through hip replacements, our hearts extended with implants. More radically still, some companies are seeking funds to upload our brains to the cloud, so that when we die as organic matter we can live on in the cyber-verse. This is not just science fiction; companies are actively seeking funding today to enable the abstraction of consciousness and its upload to computerised systems. What kind of social world would this create? How should this be theorised and understood?

Global warming is of course another existential threat to our way of life. Some scholars warn of the need for 'deep adaptation', to adjust ourselves to the fact that civilisation will likely not survive long into the future and we shall likely witness the displacement and suffering of billions of people due to manmade climate change. It is not merely the probable likelihood of such a horror, but a world where this potentiality is increasingly acknowledged, that calls for renewed urgent theorisation. If we cannot realistically offset climate catastrophe, how do we prepare for what is coming towards us?

The social world is in revolution across so many domains. For example, in the past 30 years there has been a revolution in sexual and gender identities. What will relationships look like in the future? What will families consist of? Will gender identities or sexualities be meaningful categories 100 years from now?

Clearly, social theorists have much to ponder about; the future will require new concepts, new perspectives, new theories. The importance of a critical consciousness, a form of thought which creates and refines concepts to challenge and question the dynamics driving social reproduction, will likely be more urgently needed than ever.

Reading Social Theory Today

One problem with reading social theory today is that many foundational texts bear the stamp of the social worlds of their creation. This is the case in both the ideas themselves and in the authors whose voices remain.

Typically we are left with the ideas of rich, heterosexual, white men. As such, we have to account for the reality that patriarchy, capitalism, and racism often echo throughout the texts of many canonical social theorists.

One solution to this has been to try to diversify the curriculum. This typically means introducing students to a wider variety of scholars; to thinkers who are not just dead white men. Such an approach suggests that you should try to retain coverage of many of the foundational Western social theorists but complement this by adding in other scholars with different standpoints. Diversifying the curriculum certainly has some real merits; it can enable students to learn about other experiences and this can challenge taken-for-granted biases. For instance, what is considered 'work' can be destabilised by drawing upon a wider range of perspectives, so that 'housework' is also considered to be a meaningful kind of 'labour' after having read more accounts from feminist theorists. As such, attempts to diversify the curriculum certainly have merit: concepts can be refined and limitations and exclusions within perspectives exposed.

Yet, the diversification approach risks displacing valuable insights which reside within the founding texts of social theory. Who do you get rid of for a term-long course to get more space for a more diverse cast of thinkers? For example, in this text I chose to exclude a chapter on microsociology to leave space for a chapter on the newer decolonial theory. Some may disagree with my choice. This is a particular challenge when it comes to considering which older, established ideas should be excluded, as so many thinkers, including those from beyond Europe, have built perspectives drawing upon the founding texts of Western social theory.

Further, diversifying the curriculum can ironically serve as a fig-leaf to excuse a failure to engage in the structural changes decolonial activists call for. There are many pressing forms of exploitation and discrimination that exist within society and with which universities are entirely complicit. It is all very well having more racial and gender diversity on reading lists, but it is a problem if this is done as a way of deferring actual structural material changes, such as removing student fees, dealing with the gender pay-gap, relying on racialised outsourced, ununionised cleaning or security staff, and supporting hostile visa regimes.

While there are real strengths to diversifying the curriculum, in this book I offer a critical introduction which seeks to engage primarily with the canonical thinkers of social theory. As a critical introduction I engage with these thinkers mindful of their limitations and I constantly seek to encourage you, the reader, to interrogate all ideas critically. For example, Chapter 2 discusses Karl Marx's alleged Eurocentrism and class reductionism. To me, this approach seems preferable compared to displacing foundational names who have shaped social theory for lesser-known authors. There is also a risk of fetishising or orientalising non-European scholars. There is a constant threat of neo-nativist thinking emerging when it comes to attempts to diversify the curriculum. Neo-nativism refers to the misguided belief that there is some 'pure' knowledge 'out there' beyond the tainted, colonialist West. In fact, as many postcolonial scholars remind us, post-colonies are riddled with their own discriminatory cosmologies and epistemologies (such as caste). Equally, post-colonies are often colonising themselves. As such, there is no neat binary of 'clean' and 'dirty' ways of knowing the world. As a result, a turn to find knowledge solely from the non-Western 'Other' is not desirable for multiple reasons. Rather, a balanced inclusion of new voices, alongside a considered interrogation of the established canon, is the preferred option adopted in this critical introduction to social theory. As such, there is a concluding chapter on decolonial and postcolonial scholarship as well as frequent critical interrogations of the canonical thinkers in line with the provocations offered by these emerging schools of thought. Decolonial and postcolonial theory truly have much to offer, but there is equally still merit in a critical engagement with the founding texts of social theory.

The Structure of this Book

Over the next nine chapters you will be introduced to different approaches to theorising society. Four of those approaches focus on a particular thinker: Karl Marx, Émile Durkheim, Max Weber, and Pierre Bourdieu. The other five chapters introduce a school of thought, such as the Critical Theory of the early Frankfurt School or Decolonial theory. As ever, when writing any book there is always a question of selection: who should be left out and who should be included? As alluded to above, this is an increasingly complicated question when it comes to the topic of social theory. Where I have been unable to include a chapter-long discussion on certain key thinkers due to lack of space (for example, on Anthony Giddens or Frantz Fanon) I have made an effort to ensure that they are at least introduced within other pertinent chapters.

The following chapters all have a similar structure to give you a critical overview of the core ideas of the thinker or tradition. Each chapter starts with a brief historical overview or biography before moving on to discuss five key concepts. For example, in Chapter 3 on Durkheim, we look at anomie, collective consciousness, organic and mechanical solidarity, the division of labour, and social facts. I then outline how the concepts discussed shaped subsequent social theory. For instance, in the case of Durkheim, there is a discussion of the broader functionalist and positivist traditions. At the heart of each chapter there is a critical discussion, where you are invited to reflect on the challenges which exist when turning to these concepts today. With Durkheim, we discuss how functionalism normalises conflict and exploitation and how positivism is blind to the relationship between power, rationality, and depth-psychology. Each chapter finishes by showing why the thinker/school's ideas still matter today, pointing to the all-important question: why care? After a brief conclusion, each chapter has two key further features: some discussion questions for you to reflect on and a short, annotated reading list. Here a selection of primary and secondary texts are summarised and their respective merits outlined.

Over to You

There are many other introductions to social theory. Many are longer, some are shorter. What I hope this introduction will offer you is an overview which is both accessible and critical. I hope to simultaneously get you thinking about some big ideas, possibly for the first time, while immediately inviting you to challenge them. This returns us to Marx's favourite motto at the start of this chapter. I want you to feel confident that you can get a good grasp on the key foundations of social theory and that you can interrogate their core tenets. This is a critical introduction to social theory. One which encourages you to doubt everything and to adopt a consistently critical attitude. With the rise of fake news, 'alternative facts', artificial intelligence, and machine learning, there has never been a more important time for you to develop critical skills and to take a position on key debates about society. Push yourself and challenge the ideas as they come at you. Welcome to the foundations of social theory; it is now time for you to start developing your own critical perspective.

Discussion Questions

1 What's the point of social theory?
2 Is there such a thing as society?
3 Is it right to study past thinkers even if they had views that we today consider to be unacceptable?
4 What other subjects is social theory connected to and why?
5 What is the difference between a concept, a theory, and a perspective?

chapter 2

Karl Marx: Critique, Class Struggle, and Revolution

Contents

DOI: 10.4324/9781003359555-2

While you may not have previously encountered the other 'founding fathers' of sociology, namely Émile Durkheim (1858–1917) and Max Weber (1864–1920), everyone has heard of Karl Marx (1818–83). His fame often comes from being linked to the Russian, Chinese, and Cuban revolutions in the twentieth century. Because of this, however, his name, and the scholarship named after him ('Marxism'), is at times problematically associated with the atrocities committed by the rulers of these regimes. For many people, Marx, and Marxism, become elided with these horrors. For example, on 15 February 2023, the conservative psychologist Jordan Peterson tweeted, quoting a comment by Marxist Professor David Harvey: 'Oh good. A Marxist. In academia, 100 million plus corpses not enough for you, buddy?'.

This is problematic on several accounts. First, in this chapter we are interested in understanding Karl Marx as the nineteenth-century social theorist. He obviously had no direct links with the regimes of the twentieth century: he was long dead. Equally, he would never have justified the killings and abuse these regimes perpetrated. Throughout his life Marx strove to improve the lives of ordinary working people; he would not have wanted to see millions of them murdered, imprisoned, and living in fear. Second, it is crucial to distinguish between the work of intellectuals (like Karl Marx) and the ways in which their ideas might be used by politicians. That many regimes considered themselves influenced by the work of Marx and other revolutionary thinkers (such as Lenin or Trotsky) is a real and complex issue, and to understand it one must first understand the work of those authors separately.

Nevertheless, it is important not to separate the political and the academic completely. Marx was both an intellectual and a political activist, he argued for the need to think critically as a practice of political action, and he defended revolutionary struggle towards socialism and communism. He famously wrote that historically intellectuals 'have only interpreted the world, the point, however, is to change it'. When it comes to understanding Marx, political change and academic research are closely connected. Crucially, this is very different from saying that all the groups who claim to be Marxist are actually bringing Marx's ideas into action. Finally, in response to Peterson's question specifically, and to the factually spurious numbers of deaths supposedly justified by Marxism, Marxists would respond that their approach enables a different view of history that looks instead at the far greater number of deaths caused by capitalism. These are due to the working conditions and structural inequalities particular to the capitalist mode of production. These are too often ignored by academics and politicians, and are incorrectly assumed as being inevitable and natural. In contrast, as Marx's work shows, capitalism is just one mode of production; others have come before, and others will likely come after.

Marx lived the tumultuous life of a revolutionary; stirring up trouble across Europe, being kicked out of country after country. He moved from Trier (Germany) to Paris in 1843, but was deported in 1845 and settled in London, where he lived until his death at the age of 61. Throughout his life Marx was a philosopher, a political economist, and a journalist. He finished his doctoral dissertation in 1841 and in 1843 married Jenny von Westphalen (1814–81), who supported his work and contributed to it by writing up his manuscripts and taking care of the household. Marx lived a rich (if at times scandalous) family life and was devoted to his three daughters, Jenny, Laura, and Eleanor, who also lived intellectual and revolutionary lives in their own names. Marx's most important friend, co-author, and life-long financial and emotional sup-porter was Friedrich Engels (1820–95), a Manchester-based industrial-ist. It is often difficult to separate them when discussing Marx's work, as they wrote key texts together (*The German Ideology*, *The Communist Manifesto*), and Engels, alongside Marx's daughters, edited most of Marx's unfinished works after his death. For a while Marx worked as a journalist, creating a review with Engels called the *Neue Rheinische Zeitung*, which was eventually banned in 1849 amidst a period of intense revolutionary uprisings. Marx also wrote pieces for the *New York Daily Tribune* between 1852 and 1861, before dedicating himself to a range of major works in history, political economy, and philosophy.

In spite of his many writings, Marx struggled financially all his life. As part of the bourgeois class, he tried to keep up appearances and main-tain a standard of living for his daughters. This came at a material and psychological cost for him and his wife, who were constantly living on the edge of starvation and falling into large debts, which Engels continu-ously helped to cover. Marx repeatedly had to pawn his trousers to buy food. Marx was a committed activist, especially in his earlier years. In his later life he dedicated his time to writing his unfinished masterpiece, *Capital*, of which volume 1 was completed by 1867, and volumes 2 and 3 remained in fragments, notes, and letters. Marx was unique as a social theorist in terms of the style of his writing, developing an acerbic, ironic, and diverse prose. He worked tirelessly but was also a very sociable person, who lived a full life spending his days working at the British Library and visiting another key British institution, the pub. This remains the preferred habitat for many Marxist social theorists today.

Key Concepts

Marx's most famous work, *Capital*, is an attempt to understand the emerging capitalist society. Yet, despite the overarching fame of *Capital*, many of Marx's most important concepts first emerge in other, lesser-known texts, such as *The Economic and Philosophical Manuscripts of 1844*. Throughout his many books and letters, Marx introduces and revisits a range of concepts, of which those given below – alienation, class, mode of production, commodity fetishism, and historical materialism – are only a small selection.

Alienation

Marx noted that in capitalism individuals compete for jobs and have to submit themselves to their employers' control. Employers often impose unreasonable and arbitrary working conditions, while at the same time making a profit from their employees' labour. You may have experienced this yourself. For example, you may have worked in jobs you did not want to do. You may have been forced to clean up other people's mess, or to fill in loads of pointless forms, or you may have been required to try to sell people products that you know are useless, overpriced, or harmful. You may have been treated in a demeaning, degrading, or discriminatory way by people while doing these jobs, yet knowing you were unable to fight back without putting your career at risk. You may have had to compete with fellow employees over sales, or in terms of how much you're prepared to work overtime. You may even have been asked to be a manager and effectively spy on your employees. You may have been left feeling isolated and undervalued because your ideas, or your way of life, don't fit with the way employers want you to sound or to look.

Marx argued that these processes are alienating in that they make you feel estranged from your own labour, your fellow humans, and the environment you are in. Capitalist work makes you feel alienated from more 'natural' ways of behaving in a collective and sharing community, as you would towards your family or closest friends. We let ourselves behave at work in ways we wouldn't otherwise. This alienation creates a feeling of a loss of agency and a lack of control over one's life. It leads to a series of individual and social ills, such as physical and mental health problems, and, in a world of growing 'bullshit jobs', cases of depression and anxiety increase. Marx argued that we can resist alienation by changing the world and adopting an emancipatory and revolutionary approach. This is because he believed that the alienation we feel is not a natural and inevitable phenomenon but is socially constructed and caused by capitalism. Marx thought that if you got rid of capitalism these problems could be substantially reduced.

It is important to note that for Marx labouring isn't a bad thing. Marx thought that humans are all naturally praxis-oriented creatures: that we like to do things. In this he is entirely correct: if we are not doing anything at all, even for a short time, we become frustrated, bored, or fall asleep. As such we voluntarily 'labour': we choose to play instruments, talk to friends, play computer games, play sport. These are all forms of 'labour': they are mental or physical exertions. The problem for Marx, therefore, isn't that we need to labour, the issue is that we have lost control of our abilities to do so in conditions of our choosing.

Class

Class is probably the concept most associated with Marx and Marxism. For Marx, class refers to where someone is located relative to the *means of production*. Marx argued that in capitalism there are two classes who are opposing each other: the proletariat and the bourgeoisie. The bourgeoisie owns the means of production (i.e. they are the business owners, they buy labour power). This class is very small in number and exists only by exploiting the work of the much larger class of people who are forced to sell their labour to the bourgeoisie in order to survive. Marx called this class of labourers the proletariat. The proletariat makes up the vast majority of the population. Crucially, for Marx, this class structure has not existed forever and will inevitably be changed, in time, through a workers' revolution.

For Marx the relationship between the proletariat and bourgeoisie is fundamentally *exploitative*. The exploitation of the proletariat isn't something that happens when capitalism has gone wrong; rather it is inherent to its everyday, normal functioning. Marx demonstrated this through his *Theory of Surplus Value*. This is the cornerstone of Marxist economic theory and is represented by the equation M-C-M'. Don't panic! It is actually quite easy to understand. M refers to money. C refers to commodities (i.e. stuff bought with money). M' just means more money than you started with. All nice and simple. So, for Marx, the basis of capitalist enterprise is a process where money (M) is converted into commodities (C) and somehow you end up with more money (M') than you started with.

How does this magic work? For Marx the answer is simple: the extra money the business owner makes comes from the fact that they do not pay the worker(s) enough money. All profit, therefore, comes from exploiting the worker as they are not paid enough. Let's give this an example. Imagine a capitalist wants to make chairs. They have £100 (M) and want to make more money through capitalist enterprise. They convert their £100 (M) into commodities: wood (£30), nails (£10), and labour (£60). Labour is treated as a commodity in capitalism: that's really important to remember. So £100 (M) has been converted into £100 worth of commodities (C). The commodities are put to work, the chairs are made, and then sold for £500. The capitalist has made £400 profit – how come? Where did this additional value come from? For Marx the answer is simple: the labour of the worker. The worker was underpaid. While they were paid £60, they should in fact have been paid £460. The additional value of the chair is a result of the labour that has gone into it. The fact that the capitalist ends up with profit is a sole result of the worker not having been paid fairly. The worker is structurally exploited. The extraction of this work without fair pay is Marx's theory of surplus value.

For the worker this seems a really awful position to be in. Why would you ever agree to it? It is worth stressing that capitalism needs a massive proletariat, a huge class of waged labourers, for it to function. Where did this new class come from? Historically people didn't need to sell their labour for a wage in order to survive. They worked largely as agricultural workers, farming crops and raising livestock in the countryside. Some people made goods or other foods, making things like barrels (coopers), beer (brewers), or bows and arrows (fletchers). Many people did both: working in the fields during the harvest and making stuff the rest of the time. But next to nobody, back in 1500 CE, was working for a company earning a paid wage. During the transition to capitalism the vast majority of people lost their traditional means of working and thus had no choice but to become waged labourers. Very few people wanted to become proletarians. Many farmers were kicked off their traditional lands in a brutal and tragic process known as the enclosures. The small producers (blacksmiths, coopers, etc.) found that they could not compete with the emerging capitalist factories which could make goods far cheaper. As such, the vast majority of people had no choice but to become waged labourers, hence the emergence of the proletariat. This was a vital ingredient for the birth of capitalism. Without this class of waged labourers there could be no capitalist mode of production.

Crucially, for Marx, class relations are always open to change. A key concept here is 'class consciousness'. If the working class realises what it has in common; that it is an exploited majority, they can come together and change the social structure, reconfigure class relations, and bring forth a new mode of production. The problem is that the workers do not have class consciousness but instead suffer from 'false consciousness'. This is an important reason why no revolution has happened and why capitalism, for now, remains. For Marxists this is due to the fact that most people in society have been tricked into accepting their economic conditions and believing that the social world exists as it does for their benefit. Marxists would argue that liberal theories, such as 'trickle-down economics', where everyone is meant to benefit from the rich getting richer, are powerful falsehoods which encourage conformity and which reduce the possibilities for revolution. For Marx, for society to change, the working class needs to shed its 'false consciousness', to realise the lies of capitalism, and to attain class consciousness. This would lay the foundations for the working class to come together and bring forth a fairer, more rationally organised society.

Mode of Production

'Mode of production' refers to the way in which labour is organised within society. Marx was writing while the capitalist mode of production was in the ascendancy, replacing the earlier feudal mode of production. There have been modes of production before feudalism, such as slavery-based societies and primitive forms of communism. Marx's work is largely focused on understanding capitalist society as representing a distinct mode of production, with its particular form of exploitation and with distinctive tendencies and contradictions. While capitalism is not the only mode of production to have existed and is not inevitable or natural, it is unique in its ability to reshape the entirety of the social world to serve its logics and dynamics. Capitalism is a more totalising socio-economic system than any that came before.

The concept 'mode of production' is broken down into two further concepts: the *relations of production* and *the forces of production*. The relations of production refers to the socio-cultural conditions which exist within a given mode of production, for instance, the particular class dynamics and legal frameworks. In contrast, the forces of production refers to the totality of technologies, tools, and crucially *human labour*, which are drawn upon to make the capitalist economic machine function. For Marxist theorists the particular relationship between the relations of production and the forces of production is useful for explaining how societies change over time.

Marx's approach to thinking about the mode of production is structural; he understands social relations as being determined by a variety of factors which are often, but not always, outside the control of individuals. However, he was also determined to make sense of people's agency. As Marx wrote in *The Eighteenth Brumaire of Louis Bonaparte* [1852]: 'Men make their own history, but they do not make it as they please; they do not make it under self-selected circumstances, but under circumstances existing already, given and transmitted from the past.' There is scope for resisting capitalism, but the opportunities for doing so are structured by the mode of production itself.

Commodity Fetishism

One of the complexities of Marx's approach is that it goes back and forth in discussing how things appear to individuals and how they really are. In other words, Marx's originality is in describing a new social system whose appearance is different to the reality that it obscures. Marx argued that in reality capitalism is a social relation mediated by things. In particular, capitalism is distinct in how it fetishises commodities. This means that in a capitalist mode of production individuals assume that the price and value of a commodity reflects the work that was necessary to produce it. People also mistakenly assume that all commodities have a natural relationship between themselves. This obscures the exploited labour that produced them. At the same time, and in reversal, workers under capitalism also assume that the relations between themselves (their labour relations) can also be commodified and take on the form of commodities in the form of waged labour. In other words, people turn real relations into things, and things into real relations. In *Capital Volume One* Marx wrote:

> There is a physical relation between physical things. But it is different with commodities. There, the existence of the things *qua* commodities, and the value relation between the products of labour which stamps them as commodities, have absolutely no connection with their physical properties and with the material relations arising therefrom. There it is a definite social relation between men, that assumes, in their eyes, the fantastic form of a relation between things. In order, therefore, to find an analogy, we must have recourse to the mist-enveloped regions of the religious world. In that world the productions of the human brain appear as independent beings endowed with life, and entering into relation both with one another and the human race. So it is in the world of commodities with the products of men's hands. This I call the Fetishism which attaches

itself to the products of labour, so soon as they are produced as commodities, and which is therefore inseparable from the production of commodities.

This complex idea is central to Marx's later work, which focuses on the inner mechanisms of capitalism. The fetishism of commodities helps us understand the *value theory of labour*, i.e. how value is generated by the production of commodities through labour. The value theory of labour comes from classical political economy and is linked to classical economists such as Adam Smith (1723–90). Marx studied these ideas at great lengths in order to develop his critique of them.

For capitalists to make money out of the production of a commodity, such as a car, they need to make sure they sell the car for more than what it cost to be produced. One of their major costs, in addition to investment in machines and buildings – or fixed or constant *capital* – is the wages they have to pay to workers – or variable *capital*. This variable *capital* is determined by the amount of time and skill a worker gives to their employer. If a worker can be forced to perform an operation, whether it's a complex technical design or the routine servicing of a machine quicker and better than a worker at a competing factory, then there is more surplus value available to exploit. Capitalism is thus a specific drive for profit which is based on the exploitation of wage labour and the extraction of surplus value from that labour and its production of commodities.

Crucially, it also needs to make people believe that this exploitation is *normal, inevitable, and that it benefits them* by giving them economic freedom. This is what is meant by ideology. Thus, for Marx, labour itself is fetishised as a commodity. In other words, it forces relations between people to be mediated by things, by fetishising both those things and the labour used to produce them.

Historical Materialism

Marx's approach to theorising society was based on his critical reading of the German philosopher, G. W. F. Hegel (1770–1831). Hegel's work was extremely rich conceptually but very hard to engage with. Hegel was interested in how societies evolve and how people's ideas developed. For Hegel, these two concerns are closely related. Hegel held that there was a 'spirit' [*Geist*] which permeates the world, which echoes throughout social institutions and which shapes people's consciousness. Precisely what Hegel meant by *Geist* is much debated; it is a very tricky idea to understand. It is perhaps easiest to think of it as a sort of 'social mind', a form of thinking which permeates social organisation and people's consciousnesses. For Hegel, *Geist* is always in motion, always developing. It was always constantly changing and becoming more coherent over time.

Hegel argued that the unfolding and development [*Aufheben*] of this spirit led to a more rational social order. The process through which this happened was theorised at length by Hegel as being a *dialectical* process. For Hegel, change occurs through conflict and contradiction. As ideas come into conflict new ideas emerge which reflect a compromise between the competing positions. In strict philosophical terminology, Hegel argued that a 'thesis' (idea A) meets an opposing thesis (idea B) called an 'antithesis'. The result of their confrontation is a new thesis (idea C) called a 'synthesis'. For Hegel, all social change is a result of the working through of *Geist*, as it unfolds its contradictions. This development of a synthesis out of competing ideas is at the core of Hegel's *dialectics*. For Hegel, new syntheses of ideas lead to new ways of thinking and to new, or restructured, social institutions.

Marx found Hegel's idea of dialectics convincing. He was sure that there was a constant process of societal change at work as a result of contradictions being worked through. Yet, where Hegel had his complicated theory of *Geist* shaping society, Marx saw the economic domain as central to social development. While Hegel was interested in the conflict of ideas, Marx focused on the conflict between different socio-economic classes. Therefore, where Hegel's philosophy was a form of *Idealism*, located in the world of ideas, Marx's approach was rooted in the conflict of the material world of the economy. As such, Marx's philosophy was a form of *dialectical materialism*. As Marx wrote in his book on Hegel's philosophy, *A Contribution to a Critique of Hegel's Philosophy of Right* [1844], it is not ideas which shape our social world but the social world which shapes our ideas.

For Marx the ideas of a particular person are explicitly a product of their time and place. While Hegel viewed the social world as being driven by this universal ideal realm of *Geist*, Marx focused on the specificities of the subject's historical-economic circumstances. This focus on the particular historical conditions frames Marx as a *historical materialist*. As such, Marx was interested in learning how, through the lens of political economy, different social systems led to different forms of thought and behaviour. As a result, much of Marx's work was rooted in intensely detailed study of past historical periods, including of the classical worlds of Ancient Rome and Ancient Greece. To the present day, it is worth noting that much Marxist scholarship occurs within the realms of history as well as within economics, political economy, development, international relations, and sociology.

Historical materialism is the philosophical-methodological foundation of all 'Marxist' scholarship. Marx's fundamental insight was to place the material world at the basis of social research, rather than the world of ideas, as in Hegel's work. As I discuss below, this paradigm shift impacted the entire tradition of Western thought.

How Did Marx's Work Shape Social Theory?

Marx's legacy cannot be overstated. His work provided the foundations for generations of critical social theorists to come, shaping critical theory, decolonial theory, post-structuralism, gender theory, Critical Race Theory, and many more traditions besides.

Historical Materialism as 'The Second Copernican Revolution'

Nicolaus Copernicus (1473–1543) discovered that the Earth revolved around the sun (heliocentrism) and not the other way round. This was crucial not merely because it offered a valuable correction to a false belief but because it led to a totally new way of studying space and motion. When you no longer believe that the Earth is static you can produce an entirely new model of the universe. Marx's materialist rereading of Hegel has been viewed as being of similar significance for the social sciences and for philosophy. Instead of understanding all social developments as being derived from the world of ideas, or the actions of a transcendent God, suddenly scholars could start analysing society itself as a crucial factor shaping social behaviour.

What does this mean in practice? Well, previously, social developments were largely understood to be occurring due to the unfolding of contradictions in the world of ideas. You cannot really get at this domain and subject it to scientific analysis. Abstract philosophising was as good as it got. In contrast, Marx's view was that social changes were due to what was happening within the mundane world which we can see and experience. As such, with this changed viewpoint, suddenly social systems and social transformations could be meaningfully examined, quantified, scrutinised. Marx's 'second Copernican revolution' thereby legitimated the *scientific* study of society and the economy.

Historical materialism therefore represents not merely a shift in paradigm but a justification for social scientific enquiry more broadly. Following Marx, the focus of analysis shifted from the transcendent, idealistic domain into the material economic world. In this regard, through his historical materialism, Marx did not just shape social theory; he also centred the 'scientific' study of society as a crucial requirement for making the world a better place.

Linking Theory and Praxis

This commitment to wanting to change the world really marks out Marx as different to many of his contemporary theorists. Traditionally, academics seeking social change would have adopted a two-step process. First, they would conduct some 'objective' knowledge gathering. Then they would take this knowledge and apply it to help them take part in political activities. In contrast, for Marx, and for subsequent schools of Marxian theorists, research itself can be a deeply political activity. This particular understanding of the relationship between theory and social change is referred to as the link between 'theory and praxis'.

For many critical social theorists, a substantial obstacle to reaching a fairer social world is *ideology*. This refers to the dominant ideas in circulation which perpetuate and naturalise the way things are. Important parts of capitalist ideology are the belief that running things along market lines tends to be more efficient and better for the end consumer. Marxists would argue that if you looked at the results of most privatisations (the state of British waterways, train lines, etc.) you would see the myth of this claim. As such, unpicking these lies, and showing the true nature of the social relationship which capitalism naturalises, serves not merely to gain a better understanding of our world but also to dislodge ideological forms of thought. This helps make it easier to bring forth sweeping social and economic changes.

As a result, social research in all its forms can be a deeply meaningful political project. But crucially, this also teaches us that *all* theorising is political, whether it intends to be or not. If you write using the generally accepted terms and concepts of capitalist societies, for example, you normalise the dominant system and entrench ideological conceits. As such, the idea of 'objective' or 'value-free' research is an illusion. This idea was most extensively theorised by the Frankfurt School of Critical Theory. Indeed, the entire 'Critical Theory' tradition stems from this Marxian awareness of the role of ideology in society, and within research in particular. As such, for critical social theorists drawing upon Marxian themes, it is preferable not to even pretend to be 'objective' and 'unbiased'. Rather, like Marx, many critical social theorists believe that scholars should admit what they believe in and acknowledge the partisanship of all research. Marxist scholars therefore do not pretend to be existing outside society in some ivory tower where they are immune to politics.

Marxist scholars instead explicitly seek to research in order to change the world in line with their political vision.

This awareness of the unavoidably political nature of scholarship and of concepts, combined with the belief that the critique of ideology is a vital precursor to broader social change, impacted many subsequent traditions of critical social theory. You will learn more about different critical theories which developed these insights in chapters on the early Frankfurt School, Habermas and Honneth, and post-structuralism and post-modernism.

Problems for Contemporary Social Research

While Marx's ideas undeniably shaped social theory (and many other disciplines), his legacy is contested and his ideas have increasingly been combined with those of other scholars. For many decolonial and postcolonial thinkers, Marx's work is problematically 'Eurocentric', placing European developments at the centre of global history. These thinkers typically argue that Marx's concepts need to be modified in light of this criticism. For other groups, such as intersectional feminists, Marx's work is restricted by his 'class reductionism'; that he boils everything down to competing economic classes and fails to understand the importance of other social dynamics (such as gender). Few social theorists today would claim that Marx's work is perfect or that his concepts can be deployed without any modification. As such, most Marxist-inflected social theories connect Marx's ideas with concepts from other traditions so that multiple axes of oppression can be considered. An obvious example here is Marxist Feminism.

Eurocentrism

Was Marx Eurocentric? This is an increasingly common charge. He certainly worked more on the cases of Western European states than elsewhere. But that is not problematic in itself. What may be problematic is the charge that his approach also implies that any developments in, or any struggles against capitalism, will mirror the European experience. In other words, critics claim that his analyses of other parts of the world were overly based on his European understanding of social relations.

For Bhambra and Holmwood, Marx was stuck in the era's stadial theory of societal development. This meant that Marx assumed, in keeping with the Enlightenment tradition, that all societies progressed along a particular trajectory, going through various stages of development in a pre-set order. This view is central to the philosophy of G. W. F. Hegel who was a strong influence on Marx's work. While Hegel believed that society had progressed through its various stages to reach its ideal form (as per his book *Philosophy of Right* [1820]), Marx was a staunch critic of the society of his day. Hence the title of book *A Contribution to the Critique of Hegel's Philosophy of Right* [1844]. Yet, for decolonial theorists, Marx was still problematically invested in the idea that societies will all progress through particular stages and that the pattern he identified from studying 'Western' countries could be applied universally to understand and predict developments across the entire world. Indeed, various decolonial scholars have argued that the idea that society needs to progress in a certain way for development to be achieved is itself a deeply ideological notion, with the very ideas of 'development' and 'progress' requiring considered deconstruction. Expecting all other regions of the globe to inexorably proceed through the same stages identified in Europe has been criticised as blinkered, Eurocentric, and simply wrong. Marx's work is not merely problematic at a methodological level; when it comes to his Eurocentric tendencies, it is simply incorrect historically. Marx did not predict that some societies would 'skip' certain 'stages' and experiment with worker-controlled economies (nominally, at least). He most certainly did not expect the Russian Revolution in 1917, which was entirely at odds with his stadial view of historical development. As such, Marx's belief that one could extract patterns of development from certain European countries and then apply these patterns in order to understand and predict how the whole world would function can be seen to be problematic in terms of its Eurocentric bias, but also in terms of the problematic homogeneity it predicts for how societies evolve, which history has proven to be more complicated and varied.

Class Reductionism

For many contemporary scholars, such as Critical Race Theorists and Intersectional Feminists, Marx is overly focused on class and his theories fail to show how class connects with other important social dynamics, such as racial or gender discrimination. As Marx and Engels wrote in *The Communist Manifesto*, from their perspective, 'The history of all hitherto existing society is the history of class conflict'. Their approach suggests that we need to understand social change, and indeed social interaction more broadly, through a historical materialist lens: class relations have primacy. Yet this view fails to acknowledge the importance of other forms of oppression or other drivers of history. This poses the question: is the history of all hitherto existing societies really the history of class conflict? Does this claim need to be modified and, if so, how?

Two responses can be given by those who appreciate Marx's work. One approach is that taken by Eco-Marxists and Frankfurt School Critical Theorists, which is to broadly agree with Marx and to say that yes, class antagonisms do drive social change more than anything else. These thinkers broadly say that struggles over ownership of the means of production are indeed a crucial catalyst for social transformation and they have been the dominant dynamic across all known societies. However, while Marx was right that class conflict drives societies and shapes how we come to view and understand our world, a more sophisticated social theory can be built which is also sensitive to how class interconnects with other dynamics, such as those of race, gender, and the environment. From such a perspective, capitalism is seen to interconnect with other logics, such as anthropocentricism, racism, and patriarchy. Ultimately, class and capitalism are the dominant forces in today's society; yet to understand capitalism you must also have a theory of its relationship with patriarchy and with racism. Marx's co-author, Friedrich Engels, already produced a work as early as 1884, *The Origin of the Family, Private Property, and the State*, which connected capitalism and patriarchy in important ways, and which points in this direction.

Another response is to reject the primacy of class and to suggest that all social dynamics are intersectional. For such intersectional scholars, capitalism exists and is a crucial area of study, and Marx indeed has useful insights to offer. Yet, for intersectional feminists, for example, the idea that society is ultimately all about class at the foundation level is seen to be class reductionist. For intersectional feminists, patriarchy, racism, and capitalism are all interconnected, and none have a causal primacy. In essence, while intersectional feminists would not reject Marx's concepts, they would say that the fundamental primacy afforded to class cannot be offset with 'adding' other dynamics as secondary subplots. Rather, for intersectional feminists, unless class, gender, race, caste, anthropocentrism are understood as co-eval and co-constitutive, you will fail to truly understand how society operates.

Both of these approaches are of course matched by a third response: to simply reject Marx out of hand as simply wrong on class! This is the idea presented by liberal and conservative scholars. For such authors, Marx's view on class is deeply misguided and capitalist society should be viewed as emancipatory and at the core of social progress. For example, liberal feminists would argue that the dominant challenge facing social progress today would be to overcome patriarchal oppression. For liberal feminists such as Sheryl Sandberg (1969–), capitalism and class division is not the enemy, rather capitalism needs to be protected and developed by ridding society of other logics, such as patriarchy and racism.

How are Marx's Key Concepts Deployed Today?

Marxist Schools

As discussed above, a key reason for the continuing relevance of Marx today is the very significant body of research he has influenced. Some of the following chapters are even dedicated to specific strands of Marxism, such as the theorists of the early and the contemporary Frankfurt School. But Marxism has also branched out into a broad range of theories, often mixing traditions, and has produced new perspectives such as post-colonial theory, Social Reproduction Theory, the Intersectionality of the Combahee River Collective, and Eco-Marxism. Some Marxist schools are more focused on certain disciplines or topics. For example, value-form theory focuses more on the pure economics or monetary dimension of capitalism. Dependency theory, Neo-Gramscian theories, Political Marxism, or Uneven and Combined Development (UCD) have been more relevant to studies of international relations and development. Finally, ecological Marxism focuses on the relationship of capitalism and nature, alongside the problem of climate change as a capitalist phenomenon; for example, through Andreas Malm's (1977–) work on 'fossil capital' or through Kohei Saito's (1987–) work on 'degrowth communism'.

International Relations

A limitation of Marx's work is that he failed to produce significant writing on the state. The world today is divided politically into approximately 200 states, and the sovereign state remains the main international legal entity that accords a population some independent rights. But economies are globally intertwined in unequal and contradictory ways that benefit capitalists and certain states and not independent populations. Other international legal actors – such as corporations, multi-state organisations, non-governmental organisations, and judicial bodies – are increasingly present on the international scene and can challenge the independence of states, especially those not powerful enough to do as they please. In spite of the continuation of what looks like classic geopolitical conflicts, such as the war in Ukraine, all aspects of international relations today are determined by the global political economy, i.e. the way in which commodities are produced, sold, and consumed around the world, and how the reproduction of human beings and nature are shaped by those processes. This is the continuing contribution of Marx's work. The more the world functions as an interdependent system where people in Europe consume products made in Asia and food made in South America, where corporations can escape regulations by delocalising their production centres and financial responsibilities, the more an approach that combines these factors and focuses on the struggles and inequalities they produce is going to be justified.

For Marxists, the state today serves an ideological purpose for capitalism in terms of providing the illusion of a possible limit or accountability to its so-called excesses. For many people, the state and the juridical apparatuses at its disposal provide ways of 'civilising' capitalism, of 'doing it right' so that all can benefit from growth and access to work and enterprise. However, Marx would argue that the state is part of the problem as long as it serves the interests of capital. Moreover, problems today are of such a scale, whether ecological or financial, that it is difficult to see how states can solve these challenges when conference after conference show that states remain tied to their national prerogatives or to the interests of their own elites. Greta Thunberg's famous speech to the United Nation's Climate Action Summit in 2019 summarises well the inadequacy of this structure: 'how dare you!' she screamed out. 'How dare you continue to look away and come here saying that you're doing enough, when the politics and solutions needed are still nowhere in sight'. The climate activist is powerfully pointing the finger here at the political world which acts as though it's in control, in spite of showing a total lack of action on these key issues. This is what Marxist social theory can provide, as an approach which is based on the critique of what exists, but which also uses that critique to be ambitious and creative about changing the world according to new and complex ideas.

Conclusion

Marx's approach to social theory develops new concepts to account for new social relations emerging in the nineteenth century after a process of transition from feudalism to capitalism in Western Europe, mainly from the seventeenth century onwards. This approach, historical materialism, is grounded in historical and material processes, especially those necessary for the production and reproduction of labour and commodities, while grappling with the ideological and even mystical or fetishised forms these take under capitalism. Marx's – and, very often, Engels's – work connects the concepts of alienation, class struggle and class consciousness, capital and capital accumulation, mode and means of production, and revolution in multiple ways and creates a mechanical or structural system, which aims to reflect the inner and outer workings of the social reality at its basis. For Marx, we need a social theory that can make sense of this totality, be critical of it, and reveal what it obscures.

Discussion Questions

1   Have you ever felt alienated at work or in a social encounter, and how, if at all, does this connect to capitalism? How does work make you feel?

2   Can class struggle lead to the overthrow of capitalism?

3   Considering recent changes in production – complex global supply chains, digital technologies, automation, delocalisation, and temporary migration – who is the global working class today, and how is it in conflict with the global capitalist class? Is Marx more relevant to the nineteenth-century phase of capitalism?

4   Is modern slavery today a consequence of capitalism, or is this form of unfree labour a remnant from a pre-capitalist period?

5   Is it possible to be critical *and* objective in social theory?

Further Reading

Primary Texts

Contribution to the Critique of Hegel's Philosophy of Right [1844]

In this book Marx criticises important aspects of Hegel's philosophy and politics. This book is also where Marx writes about the relationship between religion and class conflict, containing his famous discussion of religion as 'the opium of the masses'.

The Economic and Philosophical Manuscripts (or Paris Manuscripts) [1844]

This is Marx's first serious engagement with political economy, where the notion of class conflict becomes central to the understanding of society. Marx develops ideas about human nature which he later abandons, but retains analyses of what human life should be and how capitalism is a threat to it.

The German Ideology [1845]

This text, written with Engels, is often considered to mark the transition in Marx's work from his focus on more philosophical ideas such as alienation, human nature, religion, to a new scientific and materialist approach to history. This is where Marx most explicitly states that the role of philosophers is not only to interpret the world but also to change it.

The Communist Manifesto [1848]

A key pamphlet text written with Engels and containing a hard-hitting structural and international analysis of capitalism, which will be nuanced in his later work. The text contains snippets of most of Marx's key contributions, such as the approach of historical materialism and focus on class summarised by the sentence: 'The history of all hitherto existing society is the history of class struggles'. The text ends with this key quote, inscribed on Marx's grave: 'The proletarians have nothing to lose but their chains. They have a world to win. Working Men of All Countries, Unite!'

The Eighteenth Brumaire of Louis Bonaparte [1852]

In this text Marx discusses the 1851 coup by Louis-Napoléon Bonaparte or Napoleon III in France, and uses some of his most famous quotes such as how history repeats itself 'first as tragedy, then as farce'. This text displays most powerfully his approach of historical materialism, applied to a specific event, and showcases the interdependency between structure and agency. It is also a text full of the promise and disappointment of revolutionary activity.

Grundrisse [1857–8]

This is a set of notes where Marx lays out the broadest overview of his biggest unfinished project, Capital, dealing with all aspects of capitalist society.

Capital, Volume 1 [1867]

Marx's most ambitious project is an attempt to capture the essence and mechanics of capitalist society. Volume 1 is dedicated to the production of commodities, and traces this general process as it occurs inherently in any capitalist society rather than historically or geographically. The first few chapters are more theoretical and abstract, while the final chapters develop more historical analyses showcasing the processes of capital accumulation in England and its colonies. Capital is a tour-de-force in literary style, and showcases Marx's abilities as a writer to switch between styles and vocabularies, and his extensive research into a very wide range of studies.

Capital, Volume 2 [1893] and *Capital, Volume 3* [1894]

Volume 2 is focused on the circulation of commodities as opposed to their production. Volume 3 brings together these two processes. These two volumes remained largely unfinished by Marx and were edited by Engels before publication. They are therefore the subject of much debate among Marxists, and it is difficult to be sure as to Marx's intentions in them. But they remain key sources for thinking through how Marx was going to develop his analysis into the more political domains of capital.

Secondary Texts

Daniel Bensaïd, *Marx for Our Times: Adventures and Misadventures of a Critique* [2002]

This is an accessible introduction to Marx's work from an outspoken French activist and thinker, who reads Marx through our contemporary challenges.

Mike Davis, *Old Gods, New Enigmas: Marx's Lost Theory* [2018]

Mike Davis worked hard as an activist and writer to bring Marx's analysis and approach of social theory to a larger public. This text is more specifically focused on Marx's theory of revolution, and how class struggles since the nineteenth century have borne out his ideas.

Nancy Fraser, *Cannibal Capitalism: How Our System Is Devouring Democracy, Care, and the Planet – and What We Can Do About It* [2022]

This text from one of today's most important critical theorists brings together recent sympathetic critiques of Marxism's blind spots and the new hidden abodes of production, and integrates them into her Marxist analysis of today's manifestations of capitalist exploitation, focusing on racial and gender inequalities, and the ecological crisis.

David Harvey, *A Companion to Marx's Capital Volume 1* [2010]

Harvey is a geographer who developed some key Marxist concepts and became one of the key pedagogues of Marx's work. This text is the first in a series going through all volumes of *Capital*, and most recently, *The Grundrisse*.

CLR James, *The Black Jacobins* [1938]

This classic text by the multi-talented Trinidadian author is an exemplary case of tying Marx's method of historical materialism to a specific event, which Marx and Marxism ignored for a long time. This ground-breaking analysis of the Haitian Revolution of 1804 and of its leader, Toussaint L'Ouverture, set the scene for a new historical agenda revisiting the class struggle between colonisers and colonised.

Jonathan Joseph, *Marxism and Social Theory* [2006]

This is an accessible introduction to the relationship between different strands of Marxism and social theory. It is a great follow-up to this chapter.

Sando Mezzadra, *In the Marxian Workshops: Producing Subjects,* [2018]

This text develops Marx's work from an Italian autonomist standpoint. Mezzadra skilfully integrates issues of subjectivity, race, and migration, into this important analysis.

Bertell Ollman, *Dance of the Dialectic: Steps in Marx's Method* [2003]

This is a classic, beautifully written text which goes deeper into the linguistic mechanics of Marx's work, analysing his approach to concept formation and specifically how the contradictions and multiple definitions by Marx himself fit together dialectically.

McKenzie Wark, *Capital is Dead? Is This Something Worse* [2019]

This text applies Marx's method, coming to the conclusion that the ascent of big data is leaving capitalism behind. True to Marx's insights and politics, this is a provocative and accessible read with unique conclusions.

Ellen Meiksins Wood, *The Origin of Capitalism* [2002]

This short text makes the debate on the transition to capitalism, and Robert Brenner's work especially, more accessible, and introduces

students to key debates in Marxist theory. It lays out some fundamental principles for a different approach to historical materialism
grounded in a broader concept of social property relations, while arguing for a more historically specific approach to the transition based
on transformations in the seventeenth-century English countryside.

Émile Durkheim: Society Functions!

Contents

DOI: 10.4324/9781003359555-3

Unlike Karl Marx, whose life was that of an exiled rebel, Émile Durkheim's (1858–1917) biography is frankly boring in comparison. While Marx was on drunken pub crawls, evading spies, and calling for revolution, Durkheim was rigorously disciplined and unadventurous. He rarely travelled far and he worked constantly. He was born into a poor Jewish family in Épinal, France in 1858. His father was a Rabbi and his parents assumed that young Émile would inevitably follow in his father's footsteps. Even though he eventually lost his religious faith while at university, his interest in religion continued to shape his work. Durkheim's life was not only comparatively sedate, it was also rather sombre. Following the death of his father, he became particularly moody and introspective. He even told friends that he thought his grief enabled him to better understand and experience society. Whatever this 'experience' was, it was certainly limited; like Marx and Weber, Durkheim exhibited an obsessive devotion to work and study, reading and writing with excessive dedication. He was rewarded with a place at the prestigious *École Normale Supérieure*, the French equivalent of Oxford or Cambridge. Durkheim thrived at university, meeting many figures who would grow to become central to French intellectual and political life, such as the future Socialist Party Prime Minister Jean Jaurès (1859–1914).

Durkheim was noted by his peers for his staunch dislike of the starchy customs of much French academia. In place of the long, florid speeches of his lecturers, he yearned for objectivity and scientific rigour. As a result, he looked to the sciences for guidance on how best to study society. These ideas were to develop in time into his mature work, *Rules of the Sociological Method* [1895], which was to become a classic text of the social sciences, and is seen by many as a mission statement for a *positivistic* sociology. As we discuss below, Durkheim's scientific approach to studying society called for a rigorous examination of observable social phenomena, the identification of 'social facts', and unwavering objectivity.

Durkheim's work was pivotal in shaping the *methodology* people use to go about researching society; yet his conceptual innovations were equally significant in bringing about a new *perspective* for understanding society. This viewpoint was to become known as 'functionalism'. While Marxists look at the social world and see conflict, exploitation, and irrationality, functionalists look at society and think 'wow: it works!'. As such, drawing upon Durkheim's concepts, functionalists analyse how social institutions combine together in a delicate balance to maintain social harmony and stability. As a result, the functionalist perspective is typically associated with more conservative attitudes and an opposition to radical social change. Whether it is right to describe Durkheim himself as a 'functionalist' is discussed below. What is undeniable is that the concepts he developed to explore the vulnerability of the social order laid the foundations for functionalist analyses to follow.

Two events in particular shaped Durkheim's thought, both of which reinforced his sense of the frailty of the social order. These were the rise and fall of the Paris Commune (1871), during his youth, and the Dreyfus Affair (1894–1906), as a mature academic. The Paris Commune was a short-lived radical democratic community which emerged in the wake of the collapse of the French Second Empire following their defeat in the Franco–Prussian War. The French had been humiliated on the battlefield, and Prussian forces had captured Emperor Napoleon III and surrounded Paris. The Parisians were already festering a deep-seated resentment due to decades of poverty, inequality, and an authoritarian, centralised political system. The sky-rocketing food prices which occurred as a result of the Prussian blockade of the city were the final straw. On 18 March 1871, politicised workers and soldiers rose in rebellion against the faltering French government. In its place, they declared a revolutionary new system in Paris: what was to become known as the 'Paris Commune'. It was a truly revolutionary project. The communards sought worker control of businesses, a progressive education system free from religious influence, and a system of direct democracy. This was in opposition to both conservative and capitalist interests, which remained strong throughout the rest of France. The Commune was brutally destroyed after just a few months, in the so-called 'Bloody Week', where many communards were slaughtered on the orders of President Adolphe Thiers. Both the reasons leading to the rise of the Commune, and the manner of its suppression, taught the young Durkheim about the fragility of society and the overwhelming power and ruthlessness of the bourgeoisie. His concepts of 'anomie', his reflections on different types of 'solidarity', and his concern for the precarity of city life were undoubtedly shaped by living through the Paris Commune's rise and fall.

Decades later, when Durkheim was an established academic, a national scandal gripped his attention. In a climate of growing xenophobia and anti-Semitism, a French-Jewish soldier, Captain Alfred Dreyfus, was wrongly convicted of treason. This because a *cause célèbre* for many leading intellectuals and public figures, who called for his retrial and acquittal. Durkheim edited a journal, *L'Année Sociologique*, which published many pieces in support of Dreyfus. Durkheim saw the Dreyfus affair as reinforcing many of his views. It spoke of the frailty of society and of the dangers of fervent nationalism. As a Jewish intellectual himself, trying to popularise a 'science of society', he was seen by some reactionary voices as 'foreign' and 'Germanic'. As such, Durkheim could relate personally to the Dreyfus case. Despite his academic rather than political profile, and his comparatively moderate political persuasions, Durkheim was a highly divisive figure. While he had a devoted group of students and followers, he was strongly opposed by some conservative voices who saw him as a dangerous outsider, propagating a strange, alien subject.

In his later life he devoted more of his time to the topic of public education, which he thought could help engender a stable, harmonious, and moral society. He came to believe that through a carefully cultivated education system, with a tailored curriculum, governments could significantly foster moral and social progress. His various essays and lectures on education were collected and published posthumously as *Moral Education* [1925].

Durkheim is primarily associated today with a *functionalist* perspective for understanding society and with a 'scientific', *positivist* methodology for conducting research. As we discuss, his actual belief in either, as they are understood today, is questionable. Yet, irrespective of the nuances of Durkheim's personal views, both functionalism and positivism need to be critically interrogated. Both can serve to hide and normalise forms of oppression and exploitation and have been mobilised for reactionary socio-political agendas. This is an unfortunate legacy for Durkheim, who was far more socially liberal than many of his contemporaries.

Key Concepts

Durkheim viewed society as something akin to a fragile, intricately balanced organism. The concepts discussed below can all be viewed as tools he created to help understand the delicate stability of social life. From a functionalist perspective, social equilibrium is prized; the goal of the sociologist is to understand how society keeps everything in balance. As a result, functionalists stress the stabilising and harmonising role played by *all* social institutions, even those which may be criticised for being irrational or inequitable. While Marxists and feminists typically focus on conflict, exploitation, and social change, functionalists, like Durkheim, focus more on social equilibria, and see merit in existing social institutions.

Anomie

Anomie refers to a painful feeling of disconnection from the values of society. While it is experienced on a personal level (as something an individual feels) it is an important social theoretical concept, as it captures the relationship between individual actors and social norms. Durkheim argued that this sense of disconnection often happens when the shared normative order, the rules and beliefs which bind people together, breaks down, due to social changes happening too quickly. As a result, people can be left feeling adrift, lacking a socio-moral anchor. One reason such rapid changes may happen is that social institutions may have failed to retain their delicate balance. For instance, the norms of one institution (e.g. the capitalist market) may suddenly have become too strong for other institutions to offset. This can happen for many different reasons and can connect with analyses made by commentators of differing political viewpoints.

For example, socialists have commented on the feelings of loss and social disconnection experienced by many people as a result of the neoliberal revolution. This refers to the rapid change to an extreme form of capitalism which views all parts of the social world as areas that should be controlled by market forces. As a result, many people feel painfully disconnected from their social world, where education, water, and personal care were suddenly seen as 'products' for sale. For many people there was a painful disconnect between what society was now manifesting and their own values. People born during the social democratic period were raised to view healthcare, education, water, etc. as social goods, as something any decent, rational society should provide each citizen as a fundamental right. This rapid change to an extreme market society, where personal 'greed is good', led to a painful sense of disconnection and anomie. It is worth stressing that for functionalists, the market's logics of commodification and rational self-interest are not themselves the problem here. What matters for functionalists is that society is functioning, not what values it inscribes. The problem is not that certain values are 'wrong' in themselves. Rather, the issue is that an *imbalance* had set in and changes had occurred too rapidly for people to connect with, leaving them feeling anomic. This was threatening society's ability to function.

Equally, patriotic conservatives could argue that people are feeling a sense of anomie as a result of excessively fast globalisation. Such voices may contend that internationalist values and policies have been excessively prioritised over the value many people hold for the importance of their national community. For generations, people were raised to be highly patriotic, to consider their identity to be tied to their country.

For people raised to proudly connect their identity to their nation, rapid globalisation and migration can be seen to induce a real sense of anomie. The 'elite' may have moved to embrace globalisation and multiculturalism, but that doesn't mean that everyone has moved at the same time and speed. The issue for functionalists again is not that change is happening. Rather, people need to be feeling anchored within the new and changing social norms. This is not the case for everyone when it comes to increased globalisation and migration. For example, during the Brexit referendum in 2016, many people said they felt they wanted to 'take their country back', reflecting this profound sense of loss. This can be understood through Durkheim's view of anomie: changes in the normative order of society, a move away from valuing the 'national' and 'patriotism', had happened too quickly for many, typically older people, to connect with. For conservatives, the forces of liberal globalisation had not been balanced enough by the institutions which engender a sense of national social cohesion and national pride. This had induced an anomic reaction, which manifested in support of authoritarian populist movements. Again, for functionalists, neither 'internationalism' nor 'patriotism' is a problem here; the issue is the threat to society's functioning which widespread anomie leads to. We saw a social world of extreme polarisation and increasing fragmentation. The rise of anomie as a result of disconnects with socially inscribed norms posed a threat to social stability.

While the examples above present anomie as occurring as a result of sudden social changes, people can also experience anomie if they feel disconnected from long-standing traditions and beliefs which are central to how their social world is ordered. Anomie can occur not just because society is changing too fast but also because some people feel it is changing too slowly. For example, there are some ancient customs, such as monarchies, which no longer resonate with millions of social actors today. Indeed, many young people find the monarchy not merely irrelevant to their lives but consider it offensive to their own normative values, such as the importance of equality. As such, these young people are increasingly disconnected from the monarchy in British life and may feel a sense of anomie every time they witness the disproportionate media attention it receives. Here, the problem is not that society has changed too fast; rather, the issue is that, for some people, social institutions have not changed quickly enough.

While Durkheim's concept is more commonly used to refer to situations where changes have occurred too quickly, it is equally helpful to explain dynamics where people feel disconnected due to a lack of social change. Anomie is therefore a particularly rich and valuable concept which Durkheim used across his work. He developed it across several works, such as *The Rules of Sociological Method* [1895], *The Division of Labour in Society* [1893], and most famously, *Suicide* [1897]. Across all of these works Durkheim wrote that anomie is both a symptom of failing social cohesion (people only feel anomic because society is breaking down in some way) and is itself a threat to social cohesion (an anomic society can rapidly fall into chaos). Durkheim warned that rising rates of anomie can often lead to forms of violent social unrest, such as riots. From such a perspective, a riot is understood as an outpouring of frustration at a lack of societal rootedness, a collective sense that societal norms have broken down. An optimally functioning society is one with little to no anomie experienced by the population. Conversely, the more people feel anomic, the greater the chance of chaos and societal disintegration. For functionalists, changes need to be slow and steady to avoid the spread of anomie, which is a real danger to social life.

Collective Consciousness

Durkheim's concept of 'collective consciousness' is closely related to his work on anomie. While anomie refers to the *feeling* of disconnection from the normative order of society, collective consciousness captures the shared beliefs, customs, attitudes, traditions, *as well as the norms*, that serve to bind individuals together. Durkheim believed that a robust 'collective consciousness' was indispensable for ensuring a stable, functional society. Without such a shared framework of understanding, effective communication and cooperation would be impossible. Following Durkheim, functionalists argue that having some shared connection enables people to work and live together; it makes life so much richer and easier when you have things to talk about, to enjoy, to cherish as a group. But Durkheim also believed that a shared collective consciousness serves to subtly repattern our behaviours, gently moulding social actors to act and think in ways that facilitated social functioning.

'Collective consciousness' encompasses so much more than just agreeing to a vaguely similar sense of 'right' and 'wrong' as everyone else. It includes this, but pushes more further. While 'anomie' is linked to a lack of normative rootedness, 'collective consciousness' points to *everything* that binds people together through shared understandings: not just norms. Returning to the example above, anomie may set in for some people if they are forced to sign a contract to receive education as a 'product'. This may reflect a lack of shared norms. This would be seen as a loss of collective consciousness; however, collective consciousness also includes the knowledge that when people make a deal they shake hands on it, for example, or that signing a document reinforces a commitment. These forms of knowledge are equally crucial to collective consciousness.

As such, collective consciousness includes a shared awareness of cultural rituals. Shaking hands is just one example. The phrase 'cultural rituals' may perhaps sound exotic; one may think of communities far away in space and time, rather than of our community. But every society has its rituals, things that we take for granted and normalise. Our process of doing these things without thinking about them, of expecting shared practices and values implicitly: this is part of what Durkheim is referring to. For example, it is a 'cultural ritual' to eat popcorn at the cinema, to throw confetti at (Christian/secular) weddings, to drink champagne at celebratory events, to wear seemingly old-fashioned and absurd clothing at graduation ceremonies, to celebrate anniversaries and birthdays. These rituals, and the knowledge and appreciation of their significance, feed into the 'collective consciousness' and help bind people together. This is still all part of the 'collective consciousness', and for Durkheim it also captures shared stories, myths, philosophical beliefs. It refers to the entire socialised commonalities of behaviour across a society.

Durkheim underscores the importance of collective consciousness throughout several books, especially *The Division of Labour in Society* [1893] and *The Elementary Forms of Religious Life* [1912]. He argues that it underpins the formation of social solidarity among individuals, a topic we discuss next. A thriving collective consciousness is crucial for social integration and effective social functioning. For Durkheim, all social institutions are responsible for imbuing collective consciousness. As such, any drastic social changes need to be carefully considered, since they may risk harming the careful balance of social factors which bind people together. For Durkheim, the preservation of collective consciousness is intrinsically tied to the maintenance of social order and cohesiveness in a given society. Without a healthy collective consciousness, social actors will risk suffering from anomie and will lose any sense of social solidarity. Without collective consciousness, society will be unable to function.

Organic and Mechanical Solidarity

As we have seen, Durkheim was fascinated with how society functions and how society binds people together. Throughout his work, and especially in his book *The Division of Labour in Society*, he stressed that the key to such stability is the maintenance of bonds of solidarity between people. If everyone despises each other and feels entirely disconnected, society will struggle to remain peaceful and harmonious. As such, bonds of solidarity must be forged between social actors. Durkheim was particularly interested in how this worked, as the way societies cohere and the way bonds of solidarity were formed had rapidly shifted in a comparatively short period of time.

While approximately 90 per cent of French people lived in small countryside communities in 1800, by 1900 this figure had dropped to around 40 per cent. Or, put another way, in just 100 years, roughly half the French population had changed from living 'rural' to 'urban' lives. This was not simply a case of millions of people moving house and living in a new postcode. The shift from rural to urban life marked a massive change in people's entire existence. In rural life people lived as part of a small community who knew each other well, with shared customs, values, and control over their own time, often being out in the fields together. In urban life people experienced highly individualised factory work, with hours regulated by the clock, working next to someone they did not know, who they could often barely communicate with. It is worth stressing that there were many different languages in most European 'countries' at this stage, and it is only in the past 150 years or so that a dominant shared language has emerged in France, for example. Durkheim wanted to know how people stay connected despite such differences. How are bonds of solidarity forged in this new urban, capitalist world? To explore the changing forms of solidarity, he developed two different models: 'organic' and 'mechanical' forms of solidarity. In *The Division of Labour in Society* he wrote that while people had previously experienced 'mechanical' forms of solidarity in more simple, rustic communities, the new, more complicated urban social worlds were predicated on an 'organic' form of solidarity.

Durkheim argued that simple countryside communities tended to bind people together through bonds of 'mechanical' solidarity. People typically worked together for the benefit of the whole; the overall food supply of the community mattered; people were not desperate for their own personal wealth to accrue, rather resources were for the collective. There was a very strong sense of collective consciousness, there was a clear set of traditions, values, a shared language, a shared religious identity. People also typically all mucked in together to help with key forms of labour, such as taking in the harvest as a community. In these comparatively homogeneous communities, people are all connected *like parts of a machine*: everyone is experiencing the same sort of thing, working together, for the benefit of the group. There is very little individuation. As such, solidarity forms relatively effortlessly. The community all worked together like a machine, ergo mechanical solidarity.

In contrast, urban communities experienced a form of 'organic' solidarity. Instead of people being bound together like a machine, Durkheim viewed complex urban life as providing a form of solidarity where people were bound together more like the parts of a body working together. Where in simple rural life people largely all did the same thing and were very similar, in complex urban life people did very different things but were all connected together through interdependence. The analogy goes that now we have a society where some people operate like a heart, a liver, hair, skin, eyes. They live very different lives and may not be able to understand each other. However, people are crucially interdependent; they need each other to stay alive. There is a greater individualisation and a weaker collective consciousness; people have less in common and do not aspire as much for the good of the community. Yet, they remain bound together through the specialisation of their roles in society, and their functional interdependence. As such, Durkheim's work on 'organic' solidarity ties neatly into this work on *The Division of Labour*, discussed below.

The Division of Labour

In *The Division of Labour in Society* [1893] Durkheim argued that as societies modernise, workers are allocated increasingly specialised roles. This leads to greater interdependence among workers. While in the past small communities of farmers could live relatively autonomously, who among us today could survive without interacting with the *labour* of others? We do not grow our own food, or repair our own cars, we do not know how to produce our own electricity, or to make our own medicines. Without the labour of others our normal day-to-day lives would be impossible. Durkheim was already seeing this move to a greater interdependence, caused by the specialisation of labour tasks, over 100 years ago.

Just think about our world today: our skillsets are increasingly of use only as part of a larger group; administrators require people to administer, technicians require other technicians and marketing teams, marketers need something to market, etc. This creates an interdependence, binding people together, whether we are always aware of this fact or not. We cannot easily just 'drop out' of society. Durkheim was always concerned with balance and social equilibriums, and with this in mind it is perhaps best to frame the challenge of specialisation of labour as a balancing act: both excessive specialisation and excessive under-specialisation can lead to problems integrating within society. If we are capable of looking after ourselves entirely without any need to turn to others for help, our social ties are loosened. Equally, if we spend our entire lives stuck in our own offices, only ever working alone on highly specialised and isolated tasks, our connections to other people can be easily forgotten. The empirical reality of our interdependence does not inevitably mean that people will be conscious of it.

Today, we increasingly live in a world dominated by global supply chains. The ascent of these international routes is closely connected to the rise of specialised labour roles. It can be more cost-efficient to produce certain goods in particular parts of the world, or there may be a greater proximity to essential component parts in countries where certain natural resources are located. When we consider the global supply chains upon which we all depend today for our laptops, our food, our petrol, the specialisation of labour can be understood as a force binding global society as much as uniting people within national societies.

Social Facts

So far, the concepts we have introduced relate more to Durkheim's *perspective* on society, which has come to be known as functionalism. His work on anomie, on different forms of solidarity, on the division of labour in society, and collective consciousness, all helped Durkheim explore what kept society stable and bound people together. Yet Durkheim's work is equally important for the development of a *methodology* for researching society, which he presented most clearly in his book, *The Rules of Sociological Method* [1895]. Durkheim was really passionate about developing sociology as a 'science' of society, which he wanted to have a rigorous, objective, and empirical approach. There was a real urgency to his work here. Indeed, he had *The Rules of Sociological Method* published just months after he had written it; often it takes years for academic works to appear in print after they have been written. This may reflect Durkheim's desire to respond to his critics; many conservative French voices found his ideas on 'a science of society' highly distasteful. Whoever his intended audience was, *The Rules of Sociological Method* is less of a long, complicated rule book, and more a focused and concise work, which clearly lays out Durkheim's preferred method for researching society.

The concept of 'social facts' is a really important feature of this work, referring to what it is that Durkheim thinks sociologists should study. They comprise objective, observable realities, typically connected to systems, be they religious, economic, political, or legal. For example, sociologists should study how the capitalist order socialises individuals to behave in a certain way. Such work should be done drawing upon quantitative methods and the use of statistical analyses, looking for patterns, in much the same way a chemist might look at molecules in a lab. The logics of the market are held to be similarly objectively discernible and their impact on subjects ascertainable through analogous empirical research. Similarly, religious and legal systems could be studied to objectively note how they shape people's behaviour. Social facts are society-wide; they reflect patterns and dynamics which impact on large scores of the population and can be approached with objective, empirical, clinical rigour.

The concept also helps Durkheim distinguish sociology from psychology and other related subjects. While psychologists were to study people's feelings and their cognitive states, Durkheim wanted sociologists to study objective, observable social phenomena. In essence, if psychology was the study of what was happening in the minds of social actors, sociology was the study of the 'social facts' which *shape* people's thoughts, feelings, and actions. For Durkheim, these social facts exist regardless of whether people are aware of them and typically have a profound impact on people's behaviour. Whether or not you know about capitalism, it won't stop you being impacted by its laws and logics. Therefore, where psychologists may discuss feelings and the subject's self-knowledge, sociologists were to analyse the observable, objective world.

It is important to pause here. You may have noticed that something a little odd is going on. Durkheim spent his life arguing for the objective study of social logics which impact on people's lives, regardless of whether they are aware of them. He is not invested in exploring the subjective states of individuals, which he says is the task of psychology. He is passionate that sociology should be about the study of observable phenomena, using scientific methods. He wants to use scientific analyses, quantifying, finding observable, provable patterns. Yet, a few pages ago, you were reading about how anomie was central to Durkheim's approach to studying society. Anomie is very much a feeling, a subjective state. It is not something you can measure under a microscope. It would be very hard to meaningfully quantify or to understand through statistical analysis. This disconnect between Durkheim's proposed method, and his interest in studying anomie, reflects a fundamental tension for all positivistic, scientific approaches to researching society. We discuss this in more detail below. However, reading Durkheim sympathetically, one could frame his work as partly being an attempt to bridge the gap between the subjective state of the individual (anomie) and social facts, by explicitly tying the individual's experience to observable social phenomena – such as changes in socio-economic structures. This is definitely a charitable reading, seeking to find coherence between his concepts. It has also been argued by various scholars that Durkheim simply does not practise what he preaches, that while he aspires to a scientific analysis of social facts his own work pushes into territory which does not meet the rigorously positivistic standards he aspires to.

How Did These Concepts Shape Social Theory?

Durkheim's legacy lies in the development of *functionalist* perspectives for viewing society and in *positivistic* methodologies for researching the social world. As such, Durkheim's status as one of the 'founding fathers' of sociology is undeniable. He is associated with shaping a dominant paradigm for viewing how social institutions and social actors work together to keep society stable and harmonious. He is equally associated with building a paradigm for understanding what methods can produce meaningful knowledge about the social world. Both of these paradigms have shaped generations of subsequent social research and, as we discuss in a following section, continue to shape social theory and social research today.

Functionalism

The way we interpret past thinkers, and the ideas and words we associate with them, is complicated and sometimes highly ironic. For example, Karl Marx never once used the word 'capitalism' in his writings. Similarly, neither did Durkheim use the word 'functionalist' in any of his works. Yet, Durkheim was certainly invested in understanding the way society binds people together. His work is all about exploring forms of solidarity, and he was fascinated with the role of institutions in maintaining social equilibria. While there has been much debate over whether Durkheim should be viewed as a functionalist, his concepts were subsequently utilised to develop an explicitly functionalist perspective to social research.

But what actually is 'functionalism'? One way of thinking of functionalism is as a perspective to studying society driven by the belief that society 'works', that it 'functions'. The idea driving this perspective is the sense that everything in society is working as a whole, that all social institutions are in some kind of careful balance. As a result, society is stable and not in total chaos. For instance, the family and the capitalist market, while different in important ways, are viewed by functionalists as working productively together. While some of their values are at odds (for example, the market may teach competition and the family may teach love and sharing), such differences are finely balanced to create well-rounded social subjects. Yet, also, functionalists point out that different institutions bend to accommodate the needs of other social realms. Families help the market work and the market order helps families function. For example, children are imbued with values which prepare them for work in the capitalist marketplace. Parents teach children about the importance of hard work, of following justified orders, of financial responsibility, of the need to respect money. Similarly, market institutions acknowledge that workers will need certain time off to raise children or look after ailing relatives. For functionalists, while social institutions exist in harmony, this balance can easily be disturbed. Revolutionary political projects, and indeed most reformist ones, are to be avoided as the delicate balances at work risk being disturbed. From a functionalist perspective, we also do not fully understand the precise manner in which social institutions balance against each other. As such, we have a high degree of ignorance about what prevents society from descending into chaos. As such, making substantial changes would be foolish and dangerous.

This question of integration is a central concern across functionalist sociology. Durkheim argued that social institutions are beautifully positioned to provide the right amount of integration. For example, the education system is honed to enable students to discover more about themselves and to appreciate individuality, without recklessly disregarding all social conventions and rules. Yet, excessive integration can become pathological, it can prevent social progress and can cause needless suffering. Imagine a society where everyone felt they needed to wear exactly the same clothes, or could only listen to exactly the same genre of music, for example. Equally, where a society fails to sufficiently integrate people it leads to anomie, and to the potential risks of riots and chaos.

The functionalist perspective which emerges from Durkheim's work underscores both the delicate balance which exists between institutions, but also the finely honed integrative-individuating dynamics each institution enables. Functionalists therefore look at their social world and think 'it works!' and are very concerned about people who plan to make big, sudden changes. The delicate balance at work in the social world is a matter of wonder for functionalist sociologists, something to be fastidiously understood and politically defended. As we discuss below, the functionalist perspective is laced with contradictions and has been mobilised by deeply reactionary political agendas. My sympathetic presentation of functionalism in this section is not to suggest that the approach is itself either value-neutral or coherent. Rather, throughout this whole book I am keen to offer sympathetic presentations of all ideas, before subjecting them all to a critical interrogation.

Positivism

'Positivism' is the belief that research should focus solely on observable phenomena that can be scientifically analysed. This approach dismisses claims about subjective experiences or abstract concepts like 'ideology' and 'norms', or metaphysical assertions, as mere speculation, which

Émile Durkheim

should not count as true knowledge. Only observable, repeatable, and preferably calculable insights are to be given credence as legitimate sources of knowledge. Curiously, just as with Durkheim's association with functionalism, his actual personal stance on positivism has sparked debate. Nevertheless, his *Rules on the Sociological Method* has been repeatedly turned to in efforts to construct a positivistic approach to social science. In this work the fundamental tenets of a positivistic social science are unmistakably present. Yet, as hinted at above, Durkheim seems to move outside this frame of reference in his engagement with ideas such as the individual's subjective experience of 'anomie', which is not easily amenable to positivistic study. This reflects the challenges and limitations of seeking to explore society from a purely positivistic approach. In Chapter 4 we will discuss how Max Weber's interpretivist sociology, based on his concept of *verstehen*, provides an important counterpoint to Durkheim's positivism. Now, though, we discuss the defining features of a positivistic sociology, many of which directly stem from concepts and aspirations that Durkheim outlined in his *Rules of Sociological Method*.

Just as Durkheim wrote about 'social facts' as the legitimate area of study for sociologists, subsequent positivistic social scientists have focused their research on observable, objective social phenomena. Those adopting a positivistic approach to studying society typically seek to observe and measure things such as social interactions and group dynamics and how this impacts on various outcomes. For example, they may also look at the types of social exchanges present in various institutions, such as universities, or government departments, and seek to establish causal links between behaviour patterns and various outputs. This concern with causality is a key factor for positivistic sociology. In their attempt to investigate causality, positivistic sociologists use a variety of empirical methods, such as statistical analysis, controlled comparisons, or experimental studies. These are all approaches with resonances with the natural sciences. There is no space allocated to philosophical deduction or speculation within positivistic methods. Rather, positivism is all about systematic, rigorous observation, with an anchor in carefully recorded data. In keeping with Durkheim's work, positivistic sociology thus seeks to explore observable social phenomena, using methods common to the natural sciences, seeking to demonstrate clear observable patterns, causal links, and trends.

Another key feature of positivistic sociology which draws upon Durkheim's *Rules of the Sociological Method* is its aspiration to objectivity, or of being unbiased. This is presented as the ideal way to study society; the researcher should not allow their politics to shape their work. However, like the best approaches to positivistic research today,

Durkheim advocated for a form of reflexive empirical research, acknowledging that our values will always penetrate our research agenda. This is a nuanced position to adopt. To help, Durkheim distinguishes between 'facts' and 'values'. Our values can, and almost certainly will, guide our research questions. For example, why would we research things we don't care about? Yet, the sociologist's prime commitment should always be to objectively report the facts as they observe them on whatever topic they choose to engage. In essence, Durkheim says we need to aim to be neutral, but it will be difficult. To this end, Durkheim thought that the best thing to do was to ask sociologists to honestly disclose their values and beliefs, as this helps maintain transparency within the research process. Today, it is common across empirical research, positivistic or interpretivist, to see statements of a researcher's positionality and reflexivity.

Durkheim is different here to Marx. As we saw in Chapter 2, Marx was explicitly seeking to change the world through his research and made no pretension to value neutrality. It was not something to aspire to for Marx, it is neither possible nor desirable: the world needed to be changed for the better, this was why he conducted his research. As he famously declared, 'the philosophers have only interpreted the world, the point, however is to change it!'. As such, Marx's work famously included *The Communist Manifesto*, one of the world's most famous political statements. In contrast, Durkheim thought that the best form of sociological research is that which aims to be politically independent, to aim for neutrality. While such objectivity is never perfectly attainable, for Durkheim it remains aspirational. This is the view common to most positivist social researchers today.

In summary, Durkheim's work provided the foundations for positivist social science, with a commitment to empirical observation, the exploration of causal linkages, and a commitment to scientific rigour and data analysis. While Durkheim's own work sometimes strayed from these aspirations, the rules he outlined in *Rules of the Sociological Method* were highly influential in shaping generations of positivist sociologists to come. When one reflects on the subsequent generations of both functionalist and positivist social research, Durkheim's twin legacies, it is undeniable that he was one of the most impactful figures in the history of social theory.

Problems with Using Durkheim's Work Today

In this section we echo the many critical social theorists who have argued that functionalist and positivistic approaches should be avoided. We discuss how both approaches are weak intellectually, and may even work to naturalise deeply problematic social structures, such as patriarchy, racism, anthropocentrism, and neoliberalism. As we discuss below, many feminists, such as Dorothy Smith (1926–2022), have argued that to view the social world and think 'wow, it works!' is a response which will most likely emerge from someone enjoying a position of privilege. It is a response from someone who has only experienced the benefits of the status quo. To see society 'functioning', rather than to be overcome by its agonising exploitation, you have to be less attuned to the realities of the most vulnerable. Indeed, when you reflect on the knowledge that the climate is approaching a catastrophic tipping point, the idea that society 'functions' at all seems increasingly absurd. As we discuss, various Marxists have also criticised functionalism for failing to afford sufficient centrality to conflict and injustice. Critical Theorists such as Theodor W. Adorno (1903–69) and Herbert Marcuse (1898–1979) have also shown how these problems are further compounded by positivism, which fails to acknowledge how power serves to impact on not merely our conscious values but crucially the implicit tools we turn to, the words, concepts, and forms of thought we use, as we research the social world. If Critical Theorists are right, the combination of positivism and functionalism is particularly problematic. This is because a positivistic methodology serves to prevent functionalists from realising the limitations embedded within their own thought processes as they cannot be easily explored through 'objective' scientific methods. A more philosophical and interpretivist approach is needed, which positivists are principally opposed to. As such, positivists are unable to see how they are manifesting the norms of their society within their own research. This may indeed serve to normalise and naturalise the logics of exclusion and exploitation within society, which functionalism is already comparatively prone to underplay.

Functionalism Normalises Conflict and Exploitation

Feminist scholars, such as Dorothy Smith, have drawn attention to the way in which functionalism, and associated sociological traditions, reflect the experiences and voices of those in positions of power. Sociology was, for a very long time, overwhelmingly the province of rich, white, able-bodied men. Smith's *standpoint theory*, which we discuss in detail in Chapter 9, can therefore be used to provide a powerful critique of functionalism, as a way of studying society which largely echoes the viewpoints of these privileged sociologists. For Smith, it is obvious that the experiences we have had shape our responses to the social world. If sociologists are largely rich, white, able-bodied, heterosexual men, their approach to studying society will be truly limited, as there will be crucial social concerns which they will not even consider. As such, drawing upon Smith, we can return to the question: 'who looks at today's society and sees it functioning well, as a delicately balanced, healthy organism?' and (with a certain degree of oversimplification) receive the answer: 'a rich, powerful, white, able-bodied, straight man'. That is because it is far easier for such people to be ignorant of the exploitative and conflictual nature of society, since they do not see it or experience it as profoundly. Society functions just fine for rich, white, able-bodied, American functionalist sociologists.

Yet, as Smith draws out, when you turn to look at the social world through the eyes of 'multiply marginalised' subjects such as single mothers struggling to feed their families, the world won't look anywhere near as finely balanced, or as 'functional'. As such, the fundamental concerns of functionalism, of understanding and sustaining societal balance, equilibria, and harmony, emerge as the experiences and interests of the most privileged part of global society. The relative lack of concern with extreme inequality, of suffering, of exploitation, within functionalism, and not seeing the need for urgent radical political change, can be understood, following Smith, as being tied to the restrictions of the sociologist's own standpoint. The solution is to view society through a different pair of eyes, from a different position. When you begin to view the world through the eyes of a starving child, forced to relocate out of a warzone caused by global warming drying up your water source ... suddenly understanding and maintaining beautifully balanced 'social functioning' won't seem to be your main priority.

Such ideas overlap with earlier criticisms of functionalism levelled by Marxists. For example, where functionalists speak of the integrative harmony brought about by balanced institutions, Louis Althusser (1918–90) spoke instead of these institutions functioning as part of an 'Ideological State Apparatus'. This is the distinction: where functionalists speak of 'harmony', Marxists, like Althusser, speak of 'ideology'. For Durkheim, and subsequent functionalists, the challenge was to see how society maintains its delicate peace and its careful balance; both were viewed as wonderous and worthy of defending. But for Althusser, this social stability was not something to treasure. Such stability existed because capitalist ideology served to blind people to the reality of their brutal exploitation, and to teach them, without justification, that no alternative existed. As such, in contrast to the functionalists' passion for seeing delicate balances within and between social institutions, maintaining social harmony, Althusser spoke of ideological control: of the key social institutions serving to *indoctrinate* people into being willing slaves of exploitation under capitalism. This idea is common among Marxist critiques of capitalist societies; when they are comparatively stable and not in revolt, this should not be understood as the inevitable result of beautifully balanced interests keeping people happy. Rather, as Ralph Miliband wrote in *The State in Capitalist Society* (1969), the role of the state, and of any project which seeks balance and peaceful continuance of capitalist society, is to enable the continuation of efficient, smooth *exploitation*. Here we see a crucial blind spot of functionalism: its lack of a central concern with exploitation and conflict. When you focus on the fundamentally exploitative and unsustainable nature of the capitalist system, its smooth and peaceful functioning is not something to aspire to. Functionalists have therefore been criticised for being overly interested in harmony, of balance, of equilibrium. Instead, as Ralf Dahrendorf (1929–2009) argued in *Class and Class Conflict in Industrial Society* [1957], the social world must be viewed as a site of continual conflict and exploitation. Only from such a perspective can social research truly understand how and why people are acting as they do.

In summary, the functionalist perspective moves the focus away from looking at social conflict. This is bad enough; in a world of such brutal exploitation and inequality, surely this needs to be at the forefront of our sociological research agenda. But, even worse, functionalism obscures the role of key institutions in *normalising* these logics of exploitation. Further, the functionalist approach finds undue value in social cohesion and harmony, both of which, when approached through a Marxist lens, are seen as ideological supports to maintain ruthless exploitation. Whether it is good for a system to function smoothly is not sufficiently asked. Do we want a system to function smoothly that is based on the constant unjust exploitation of certain bodies and minds? Do we want a system to run smoothy which, as ecological critics of functionalism point out, is destroying the conditions for life on Earth? Do we want a system to be running smoothly when people are simply not living happy, unalienated lives, and are tricked into believing this is as good as it could be? As Smith's standpoint theory suggests, these questions are less likely to be asked by those for whom the system is creating a comparative life of privilege: they have less reason to ask these questions.

Positivism: Blind to Rationality and Depth-Psychology

The problems with adopting a functionalist approach to social research were always quite evident. We can see the tragic effects of global warming around us. It is a world of such needless suffering. As such, adopting an approach which admires stability and which downplays conflict and exploitation was always going to be a problem. Yet, how can preferring an approach to social research which prioritises observation, statistical analysis, and scientific rigour be bad for society? Yet Critical Theorists, such as Adorno and Marcuse, who we discuss in depth in Chapter 6, have written passionately about the *political* dangers of positivistic methodologies, not merely for producing poor quality research but for obscuring social injustices and irrationalities.

Durkheim's method calls for sociologists to only focus on what can be observed and to distance their own opinions or beliefs from their research. Sociology should be about the objective analysis of social facts. Because it is never possible to fully ignore one's values, Durkheim argued that sociologists should admit to their feelings, thoughts, values at the start of their research, so that any potential bias can be offset; the reader can take the researcher's biases into consideration. Yet, as Frankfurt School scholars have argued, this is simply not how our thought processes work. It is not simply the case that there are 'values' and 'facts' as Durkheim said. It is much more complex. For Durkheim, we can try and stop our 'values' impacting on our engagement with the 'facts', and do our best to be objective. In contrast, Frankfurt School theorists combined the work of Hegel and Marx and demonstrated that the way we think, the forms of reasoning we use to make sense of our world, is deeply connected to the dominant forms of social power. People who are born and raised within a racist, capitalist, patriarchal society will inevitably adopt a form of reason which betrays the striations of such a social world. It is therefore impossible to be objective or neutral. Such an appeal to objectivity is simply futile, and its attempt is problematic. It is the *way* we think, the form of *rationality* we use when researching the social world that needs to be investigated.

This may sound a little whacky. How can capitalism, for example, shape the very way in which we think? It is easier to see how a capitalist world could make us want certain things, such as money, or possessions; but the idea that capitalism shapes the very form our thought processes take is much more complicated to grasp and is even a little scary. Yet, this is exactly the claim put forward in the classic texts of the Frankfurt School, such as Adorno and Horkheimer's *Dialectic of Enlightenment*, or Marcuse's *One Dimensional Man*. The early Frankfurt School explored how capitalism makes us try to experience and rationalise everything in terms of numbers, and place our world into rational-efficient logics. Our way of viewing the world and way of reasoning has been reshaped so as to see a world of static objects to be organised and reshaped to enable goals to be achieved. These forms of thought have been fundamentally normalised and the social researcher cannot simply place them to one side when they go about their work. We have had our consciousnesses penetrated by capitalist, racist, and patriarchal logics.

As such, all social research betrays the dominant power structures at work within society.

This is a fatal problem for positivism. If your entire philosophy to research is that you are only focusing on what can be scientifically observed, how do you deal with the problem that your subjective thought processes, which are invisible and inaccessible, can themselves have been corrupted? Positivists are left unable to even study the problem which impacts on their attempt to research the social world, let alone to offset it.

A further challenge for positivistic approaches is that they are unable to access the depth-psychology of social actors. This refers to the forms of desire and anxieties that are held in the subconscious which are a direct result of social experiences. This critique of positivism, which the Frankfurt School also made, draws upon the work of the founder of psychoanalysis, Sigmund Freud (1856–1939). The social world not merely shapes how we think, the forms of reason we use, the manner in which we experience our world, but it also impacts on our sense of desire. Capitalism and patriarchy teach us what to want. We desire our sexual partners to look and to dress a certain way, we desire a certain form of status or prestige; and if we don't achieve these goals, it can do fundamental damage to our ego. The depth-psychology of subjects, their deep subconscious responses to social experiences, has been shown by countless studies to offer crucial explanations for everything from the rise of fascism (Adorno and Fromm) to the rise of eating disorders (Hilde Bruch). Positivism is simply unable to access this entire site of human social activity: our drives and our anxieties cannot be accessed through positivistic methods.

This is a fundamental challenge to exploring Durkheim's key passions: social stability and social functioning. As discussed above, for many Marxists, social institutions serve to instil an ideological way of viewing the world into social actors. This is crucially how stability is maintained, despite the irrational and exploitative nature of modern societies. Ideology is therefore a crucial part of the modern world to try to understand. Yet, without recourse to depth-psychology or social epistemology, positivists are simply unable to explore these areas.

As such, positivistic methods for conducting social research serve to ignore the fundamental ways in which research is shaped by social structures. This leads to social research which maintains the shape, form, and interests of the existing social world. This is politically highly problematic: any attempt to explain racism, for instance, through a strictly positivist methodology, will inevitably fail, as it cannot capture the way 'racism' is encoded in thought processes, forms of reasoning, and ideology. They are invisible to positivistic methods. As such, positivism needs to be considered a limited, and potentially dangerous, way of exploring the social order, which will produce analyses and invite policy responses which are unsophisticated and likely to be ineffective, as they will fail to connect with the more complex nature of human experience and the impact of constitutive power on the subject.

How Do Durkheim's Ideas Impact on Social Theory Today?

The most famous reworking of Durkheim's ideas is the 'structural functionalist' approach developed by American sociologist Talcott Parsons (1902–79). Like Durkheim, Parsons wanted to explore how different social institutions worked together to maintain social cohesion. Parsons extended Durkheim's work, providing a systems perspective, looking at how different social structures were interconnected and interdependent. His book *The Social System* [1951] provides the most famous overview of his structural functionalism, and his approach achieved real popularity in the 1950s, especially in the USA. Yet, over time, structural functionalism, and functionalism in general, has become comparatively less popular. This is partly due to the various criticisms we identify above being taken seriously across the academy. Today, Durkheim's main impact on contemporary social theory is in providing insights on social integration as part of broader social theories. We can see Durkheim's concepts clearly living on in this regard in the work of Anthony Giddens. This is not to say that he is explicitly 'Durkheimian'. Rather, we can continue to see Durkheim's insights at work within his approach.

Anthony Giddens: Structuration Theory

One of the fundamental challenges which has run throughout social theory is to try to understand the balance which exists between structure and agency on shaping people's behaviour. In this context, 'structure' refers to how social institutions shape the behaviours, thought processes, and tastes of social actors. In contrast, 'agency' refers to the capacity for independent, volitionary behaviours, which are not merely reflex responses to social conditioning. Anthony Giddens' 'structuration theory' offers a new approach to this question, seeking to provide a balance between structure and agency. For Giddens there is a 'duality of structure'; it doesn't make sense to think of structure and agency as being fundamentally different and disconnected. Rather, structure and agency are in constant interplay; people's agential choices serve to reinforce structures, while structures shape the choices people make. While Giddens' structuration theory does not provide an unmediated application of Durkheim's concepts, he offers an extension and combination of many of the key themes which Durkheim's work introduces.

For example, one of the key concepts Giddens creates is that of 'modalities'. This is used by Giddens in *The Constitution of Society* [1984] to refer to the taken-for-granted norms, values, and assumptions which permeate society. These modalities are crucial for the structuring of society; people need to have these shared values for society to coalesce and operate within particular dynamics. Without them, integration would be impossible. This clearly reflects Durkheim's concept of the collective consciousness and its importance for social functionality. As we discussed above, collective consciousness guides social behaviour and enables communication and exchange. Yet, Giddens does not simply take Durkheim's ideas and give them a different name. Rather, his concept of modalities, while having clear echoes of Durkheim's work, is developed in a way which reflects contemporary sociology's increased concern for allowing space for individual agency. There is more space in Giddens' concept for a dynamic interplay between society-wide values and norms and individual choices and behaviours. This again reflects Giddens' investment in finding a balance between structure and agency. Hence, we can see central ideas and insights from Durkheim being updated and brought forward in the new social theoretical climate.

Conclusion

Durkheim is a confusing and frustrating figure. While he is associated with functionalism and with positivism, his relationship to both is complicated. Many of the criticisms of functionalism point to its conservative tendencies, its underappreciation of social conflict, and its overinvestment in social stability. Yet, Durkheim had many socially liberal tendencies; he was certainly not a straightforward conservative. Indeed, all of his political and theoretical views were nuanced, if perhaps at times somewhat contradictory. His commitment to a positivistic approach was certainly not seen as conservative at the time; rather, he was invested in developing a scientific and empirical method for understanding society, rather than relying on established traditions or dominant beliefs. Similarly, his study on suicide was a groundbreaking work, suggesting that mental ill-health was not merely a personal pathology, or mark of deviance and poor character, but was deeply connected to social processes.

When we return to classical thinkers, we are confronted with both the confusing mess of their own lives and works as well as the legacies which they leave. Untangling both from their mainstream receptions is a complicated task and is not one we have attempted with much granularity here. Rather, in this chapter we discussed how Durkheim's concepts enabled an examination of the social world which was anchored in an interest of social stability and the roles of institutions in maintaining a purportedly stable and harmonious society. We also drew out how his *Rules of Sociological Method* and his commitment to the analysis of social facts provided a mission statement for positivistic approaches to come. While today functionalism is far less central to the sociological tradition than it was just a few decades ago, positivism remains a central feature of much social science. As we have discussed in this chapter, positivism can serve to reinforce dominant values and norms, even when researchers are unaware of them and may be actively seeking to overcome them. A critical overview of Durkheim, assessing his relevance and impact today, needs to reflect on the challenges of engaging with positivistic methods. As Chapter 4 on Weber shows, an alternative interpretivist tradition may have much more to offer.

Discussion Questions

1   What are the key differences between Marx's and Durkheim's social theory?

2   Does functionalism seek a more just and more rational social world?

3   Is there a contradiction between Durkheim's work on anomie and his commitment to a scientific sociology?

4   What are some of the limitations of the positivistic approach to social research with which Durkheim is associated?

5   How does Durkheim's aspiration to an 'objective' science of society compare with Marx's claim that the 'philosophers have only interpreted the world, the point is to change it!'

Further Reading

Primary Texts

The Division of Labour in Society [1893]

Includes a discussion of the two different kinds of solidarity: organic and mechanical, associated in turn with modern and traditional societies.

The Rules of Sociological Method [1895]

This is where Durkheim most clearly presents his preference for a 'scientific' approach to social research which calls for an objective focus on 'social facts'.

Suicide: A Study in Sociology [1897]

Groundbreaking study which approaches suicide as a social problem rather than an amalgam of various individual pathologies. Demonstrates both Durkheim's empirical method and also the use of his concept 'anomie'.

Elementary Forms of the Religious Life [1912]

Explores religion as a social institution. Durkheim's argument is that religion serves a crucial social function, binding people together, serving to reinforce the norms within society.

Moral Education: A Study in the Theory and Application of the Sociology of Education [1925]

Focuses on the role of education in reinforcing social norms. This became a concern for Durkheim which moved beyond academic study; he actively campaigned for moral public education.

Secondary Texts

Jeffrey C. Alexander and Philip Smith, Eds., *The Cambridge Companion to Durkheim* [2005]

One of the few anthologies focusing solely on Durkheim. Includes an important contribution from Zygmunt Bauman, 'Durkheim's Society Revisited'. For more advanced readers.

Steve Fenton, *Durkheim and Modern Sociology* [2009]

A more accessible and much shorter text, compared to the books by Lukes or Fournier (below). Fenton's focus is more on showing Durkheim's continuing relevance for contemporary sociological topics.

Marcel Fournier, *Émile Durkheim: A Biography* [2012]

Another massive text on Durkheim. Exceptionally detailed. The focus is more on his biography than his ideas compared to Lukes' book. More suited for postgraduate students and students seeking to complete an undergraduate dissertation focusing substantially on Durkheim.

Robert Alun Jones, *Émile Durkheim: An Introduction to Four Major Works* [1986]

Focuses on the substantive content and the socio-historical context and impact of four of Durkheim's key works: *The Division of Labour in Society, The Rules of the Sociological Method, The Elementary Forms of Religious Life*, and *Suicide*.

Stephen Lukes, *Émile Durkheim: His Life and Work a Historical and Critical Study* [1973]

A massive text, incredibly detailed, engaging in great depth with Durkheim's thought.

Talcott Parsons, *The Social System* [1951]

Explores social functioning and stability and has become associated with 'structural functionalism'. Demonstrates how Durkheim's ideas resonated in later texts. For more advanced readers.

W. S. F. Pickering, Geoffrey Walford, Eds., *Durkheim's Suicide: A Century of Research and Debate* [2000]

Focuses on Durkheim's famous study of suicide and its impact on subsequent sociology. Accessibly written, suitable for undergraduate students wishing to explore this work in more detail.

Max Weber: Meaningful Social Action

Contents

DOI: 10.4324/9781003359555-4

Max Weber teaches us that to truly understand society we need to consider its *subjective* dimension. Social research needs to capture the meanings people give to their lives and behaviours, and we need to consider people's hopes and feelings as part of any analysis of how and why society works. A whole tradition of sociology emerged based on this insight, called *interpretivist sociology*. Interpretivists argue that social theory must be sensitive to actors' internal worlds, to their subjective lives, or our social research will be forever limited, offering only partial, unfulfilling explanations. This is in direct challenge to the *positivistic* approach discussed in Chapter 3. Remember that for Durkheim 'social science' should focus on observable and measurable phenomena. A positivist approach to sociology takes social institutions and places them under a microscope: observing patterns, movements, looking for causal relationships. Positivistic researchers might run particular experiments, changing variables, looking at different outcomes, looking at observable human behaviour. As we discuss in this chapter, Weber's work teaches us that the problem with adapting such a natural science approach to studying society is that this risks treating people like dead atoms, like parts of a chemistry experiment. People just aren't like that! If you put Hydrogen atoms and Oxygen atoms together, in certain conditions, a chemist can work out what will happen with absolute certainty. A Hydrogen atom will never *decide* it won't bond today because it doesn't feel like it; because it is against its religion, or it just 'isn't ready for that kind of commitment'! Humans, in contrast, have so much going on in their heads; society is messy and contingent. Weber's social theory reminds us that there is such subjective richness to social life and that if you cannot access the stories, meanings, and feelings which drive social action, you cannot hope to fully understand society.

As we shall see in this chapter, Weber's interpretivist sociology gives us concepts that help us do just that: to centre how meanings shape how people act within, and constantly reproduce, their social worlds.

While in the natural sciences, universal equations can be written and diagrams can be sketched with total confidence, Weber argued that with social science we require a different, 'softer' approach. We cannot aim for such certainty or consistency from social actors, or from our social research. People behave in different ways at different times, for complicated reasons. As we shall see, for Weber, the sociologist needs to try to sympathetically interpret the reason why people do things, mindful that such conjecture is always partial and limited. He was also aware that each situation is unique and that if we want to make any wide-ranging claims we need to work with representative abstractions, which he called 'ideal types'. As such, Weber's approach to studying society was built around exploring *meaningful social action* with a sensitivity to the benefits and limitations of working from abstractions.

Weber's work was very much shaped by his early experiences. He was born in Erfurt, Prussia in 1864 to a devoutly Protestant mother, Helene, and a politically ambitious father, also called Max. Our sociologist, Max Jr., had an unhappy childhood, marked by constant battles between his parents, many of which were rooted in their differing approaches to faith and religion. Weber's mother was a staunch Calvinist, while his father was far less devout. The impacts this had on their respective approaches to life, and the passion with which they held to their respective positions, was to filter through into Weber's later writings on religion and society. As well as sparking insightful sociological research, the religious conflict he experienced within his family was to also impact on his mental health, which was to be a lifelong torment. Escaping the arguments between his parents, the young Max found role-models in his wider family, and spent much time with his intellectual father figure, his uncle, Hermann Baumgarten. It is worth noting that Max Weber was not the only noted academic to emerge from the family; his brother, Alfred Weber (1868–1958), was also to become an influential economist and sociologist in his own right.

Like many young academics today, Weber struggled to pay the bills. He started working both as a lawyer's assistant and in a lowly university post. This exposed him to stifling bureaucratic procedures, a theme which would also emerge in his later writing. Through remarkable self-discipline, a supportive, intelligent wife (Marianne Schnitger (1870–1954), who would go on to become a pioneering sociologist herself), and a strict writing regime, Max Weber enjoyed an exceptional career trajectory. His Ph.D. was on farming communities in ancient Rome and early trading societies; ideas which he returned to in a famous speech in Freiburg (the 'Freiburg Address'). While Max Weber Sr. represented the pro-Bismarck National Liberal Party, the young Max was highly critical of the German aristocratic Junker class. His Freiburg Address drew upon his wealth of knowledge on past agrarian societies to point to the inefficiency of the ruling Junker elite. Yet, Weber's possibility of entering politics more permanently was hampered by his poor mental health. He spent the years 1890 to 1903 avoiding public speaking, and he even resigned his professorship.

When his health returned, his research blossomed, with the ideas which would make his legacy pouring out. Most famous is his *The Protestant Work Ethic* [1904]. Here, Weber presented a comparative historical sociology, seeking to explain why capitalism emerged where and when it did. In this famous founding work of sociology, Weber linked an analysis of why people behaved the way they did with religious-cultural patterns. His next project was to focus on different forms of authority within society, which occupied him for many years. Ultimately, these writings were combined and published posthumously as *Economy and Society* [1922]. This work united Weber's insights on social action, bureaucracy, religion and economics, and the different foundations for authority. Weber's final years saw him consciously striving to raise the profile of sociology as a subject, distinct from philosophy and economics. He believed that sociology should be defined by analytical rigor and comparative analysis. Outside of academia, Weber's last years were marked by his shifting attitudes to the First World War. Initially he supported German involvement, even signing the infamous 'Manifesto of the 93' (a statement of support for the war by prominent German thinkers). Yet, by 1916, he had changed his mind, and was arguing against any involvement in a war of expansion. Following Germany's defeat he contributed to the drafting of the new Weimar condition. He died in 1920, almost certainly as a result of the 'Spanish flu'.

Key Concepts

Weber made important contributions across many areas of sociology. As a result, his concepts will crop up across different fields in your wider readings and may seem unconnected. However, his concepts were all developed in the process of his central research project: to explore society with a focus on the meanings and thoughts in the minds of social actors; and to draw upon people's internal worlds to provide a more well-rounded form of social research. As a result, some of Weber's key conceptual contributions speak to types of authority, rationalisation, and disenchantment; themes that are deeply societal but always individually experienced and impalpable. To explore such themes he developed 'ideal types', which enabled him to make comparative statements across space and time. For Weber, comparative rigor was a primary virtue for all sociologists to aspire

Max Weber

to, yet his commitment to precision never led to a certainty of the ideas he presented. His work pointed consistently to the need for *interpretation* and of the need for sensitivity to multiple meanings.

Verstehen

Key to Weber's approach to studying society is the concept of *Verstehen*. This can be translated as 'interpretive understanding' and became a cornerstone of the interpretivist tradition. *Verstehen* analyses sit in direct opposition to the positivistic perspective to studying society described in Chapter 3. A *Verstehen* approach points to the need to consider the subjective position of each social actor as a crucial part of trying to work out how social institutions develop and perpetuate. Such a perspective calls for sociologists to work to understand the meanings, feelings, and significance actors place on their social conduct. From such a viewpoint the sociologist is not a natural scientist contemplating abstract mechanical rules, mapping human behaviours through simulations and charts. Rather, there is a greater concern with the inner worlds of social subjects. For Weber, it is through *Verstehen* that sociologists can access the true beauty and complexity of social life; they can move beyond mere description of society as a world of interacting particles, and explore the deeper levels of sociality. For Weber, the aim for the sociologist is to grasp the subjective meanings of action.

Such an approach requires sociologists to familiarise themselves with the context in which their research is taking place, to engage with the cultural practices of the society, including its traditions, values, religious beliefs, and economic practices. A *Verstehen* approach necessitates a great deal of sensitivity from the sociologist, who will need to work hard to locate their analysis within the socio-cultural context. Crucially, Weber said that this requires the sociologist to distance their own ideas, values, politics, and prejudices from their research. Weber's view is that it will be very hard to contemplate the subjective state of other social actors if you approach their world full of your own biases. In essence, Weber's argument is that to study the subjective worlds of social actors, the sociologist needs to attempt, as best they can, to approach a form of objectivity with their own research.

The *Verstehen* approach is not only important to the interpretivist tradition within sociology but is central to qualitative methodologies across social research. As Weber framed it, seeking to demonstrate the fundamental centrality of meaning to social action, the challenge for the social scientist 'is to explain those events and sequences of events within a society that are produced by the actions of individuals, and particularly those individual actions which themselves can be understood only as results of an interplay of meaning'.

Ideal Types

The concept of 'ideal types' is equally important to Weber's approach to studying society. Recall that for Weber, methodological excellence in sociology takes the form of rigorous comparative analysis. But how can you compare multiple different societies or institutions? Surely every society is fundamentally different and every person views their own world differently. As such, how can one compare? Surely this is even harder when you adopt a more interpretivist approach, where you are interested in exploring the subjective states of social actors. This is where the notion of the 'ideal type' comes into play; it helps make such richness and complexity amenable to comparative sociological research.

As Weber wrote in *The Methodology of the Social Sciences* [1922], ideal types make particular, concrete phenomena understandable by presenting them as particular manifestations of a more general concept. Put in other words: to help enable comparisons, each occurrence of some social event can be understood as one particular incidence of a broader set of 'ideal-typical' social phenomena. For example, when we talk about 'capitalist societies', as social theorists, what we think of is an 'ideal-typical' capitalist society: an abstraction based on accentuating the core features we associate with all capitalist societies. For example, the UK in 2023 is one empirical reality of a capitalist society. Yet, when we want to research 'capitalist societies', and to explore how people think and feel as they do within them, we reflect more on these 'ideal types' rather than on a particular historical instantiation. For Weber, it is the ability to engage with societies at this level of abstraction that is so essential to good sociological research.

Weber writes about 'ideal types' across several texts. In *The Methodology of the Social Sciences* [1949] he states:

> An ideal type is formed by the one-sided accentuation of one or more points of view and by the synthesis of a great many diffuse, discrete, more or less present and occasionally absent concrete individual phenomena, which are arranged according to those one-sidedly emphasized viewpoints into an unified analytical construct.

What he means is that when we build our ideal types, we look at a wide variety of different examples and work out the most common and most important features across the whole sample set. There will, inevitably, be variation within the empirical manifestations. For example, returning to the case of capitalism, different 'capitalist' societies will have different features, yet we still think of them as capitalist, despite their particularities. For example, Singapore, Sweden, and the USA are all capitalist, but they are all very different in terms of their approach to social welfare or to liberal-democratic values.

Ideal Types of Authority; Ideal Types of Social Action

Weber utilised ideal types in many of his studies. A particularly famous use of ideal types was in his work on different types of authority and social action, which themselves went on to inform generations of subsequent scholarship. Let's discuss his ideal types of authority first. Weber was interested in how authority was established and legitimated in different societies. His studies of authority combined the concepts discussed above, his interest in understanding the subjective mind of social actors (what do people think and why?) with his comparative approach through the use of ideal types (encapsulating abstracted commonalities in the ways in which authority can be held and sustained).

Weber famously wrote about three particular types of authority: traditional, charismatic, and legal-rational. Traditional authority is connected to forms of conservative social behaviour: people follow certain customs and traditions because they always have done. The legitimacy of traditional authority derives from its constancy and its heritage. In keeping with conservative justifications for established institutions, such as respecting the monarchy in the UK, traditional authority derives from a sense of stability and permanence, in contrast to the chaos and impermanence of human emotion and political strife. The authority that will still reside with an uncharismatic, incompetent monarch, on the basis of the monarchy's centuries of tradition, would be a classic example of 'traditional authority' at work.

Charismatic authority, in contrast, derives not from millennia of custom but from the personal attributes of a particular leader. It may be manifest through their chutzpah, panache, strength of personality; through great speeches, or simple demagoguery. Populist or reactionary leaders can hold charismatic authority just as much as liberal, progressive figures. Indeed, possibly the most famous examples of charismatic leadership would be Hitler, or Trump, figures whose authority derives not from tradition or competence, but from their personal manifestation of a particular vision or energy. As with both Trump and Hitler, this charismatic authority is invested within a particular figure, and movements built around such people struggle to survive when the charismatic leader is deposed.

Finally, there is legal-rationality authority. Here, the authority derives from a system, a set of rules, of due practice being followed. This can be the result of an election having been won, or other legal practices upheld. Legal-rational authority also derives from a sense of respect for predictability, reliability, and due process. This links to Weber's further studies on the role of the bureaucracy, which is held as being an ideal type of legal-rational authority.

These types of authority share some commonalities with the four ideal types of 'Social Action' which Weber outlines in *Economy and Society*. Recall that for Weber the task of the sociologist, through *Verstehen* methods, is to understand the reasons for social action through a sensitivity to the subject's emotional and interpretive frameworks. The four ideal types of social action Weber describes are: instrumental-rational, value-rational, affectual, and traditional. For Weber, instrumental-rational action is fast in the ascendancy, coming to dominate as the primary cause of social action. Modern organisations, bureaucracies, capitalist institutions such as the market, are all held to inculcate instrumental-rational forms of behaviour and to encourage instrumental-rational social action. The space left for value-rational, affectual, and traditional social action is shrinking fast.

The Iron Cage

This idea that instrumental-rationality is colonising the social world is famously presented through Weber's concept of the 'iron cage'. While this phrase is associated with Weber, he did not actually use the phrase directly. Rather, in *The Protestant Ethic and the Spirit of Capitalism* he uses the term '*stahlhartes Gehäuse*', which means 'steel-hard casing'. The passage itself is particularly beautifully written. Weber warns of the total bureaucratisation of the social world, so that all decisions are made solely with recourse to the most efficient, most 'rational' way of living. For Weber this risks an inhuman existence, which he describes as a 'polar night of icy darkness'.

But what does Weber mean by this? Weber is warning of the loss of individual humanity, the destruction of human feeling, which would be displaced by the rise of a desire for certainty, predictability, and reproducibility in modern societies. In practice, this is held to be typified by the rise of bureaucracy, a central concern in Weber's writings. The bureaucracy is the essence of the legal-rational social formation. It is a form of organisation in which the sole objective is standardisation, efficient management, and predictability. With capitalism, and with the form the modern state apparatus takes, we live in a world of standardisation, increased quantification, and the decline of 'qualities'. Bureaucracy increasingly mediates our social relationships. Yet, while bureaucratic processes can be truly efficient, they lack humanity. As you will know, the experience of filling in forms, of engaging with call centre-style 'press 1 for this, press 2 for that' is an alienating, life-destroying experience. For Weber, what makes us human, our capacity for emotion, for individuality and creativity, is at risk of being structurally and systematically eroded by this rise of instrumental rationality. We risk being trapped in the iron cage of bureaucracy, where we are unable to express ourselves in public life beyond the form accepted by the bureaucracy. Our feelings and experiences are reduced to '0–5' on surveys, quantified, standardised, dehumanised.

Disenchantment and the Protestant Work Ethic

This terrifying ascent of instrumental-rational action is a key feature of Weber's understanding of modernity. Crucially, he connects it to modernity more broadly rather than just to capitalism. This distinguishes his approach from most Marxist social theories, which place a centrality on the capitalist system. This does not mean that capitalism is not also important to Weber's work. Indeed, Weber's best-known book, *The Protestant Work Ethic* [1905], offers his analysis of the origins of capitalism. This text unites many of the concepts discussed already: ideal types, *Verstehen* analysis, types of authority, and social action. We also see in this book a sensitivity to religion as a driving force in human action. For Weber, the values embedded within religion can continue to shape societies, even long after secularisation has set in. Throughout *The Protestant Work Ethic*, values which emanate from Calvinism, and which persist in a 'disenchanted' world, are held to be crucial to explaining both the rise of capitalism and the dominance of instrumental-rational action.

Weber's thesis is that the virtuous status attributed to hard work and to thrift, central to Calvinist Protestantism, facilitated the rise of capitalism. A central Calvinist belief is 'predestination': that those who were to be saved by God had already been chosen. Who would attain salvation was not down to human agency, God was solely responsible and had already determined who would enter heaven. In an ironic response to a worldview in which agency seemed less central (as God had already predetermined what fate was in store), people actively sought 'signs' of whether they had been chosen by God, paying attention to how much material wealth they accrued, for example. This 'seeking signs' was not merely a passive search, however; rather, it altered the behaviour of the subjects, who worked with tremendous devotion in the material domain, seeking assurance, in the form of earthly riches, that they had been 'saved'. As such, Calvinist Protestantism created an environment in which the valuation of labour, thrift, and viewing wealth as a sign of goodness flourished.

Over time, this propensity for thrift and hard work led to increased rationalisation and ascetism. People did not 'splash the cash' on luxuries. Instead, they lived disciplined lives and invested their money with extremely methodical care. For Weber, the desire to invest, to expend resources on the basis of seeking a greater financial return through returns on investment, laid the foundations for capitalism to flourish.

As ever in his work, Weber does not state that there is a clear, unequivocal iron law at work between the presence of Protestantism and the rise of capitalism; instead he stresses how it created a fertile environment for it to emerge. This is further supported, through his comparative method, by explaining in other works how the religious systems in China, for example, were less suited to fostering the development of capitalism. While Weber argues that the conditions which suited the rise of capitalism were provided by Calvinism, he does not believe that capitalism requires Calvinism to continue. Rather, capitalism is itself a driving force of secularisation and disenchantment. Yet, crucially, the valorisation of thrift, labour, and the attribution of self-worth relative to financial wealth were retained in the increasingly secular society. As such, in Weber's analysis, Calvinism helped create the conditions for capitalism's birth, which, as an ideal type, is structurally programmed to increase secularisation. Yet, the values which capitalism depends upon continued to impact on social behaviour, as they were retained in the modern era in a secularised form.

We are thus left with the 'disenchantment of the world' in which the religious forces that birthed capitalism have waned, while the instrumental-rational action which capitalism inculcates serves to erode the breadth of human experience. For Weber, that 'polar night of icy darkness' threatens us: a world of inhumanity, technical-rational communication, instrumental action, standardisation, and a total lack of feeling. The subjective features of society, which Weber places as central to his *Verstehen* sociology, risk annihilation.

How Did Weber's Concepts Shape Social Theory?

Weber's work had a profound and lasting impact on social theory and on the social sciences and humanities more broadly. While his influence can be identified by pointing to clear changes in the methodologies researchers use to study the social world, it is more accurate to suggest that his work brought forward an entire 'paradigm shift', reflecting a new mindset for exploring society. Following Weber, interpretivist approaches became a crucial counterpoint to more positivistic approaches and were developed in various ways, which we discuss below. Weber's concepts also spurred particular foci for research, as well as providing methodologies through which such research can be conducted. In particular, his concepts, such as the 'iron cage', 'rationalisation', and 'disenchantment', served to inspire various subsequent traditions to explore the relationship between economic logics and subjectivity.

Interpretivism

Weber's work catalysed the interpretivist tradition across sociology which, a century later, remains central. In this regard, his greatest impact was to offer an entirely different approach to studying society; one which did not turn to the methods of the 'natural sciences'. In contrast to seeking 'social facts' and a scientific certainty, Weber's use of 'ideal types' and his *Verstehen* approach acknowledged the complexity and comparative inaccessibility of much of the social world. New tools were needed, entirely distinct from those offered by the natural sciences. While Durkheim's approach lent towards a quantitative, statistical analysis of society, Weber's approach inspired a more qualitative inquiry, valuing empathetic understanding over quantitative certainty.

It is worth clarifying the difference between the words '*verstehen*' and 'interpretivism' here. While the two words are often used interchangeably, when looked at more precisely, it is clear that they relate to two subtly different things. Interpretivist methods predate Weber and stretch far beyond sociology. For example, there is a branch of philosophy, called hermeneutics, which is all about interpretation. For scholars of hermeneutics, such as Friedrich Schleiermacher (1768–1834), the focus was more on interpreting texts (such as the Bible). However, the importance of interpretation was clear. In contrast, Weber's *verstehen* approach is a particular way of exploring society and focuses on understanding the subjective lives of social actors. A *verstehen* approach will typically lead to qualitative research methods in an attempt to achieve empathetic understanding of the social actor. In contrast, interpretivism strictly refers to a more philosophical, more abstract notion about the complexity of the social world, and the awareness that multiple interpretations of reality exist. *Verstehen* is therefore one way of actively attempting to interpret the social world. It is perhaps helpful to think of it as a subfield (and the dominant subfield) of interpretivist sociology.

Such a *verstehen* approach can be seen as having informed symbolic interactionism, historical sociology, phenomenological sociology, cultural sociology, as well as the entire development of qualitative sociological approaches. Weber's importance cannot be overstated: the idea that we should study society with an empathetic sensitivity to the subjective worlds of social actors has impacted on sociology, social theory, and Critical Theory. This has particular salience for the work of the Frankfurt School, as we discuss below.

Linking Economy, Society, Subjectivity

Weber's work also inspired an entire tradition of sociologists to focus on the relationship between the economic dynamics in society and the subjective experiences of social actors. Weber can here be viewed as spurring an interpretivist sociological study of early Marxian insights. It was, of course, Marx, and not Weber, who argued that our substantive thoughts, and the very ways through which we think, are substantially impacted by our economic conditions. However, Weber's interpretivist sensitivity and his focus on forms of authority and rationality enabled the operationalisation of these insights in sociological study.

One of the most significant studies of how social actors' subjective lives were reshaped by the economic order was offered by the Frankfurt School of Critical Theory. This group of researchers combined various disciplines and insights, learning from philosophy, sociology, and a study of the economy to explore how the inner lives of subjects had been reshaped by the market to enable the survival of capitalism. In particular, Frankfurt School thinkers, such as Theodor Adorno, Max Horkheimer, and Herbert Marcuse, drew upon Weber's work on 'rationalisation' and 'instrumental-rationality' to explore how the advanced technological societies had become homogeneous and opposed to free, human thought. One can read much of the early Frankfurt School's work as arguing that with the ever-greater normalisation and extension of capitalist forces, Weber's 'iron cage' was trapping our minds and suffocating our capacity for critical and non-instrumental social action.

Michel Foucault was another thinker whose work elided disciplines. Like the Frankfurt School theorists before him, Foucault was interested in how subjective experience was shaped by social factors. Yet, unlike the Marxist-inspired Frankfurt School, which was consistently focused on, and opposed to, capitalism, Foucault's relationship with neoliberalism was more complicated. However, through his work, Foucault was sensitive to how the economic systems shaped subjective experiences. In particular, neoliberalism was shown to create social actors whose subjective experiences were marked by self-regulation, instrumental-rational action, a valorisation of their productivity. The process through which these values are normalised are discussed by Foucauldian scholars as the rise of 'neoliberal governmentality'. The neoliberal worker understands their actions through categories and norms which directly support the way of thinking which is built into the modern capitalist economy. The Foucauldian notion of an increasingly totalising neoliberal governmentality has clear resonances with both Weber's interests in the impact of the economy on the subjective experiences of the social actor and also with Weber's idea of the 'iron cage' induced by rationalisation.

In Chapter 6 we discuss the work of French sociologist Pierre Bourdieu. His work is also interested in exploring the subjective stances of social actors and how this is related to their economic position. As we discuss, Bourdieu develops a notion of 'habitus', of internalised dispositions. These are shown to be closely linked to broader socio-economic factors. Bourdieu's sociology follows in Weber's footsteps in that he focuses on how people's internalised dispositions reflect internalisations of class cultural traits and patterns.

As we have discussed, Weber's work informed both the direction which social research took, but also the methods through which social life was studied. The core lessons to take away are that Weber provided a new way of studying society, focusing on the lived experiences of individuals. Many social researchers who followed him drew upon this insight, and paid particular attention to how subjective experiences are shaped by socio-cultural and economic factors, in such a way that enables smooth social reproduction.

What Are the Problems for Social Theorists Engaging with Weber's Work Today?

Marxist social theories have been accused of being Eurocentric, of viewing the world from a limited, Western perspective. As we discussed in Chapter 3, Durkheim's ideas have also been criticised for normalising and justifying various oppressive and exploitative social relationships. We now discuss why Weber, too, must be read critically. However, as I argue throughout this book, the best way to engage with social theory is to learn what has driven the field's development, to understand the core ideas which Weber has given to the tradition, and to be able to read them critically, with a knowledge of their limitations, as well as learning the importance of his contribution. Over the past five years, one central question has hovered over Weber's life and work, and which we now turn to head-on.

Was Weber Racist?

The question of Weber's racism has been discussed a lot more in recent years, after Weber's writings on Eastern European societies were rediscovered. It is worth stating that nobody is suggesting that Weber was a 'biological racist' in the manner of some of his contemporaries. Actually, Weber had a public disagreement about 'scientific racism' with the eugenicist Alfred Ploetz (1860–1940). Unlike the eugenicists, Weber did not believe there was an explicit biological hierarchy of races rooted in genetics or biological laws. Yet, Weber's work does undeniably reinforce various racist traits, essentialises various groups of people, and makes explicitly derogatory comments about various 'racial' communities.

In particular, recent rereadings of Weber's work have shown how he held Polish people to be in need of 'civilising' and he viewed Germany as capable of leading such a 'civilising mission'. In one text he wrote that 'a few dozen villages with a dozen German farms in each will eventually *Germanize* many square miles'. Due to his vision of the 'backward' nature of the Poles, Weber did not want Polish people to be in Germany in great numbers. This was not merely a private prejudice; Weber was involved in various anti-Polish political activities, giving lectures to both students and clergy about the need to solve the so-called 'Polish problem': the issue of the displacement of various Germans by Polish people east of the Elbe. This was not a fringe issue for Weber either; he spoke about it passionately at his inaugural lecture at Freiburg University. Nor is this some freak aberration in Weber's otherwise liberal social theory; rather, Weber held that societies do not work best when they are pluralist, when they are combined of various different socio-cultural groups. This sentiment led him to also write texts criticising the presence of Catholics in Germany, and, after 1911, several texts where he expressed views which would today be read as anti-Semitic.

Other voices have criticised Weber's broader approach for being structurally racist, arguing that Weber is guilty of a Eurocentric bias and a clear Ethnocentrism. There are parallels here with the criticisms of Marx as being Eurocentric in Chapter 2. The criticism is that by placing Western Europe at the centre of the social universe, Weber reproduces racist biases. Such a problematic attitude remains powerful today and needs to be carefully considered when reading Weber's work. Edward Said (1935–2003) discussed how Weber has 'Orientalist' tendencies which are clear in his discussion of non-Western societies. This means that Weber has a tendency to 'exoticise' and 'Other' in a manner which can lead to stereotyping, oversimplification, and dehumanisation. This can subtly feed into racist forms of thought which continue today.

It is always challenging to reflect on the prejudices of past scholars when evaluating their research. Different approaches have been taken by various scholars, and students should be encouraged to come to their own conclusions. My preferred approach in this book is always to

Max Weber

evaluate whether Weber's racist views filtered through into the ideas which informed subsequent social theory, and which continue to impact on our study of the social world today. I offer, but certainly do not 'preach', a nuanced separation of 'theorist' and 'theory'. This is not to suggest that Weber's own views on Polish people, or his reproduction of other racist tenets, is merely incidental to his theory. Rather, our task here is to focus on Weber's concepts and methodology, and to see to what extent they are tainted by, or risk reinforcing, racist or prejudicial values. There is yet to be a definitive answer on this question within the literature, and as social theory grapples with these challenges it is likely to be an important topic of consideration for years to come.

How Do Weber's Ideas Inform Sociology Today?

Weber's concepts have long been combined with those from other thinkers (such as Marx) to help explore the social world. In this section we discuss one substantive study which draws heavily upon Weber's concepts. This is George Ritzer's *The McDonaldization of Society* [1993]. While this was written several years ago now, the concept of 'McDonaldization' itself continues to inform current sociological studies. We then discuss the enduring importance of Weber's concept of 'stratification', which for many political and social scientists is the term they would primarily associate with him.

The McDonaldization Thesis

It has been over a century since Weber warned that the 'Iron Cage' of instrumental rationality was tightening around the social world. The passing of the years, with their rapid technological advancements, has underscored the prescience of Weber's warning. One particular work which draws explicitly upon Weber's analysis of rationalisation and applies it to late capitalism is George Ritzer's *The McDonaldization of Society* [1993]. In this influential book, Ritzer argued that all social interactions and experiences are increasingly taking the form characterised by hyper-rationalised fast-food restaurants. As such, we are all experiencing a flattening of our lived experiences caused by the instrumental-rational standardisation of all social domains.

Ritzer's work is highly critical of prevalent social tendencies. He shows that the key principles which are guiding social development – efficiency, predictability, repeatability, controllability – are producing a stale and lifeless social world. The McDonald's phenomenon, the spread and reach of the fast-food chain, is remarkable in and of itself. Ritzer's point is that such success is due to its embrace of a hyper-rationalisation. Consumers know what their experience will be when they enter a McDonald's, whether it is in Hyderabad or Hemel Hempstead, Honolulu or Hong Kong. You know you can order at a machine from a set range of products with familiar branding, with regional variation only in the form of 'glocalisation'. Yet, crucially, social actors have grown to desire this experience. While the style of consumption which McDonald's provides may not be to everyone's taste, it appeals to hundreds of millions of people across a global network.

What is less appealing to people, however, is when the principles of predictability, efficiency, and standardisation start to colonise other areas of our social lives. This is central to both Weber's prophetic warning of the 'iron cage' and Ritzer's more recent work. It is not just the success of McDonald's which drives Ritzer's analysis. Rather, it is the spread of the hyper-rationalised and standardised model of consumption which McDonald's epitomises to all social domains. It is the *McDonaldization* of society rather than the rise of McDonald's restaurants. We have all experienced being told to 'press one for X', 'press two for Y'. We are used to being asked to give 'customer feedback' with options on a scale of one to ten. We are trained to think in quantifiable measures of success or failure. We have become immune to the standardisation required of us in our jobs; the degree of strict control placed on our behaviours to enable predictability for both our employers and our customers when we work. Ritzer's text serves to show the salience of Weber's concepts and to reinforce his warning of the life-flattening experiences of bureaucratic forms of thought colonising the social world.

Social Stratification

As stressed throughout this chapter, Weber worked to comprehend the subjective worlds of social actors, to grasp and understand the meanings and feelings driving their social behaviour. To help in this regard, one of the concepts he developed was the notion of 'social stratification'. This refers to how society is organised with regard to the differentials of power, status, and wealth which exist between different groups of people. This concept links in with Weber's interest in how hierarchies were maintained and understood by people in society. How does one's place in society impact on how the subject views their social life? How do people experience social hierarchy itself? Weber's interest in understanding social stratification also connects with his broader interests in authority and bureaucracy.

Weber presents a model of social stratification which is more complicated than the classic Marxist division between 'bourgeois' and 'proletariat'. In Weber's model, there are three key things to consider: (1) class, (2) status, and (3) party. By 'class', Weber refers both to the individual's relationship to the means of production (as per Marx) but it also refers to their wealth, their particular income, and the nature of their occupation. By 'status', he refers to the social recognition the individual is awarded, be it in forms of honour and prestige, or their obverse. By 'party', Weber refers to whether the individual is part of an influential group in society, whether they have powerful contacts, or whether they are part of a significant network.

Weber's stratification model was developed by various social scientists. For example, John Goldthorpe (1935–) and Annette Lareau (1952–) both draw upon Weberian approaches to stratification to explore economic inequality. In terms of social theory, it was in the work of the French sociologist Pierre Bourdieu (1930–2002) that the idea of the complex nature of individual social power corresponding to multiple vectors of privilege was most famously developed, through his accounts of different types of 'capital' at play across different social 'fields'.

Conclusion

Weber's status as a 'founding father' of sociology will continue to bring new readers to his texts and new students to his concepts. As we have seen, his desire to understand the subjective worlds of social actors echoes through the concepts and methodological innovations he produced. Alongside Marx and Foucault he sits as the most remarkable revolutionary figure, who offered an entirely new way of engaging with the social world. The entire interpretive tradition of sociology is indebted to Weber's insights. When we think of the social world, we simply take many of Weber's insights for granted. We make ideal types, we care about the subjective worlds of social actors. We focus on how the institutional, and particularly the economic lives of social actors, shape how they view their worlds and understand their social actions. Just as we now accept Marx's materialist inversion of Hegel, and acknowledge that our ideas are shaped by our social world, so, too, do we accept Weber's insights, that good social theory needs to provide space for the subjective world of social actors to be explored. The social world is not a chemistry lab; meaningful social research requires us to transcend, or at the very least enrich, the methods of the natural sciences. Weber teaches us that in order to connect with what is truly unique about the social world we need to be open to uncertainty, interpretation, and to the need to conduct social research with empathy; seeking to understand the subjective worlds of social actors as central to all social conjunctures.

Discussion Questions

1 What are the similarities and differences between Weber's and Marx's social theories?

2 What are the differences between an interpretivist and a positivist approach?

3 Are we living in Weber's 'Iron Cage' today?

4 What is the role of religion in Weber's social theory?

5 What are the strengths and weaknesses of using 'ideal types'?

Further Reading

Primary Texts

Objectivity in Social Science and Social Policy [1904]

This essay discusses the question of 'neutrality' in social research. Weber's view is that researchers should aim to be objective while studying society; they should try to prevent their personal values creeping into their work.

The Protestant Ethic and the Spirit of Capitalism [1905]

One of the most important works in sociology and definitely Weber's most famous book. Weber was interested in why capitalism emerged where and when it did. His argument is that the values which are at the core of a particular form of Protestantism, called Calvinism, provided the foundations for capitalism to thrive.

Science as a Vocation [1917]

This essay emerged from a lecture Weber gave and is short and readable. Weber focuses on the importance of science in modern society. Some of the themes present in *Objectivity in Social Science and Social Policy* are here too, such as the need for objectivity and the difference between 'facts' and 'values'. Weber's position is that scientists should be aware that they have values; they should not try to deny it. Rather, scientists should all reflect on their values and consciously try to limit how this may skew their research.

Politics as a Vocation [1919]

A twin piece to *Science as a Vocation*, both emerging out of lectures, and both similar in style. This essay includes a discussion of many of Weber's core themes, such as bureaucracy, the types of authority, and comparative historical sociology. In terms of his substantive thoughts on politics as a vocation, Weber draws a distinction between two different ethical requirements of politicians: an 'Ethic of Moral Conviction' (unshakeable values) and an 'Ethic of Responsibility' (pragmatic decisions to enable social functioning).

Sociology of Religion [1920]

One of many texts published after Weber died. The focus of this book is on the relationship between religions and economic systems, a common theme throughout Weber's work.

Economy and Society: An Outline of Interpretive Sociology [1922]

After *The Protestant Work Ethic* this is the next most famous work written by Weber. The book is a compilation of his various notes, lectures, and essays. It was put together by his wife, Marianne Weber, after his death. All of his key topics feature here, with discussions on methodology, historical sociology, law, politics, and religion.

On the Methodology of the Social Sciences [1949/1922]

A collection of Weber's essays on method written between 1903 and 1917.

Secondary Texts

K. Allen, *Max Weber: A Critical Introduction* [2004]

This work offers an introduction and critical analysis of Weber's main concepts. It is not just a summary of Weber's ideas, Allen presents an argument too: that Weber's work was influenced by his position as a 'class-conscious bourgeois' individual and that his entire sociological output reflects his class-anchored outlook.

J. Radkau, *Max Weber: A Biography* [2005]

The focus here is more on Weber's life and times than his ideas; however, if you wish to understand his life story and how it shaped his work, this is a great book to turn to. It is a massive text, coming in at nearly 700 pages. It is a good resource for postgraduate students or for undergraduate students considering writing a dissertation on Weber.

J. Rehmann, *Max Weber, Modernisation as Passive Revolution: A Gramscian Analysis* [2016]

This work shares many of the themes with Allen's book (above). Rehmann argues that Weber should be read as existing with the ideological world of his time. As such, while Weber is advocating for 'value-free' scholarship, this is in part a reproduction of the dominant bourgeois values of his day.

F. Ringer, *Max Weber: An Intellectual Biography* [2004]

This is a medium-sized, highly readable intellectual biography of Weber. Much shorter and easier to read than Radkau's, ideal for undergraduate students.

G. Ritzer, *The McDonaldization of Society* [1993]

This work draws upon Weber's framing of rationalisation to show how the fast-food chain has become the model for many areas of modern life. This is a very readable book, a core text of contemporary sociology, and a great example of Weber's ideas resonating today.

M. Weber, *Max Weber: A Biography* [1926]

A biography of Max Weber written by his wife, who was herself an important figure in the history of sociology.

chapter 5

The Early Frankfurt School: What Happened to the Revolution?

Contents

DOI: 10.4324/9781003359555-5

The 'Frankfurt School' refers to a unique research centre, the Institute for Social Research, which opened in 1923 in Frankfurt, Germany. The thinkers who originally gathered there focused on one fundamental question: why had the socialist revolution which Karl Marx had predicted failed to happen? To this end the Frankfurt School provided an interdisciplinary study of late capitalism, based on a rigorous sociological analysis. Marx had written about capitalism in tremendous detail and with remarkable foresight. He had predicted its ascent, anticipated its crises, and identified many of its contradictions, tendencies, and laws, all while capitalism was still in its infancy. As discussed in Chapter 2, many of the ideas and concepts which Marx developed are still used in social research today. Yet, in one important regard Marx was unequivocally wrong: he believed that capitalism would be replaced by a different system entirely and that this would happen relatively quickly. This was due to occur through a series of revolutions, and Marx was reasonably confident that these would occur in Germany and/or England. However, as we all know, these revolutions simply didn't happen. To the thinkers gathered at the Frankfurt School it looked like capitalism was here to stay for a long time; the locomotive of history was sat at a standstill. If anything, from a Marxist perspective, things seemed to be looking worse every passing year of the 1930s, 1940s, and 1950s, with the rise of rival forms of totalitarianism, soul-destroying consumerism, and the threat of a nuclear apocalypse. An emancipatory 'socialist' society seemed further away than ever. The thinkers of the Frankfurt School were therefore all united in contemplating the question, best framed by Theodor W. Adorno: how come, instead of entering a 'truly human condition', humanity was moving ever closer to 'barbarism' and disaster?

The Frankfurt School was inspired by Marx's ideas. Like Marx, Frankfurt School scholars were fascinated by questions of social change ('dialectics') and the relationship between power, the economy, conflict, and the world of ideas ('ideology', 'reification'). However, despite their passion for Marx's work, they accepted that on a fundamental point Marx had been wrong; the socialist revolution he had predicted had not happened. As a result, the Frankfurt School thinkers wanted to draw upon a range of ideas in addition to Marx's to work out what had happened. Capitalism had been as chaotic and irrational as Marx had foreseen – how was it still surviving? To investigate this question they constructed concepts and theories which linked Marx's work with various other traditions such as Sigmund Freud's psychoanalysis, Hegel's philosophy, and Max Weber's interpretivist sociology. This unique blend of ideas gave the Frankfurt School some of the most important tools and approaches for social research which continue to fascinate scholars and which underpin cutting-edge research today.

With their mix of ideas, the Frankfurt School thinkers slowly came to an answer to their question as to why the revolution had failed to emerge. In short: Marx had not foreseen the extent to which capitalism could capture how people thought, reasoned, and what they desired within society. In part, Frankfurt School scholars such as Theodor W. Adorno (1903–69), Erich Fromm (1900–80), and Herbert Marcuse (1898–1979) argued that this derived from Marx's failure to adequately engage with the 'superstructure' of the social world: the realms of culture, arts, education, consumption; the social totality which arose out of the capitalist 'base'. This 'social' world was seen as largely inconsequential for many 'crude' or 'Soviet' Marxists, who viewed the 'economic' base as their primary concern. The Frankfurt School theorists saw the need to see beyond the workings of this economic 'base' and to look in far more detail at 'the superstructure' as a stabilising force, counterbalancing the contradictions of the economic logics of the market. The Frankfurt School accepted that contradictions of the economy still existed, just as Marx saw, and they agreed that society was irrational and unequal. Yet, the 'superstructure' of society; the worlds of culture, politics, consumption, were able to reinforce modes of thinking and being which helped keep capitalism going and which prevented critical thought and revolutionary action from flourishing. With this insight, the work of the Frankfurt School sought to identify how capitalism had achieved this. How had capitalism deformed the way people thought, and shaped people's desires? How had capitalism impacted on the depth psychology and consciousness of the working people upon whose exploitation the entire system was built?

It is 100 years since the Frankfurt School was founded and, as with any research group, ideas and interests change with time. In this chapter I introduce the ideas of the early Frankfurt School thinkers, commonly referred to as the 'first generation' of the Frankfurt School. Key names that will be discussed include Theodor W. Adorno, Max Horkheimer, Erich Fromm, and Herbert Marcuse, although the full cast of characters is vast, including thinkers such as Walter Benjamin (1892–1940), Friedrich Pollock (1894–1970), and Ernst Bloch (1885–1977). This 'first generation' of Frankfurt School thinkers was later slowly replaced by the ideas of Jürgen Habermas (1929–) and the so-called 'second generation' of the Frankfurt School. In time, Habermas's own ideas were built upon by Axel Honneth (1949–) and the 'third generation' of Frankfurt School theorists. Both Habermas and Honneth are discussed in Chapter 7. In this later chapter we will discuss how the Frankfurt School's approach has changed over the generations. Here, our focus in this current chapter is on exploring the key ideas and concepts of the early Frankfurt School and showing how and why these ideas still matter for social research today.

Key Concepts

While 'crude' Marxists concentrate on Marx's 'economics', the radical director of the Institute for Social Research, Max Horkheimer, was adamant that this was not good enough to understand capitalism. Horkheimer even wrote that such economistic scholarship was only done by people who had 'badly understood Marx'. What was needed, he declared, in his now famous opening address to the research institute, was an exploration of:

> the connection between the economic life of society, the psychological development of its individuals and the changes within specific areas of culture to which belong not only the intellectual legacy of the sciences, art and religion, but also law, customs, fashion, public opinion, sports, entertainments, lifestyles, and so on.

This was clearly a massive undertaking requiring the assembly of a new and creative toolkit of concepts and theories, which would ultimately birth a new interdisciplinary sociological tradition. What can clearly be taken from Horkheimer's speech was the need to look beyond the contradictions in the economy to understand how capitalism worked. These economic considerations remained important; however, capitalism was now viewed as an entire form of life which needed to be explored in its entirety to understand how it had managed to survive despite its fundamental contradictions.

Traditional and Critical Theory

In the same opening speech, Horkheimer also spoke of the distinction between past 'traditional' theory and a form of 'critical theory' that he wanted the Frankfurt School to pursue. As a result, the Frankfurt School thinkers are today often referred to as being 'Critical Theorists'. For Horkheimer, 'Critical Theory' was superior to 'Traditional Theory' for two key reasons. First, so-called 'traditional theory' was based on a falsehood: that one could produce neutral, apolitical research. Such past research on society, 'traditional theory', sought independent knowledge of the world, believing one could detach oneself from their values and preferences and come up with some God's-eye, unbiased 'facts'. Horkheimer showed that this was simply impossible; following Marx, he argued that everyone's thinking is always shaped by their environment. The questions we choose to ask, the language we use to ask them, the forms of reasoning we use to process our information; these are all a product of the society in which we live. Further, if capitalism was to be understood now as shaping how people thought and what they desired, all research, including that done by sociologists, would keep the 'inherited form' of the 'capitalist system'. There was therefore no objective God's-eye view possible. Instead, researchers needed to be mindful that their work was a product of their capitalistic society, which shaped the very questions they addressed as much as the conclusions they reached.

Critical Theory was further distinct, relative to 'traditional theory', in that it not merely acknowledged the political nature of research, it explicitly embraced it, viewing research as a means of changing society. Critical Theory was 'critical' in that it sought to identify problems with the social world, but it was also 'critical' in a second sense, in that it brought about social change. By the very act of disclosing social problems, such as distorted means of thinking, of the deceptive power of forms of culture, Critical Theorists were destabilising capitalism, chipping away at the supporting latticework which kept the irrational socio-economic order functioning. 'Critical Theory' was therefore uniting scholarship with politics: by doing critical theory, by their very research, the Frankfurt School saw themselves as engaging politically. Their critique of society disclosed the contradictions which held the social world together. By bringing these contradictions to light the social system immediately became less stable; a clearer form of consciousness was induced, and the socio-economic logics which exploited people's labour and deformed their consciousness were slightly ameliorated. This approach may be seen as a continuation of Marx's argument against abstract philosophising, captured in his famous quote: 'the philosophers have only interpreted the world, the point, however, is to change it'.

Horkheimer's injunction to do 'Critical Theory' made it clear that social research is always enmeshed with the views of the day; we cannot help it if ideas and values creep into work. As such, he encouraged the

Frankfurt School not to shy away from partisanship; to embrace the political nature of research. This fundamental insight is foundational to understanding the concepts and ideas which the Frankfurt School have developed and deployed right up until the present day.

Reification

For Critical Theorists, capitalism was impacting on how people thought. Crucially, it was doing so in a manner which both naturalised and obscured the exploitation upon which capitalism was based. As a result of this reshaping of people's consciousness, for its own ends, capitalism was able to survive, and Marx's predicted socialist revolution had been indefinitely delayed. The key way this deformation of thought has been understood by the Frankfurt School is through the concept of 'reification'. The word 'reification' literally means 'thing-ification', with 'res' being the Latin word for 'thing'. Put simply, Critical Theorists argued that capitalism had made people view the entire world as being made up of 'things', of 'objects', rather than of living people and the natural world, of passions, dreams, and emotions. This objectification of everything made it much easier to imagine the world as full of things for sale and to use to make money; to view the world in a way which suited the market system.

The idea of 'reification', while developed and deployed by Critical Theorists, actually has its roots in the work of a philosopher who was never part of the Frankfurt School. It derives from the work of a Hungarian Marxist György Lukács (1885–1971), who presented the idea in *History and Class Consciousness* [1923]. For Lukács, 'reification' emerges when the world is structured according to the 'commodity form', which is central to Marx's analysis of capitalism. Viewing the world as made of 'things' corresponds to a world which is based on an economic order which views everything as 'commodities'. 'Reification' is presented as being a pathology of consciousness which emerges as a result of the market system. For Lukács, with the spread of capitalism, reification spreads accordingly. As more and more areas of the world are turned into capitalist systems, there becomes no area left where reification does not also take hold. As Lukács wrote, there is now 'no way in which man can bring his physical and psychic "qualities" into play without their being subjected increasingly to this reifying process'.

The Frankfurt School theorists, most notably Adorno, Horkheimer, and Marcuse, brought the idea of reification into conversation with ideas from Max Weber, Sigmund Freud, and G. W. F. Hegel. In their work this idea that people were increasingly viewing their labour, their time, the natural world, even their thoughts, as 'dead matter' and as 'a heap of things' helped naturalise the absurdities of capitalism. Reification was so important because capitalism is based on the ability to reduce all commodities to a common denominator: money. In a capitalist world, £100 is able to buy X kilos of chicken breast, or Y amount of cinema tickets, Z minutes of an Uber driver's time; or, on the dark web, Q amount of pornography, or explosives, or even human organs. At a fundamental level, capitalism is based on a 'false equivalence', that £100 of chicken is, at some level, of equal value to £100 of human labour. This is an absurdity of capitalism based on the dominance of exchange logics across society. Critical Theorists utilised the concept of reification to help understand how this essential logic of capitalism was naturalised and accepted. When people view the entire world as made of 'things', a world of equivalences is much easier to accept and much less likely to be challenged.

Instrumental Rationality

The idea of reification, as discussed above, is fundamentally linked to *consciousness*, to how people experience their world. Yet, this is not the end of the story when it comes to reification. The way people experience things is itself linked to how people *reason* through problems and think about their existence. A reified form of consciousness will lead to problematic forms of thinking and reasoning. The concept of reification is therefore important in understanding the Frankfurt School's groundbreaking theories on rationality.

It is worth remembering that reason and rationality were important to Marx and to his key predecessors, Hegel and Rousseau. The Enlightenment injunction, 'dare to know!' [*sapere aude*] encapsulated the idea that through tireless and brave searching for the truth the world would become a better, more rational place. In this regard, the movement from feudalism, to capitalism, to socialism, to communism was seen as the development of an ever more coherent social order. Marxists were thus invested in reason, in creating a more rational society. Yet, for Critical Theorists, it became clear that capitalism had pathologically shaped how people were reasoning within society. Reason itself suddenly needed to go under the microscope. A core insight of Frankfurt School theory is that an 'instrumental' form of rationality, which was linked to capitalism, had come to dominate society at the expense of other important forms of thinking. What was required, therefore, was a more nuanced engagement with reason by Marxist-inspired sociologists; what was required was a *rational critique of irrationality*.

This idea that a problematic way of reasoning had come to dominate was most famously presented in a complicated and idiosyncratic book co-authored by Adorno and Horkheimer, *Dialectic of Enlightenment* [1944]. In a far-travelling discussion the pair argued that today all social domains had been colonised by this instrumental form of thinking which had many diverse and negative social impacts. Such instrumental rationality focuses on efficiency, on achieving the desired outcome as quickly as possible. The problem with this approach is that there is less space for critical reflection, for asking 'why are we doing this in the first place?' and even 'is this morally right?'

The co-authors reflect on how this instrumental form of thought enabled both the rise of the consumer society in America, but also enabled the Holocaust in Germany. Here we can really see the fusion of Marxist ideas with Weberian and Hegelian themes within Critical Theory. In both instances, mindless consumerist behaviour and the perpetration of the Holocaust were understood as being abetted by the solidification of an 'iron cage' of means–ends rationality. To understand such horrors researchers needed to focus on the self-understanding of the actors in question (Weberian *Verstehen* research) and connect this with the forms of rationality which were shaping institutions and subjectivity more broadly (Hegelian-Marxism).

The Holocaust is a constant theme running throughout *Dialectic of Enlightenment*. Even with the barrage of Nazi anti-Semitic propaganda, itself building on centuries of Vatican-promoted anti-Semitism, surely the thousands of men and women who were needed to facilitate the extermination of millions of innocent civilians would have felt some pangs of guilt, of uncertainty. To help explain how the Holocaust happened, Adorno and Horkheimer focus on how instrumental rationality, which rose to total dominance with modern capitalism, obscured questions of 'right' or 'wrong'. The Holocaust was explicable as a result of actors taking instrumental decisions, with the people who suffered such tragic consequences 'reified' and dehumanised. The decision to pack innocent children onto cattle trucks, for instance, was a calculation based largely on maximal efficiency. From a 'means–ends' perspective, it was a 'rational' decision. The total dominance of instrumental rationality and the loss of a critical perspective reduced the enormity of the Holocaust to a procession of instrumental calculations with obvious logical answers. The questions of humanity, of ethics, of civilisation itself, were simply negligible to the cost-benefit calculus of instrumental rationality. Reason itself had gone wrong. For Adorno, with the rise of instrumental thought 'progress and barbarism' had become 'matted together'.

Culture Industry

The idea that people's critical capacity had been lost, and that everything was increasingly organised around a *rationally irrational* calculus of efficiency, served as an important starting point for researching the emerging consumer society. Throughout the 1950s, a raft of technological innovations hit the market, especially in the USA, with cars and refrigerators available for mass purchase for the first time; suddenly pretty much *everything* was available for sale. More people started to travel overseas for leisure, and the 1950s saw a 'post-war boom' where seemingly everything was on offer. Yet, when everything was on sale, this meant that for theorists such as Adorno, Horkheimer, and Marcuse, instrumental rationality, like capitalism itself, was increasingly *everywhere*. The space for critical thought, for a non-instrumental form of rationality, was increasingly being lost.

To illustrate how capitalism was colonising all spheres of social life, the Frankfurt School focused on the changes which had occurred within the realm of arts and culture. This led to their important concept of 'the Culture Industry'. Since antiquity, the arts and culture had been held to be this place for reflection, for thinking about the big questions, for the appreciation of beauty and wonder. Art and culture were not simply about how to make money. Indeed, if anything, the work of art, such as great novels, showed the futility and absurdity of the contemporary form of life. This, however, claimed the Frankfurt School, was no longer the case: in the twentieth century the worlds of art and culture had been fundamentally captured by capitalism and had become just another sphere of market society. The space which once existed for meaningful social critique had substantially diminished. Culture had become just one other avenue for the making of money and the reproduction of capitalistic forms of thinking.

The idea of 'the Culture Industry' captures this sense of the totalising nature of instrumental rationality and the collapse of all areas of public life into the logics of the market. The framing of the Culture Industry was presented at length as a part of Adorno and Horkheimer's *Dialectic of Enlightenment* and was expanded upon repeatedly in subsequent works by later Critical Theorists. What is central to the idea of the Culture Industry is not merely that art has lost its critical function. Rather than going from 'critical of the system' to 'neutral' relative to capitalism, culture is now shown to be an active participant in reinforcing capitalist norms. As such, Adorno writes, 'movies and radio no longer pretend to be art', and cinemas boast of their box office figures, which is itself presented as a direct proof of the 'success' of the production. A movie is a 'flop' when it fails to make money, not whether it has been judged to be insufficiently affectively moving or lacking in beauty or poignancy. The space for critical thought had been lost and has itself become a site for furthering capitalist values.

Crucially, even art which was critical of capitalism was now being captured by capitalist logics. This very page I am writing *now* will form part of a book which will be sold. The majority of the money you have spent to be able to read this very book will end up with a big capitalist company called Informa, who, as well as publishing textbooks, also offers "business intelligence" services. This book, despite containing many pages all about ideas critical of commodities, is itself a commodity like any other, to be bought and sold at the price instrumentally determined to achieve maximum profit. It will likely appear on Amazon alongside the whole world of other items for sale. Likewise, when you sit in your seminar room, or your lecture theatre, and discuss these ideas, you are paying money through capitalist logics, reinforcing capitalist norms.

What is most striking about the concept of the Culture Industry is that it is often art/ideas that show a certain degree of criticism of capitalism ('realistic dissonance') which are famous successes *for* capitalism. Think about the success of *Black Mirror*, a TV series critical of modern technology and capitalism … which makes money for capitalist companies through its use of modern technology. Think of 'Welcome to the Machine' by Pink Floyd, a song about how the music industry only cares about making money … which made loads of money for the music industry. Think of Bob Dylan, Charlie Chaplin, NWA. Also: note how we have normalised the term 'industry' when it comes to the 'music industry'. An 'industry' is a word which makes more sense in terms of an 'industrial estate' or 'heavy industry'; making and building things to sell. The Frankfurt School idea of the 'Culture Industry' is that the arts and culture are as much a business as the making and selling of any commodity. Artists of all stripes are measured in terms of success or failure through the same numerical, quantitative calculus of profit and loss. The actual content of the work of art is negligible. It can be 'written off' as simply irrelevant. The market simply doesn't care.

Freudo-Marxism: One Dimensionality and Pathological Normalcy

Importantly, the Culture Industry does not solely offer a commodity for sale, and, through doing so, reinforce reification and instrumental rationality. Rather, at a fundamental level, the Culture Industry teaches us what to *desire*. Returning to the 'Welcome to the Machine' song, critical of the music industry, a key lyric screams: 'It's alright, we told you what to dream'. This idea that people's fundamental desires are recoded by the Culture Industry connects with the fundamental insights of the early Frankfurt School. Magazines, cinema, radio, advertising … a singular understanding of success is presented which penetrates the subject's sub-consciousness. The hero of the age is a rugged individual, with his car, his suit, his briefcase. This is not merely 'native advertising'; it is the system-atic imprinting of a notion of success and achievement through the reproduction of a ubiquitous narrative of recognition attained through individual effort and corresponding financial reward. Whereas we may (or may not) note the Heineken bottle Daniel Craig ostentatiously sips from in *No Time to Die*, we forget that we become enamoured by the suit, the car, the smooth worktops of the hotels, the international travel. The rugged individualism.

This idea that the superstructure increasingly dictates what counts as 'success' and 'failure' and accordingly recodes our desires is central to the work of Herbert Marcuse. In his *One Dimensional Man* Marcuse fused insights from Marx, Hegel, Heidegger, and Freud, and produced a series of concepts which became crucial to subsequent Freudo-Marxist research, such as 'repressive desublimation'. For Marcuse, capitalism has served to rob us of our creativity and impeded our ability to think criti-cally as it prescribes our modes of resistance. Frustrated by your lousy day at work and your boss speaking to you rudely? Consume our prod-ucts: go to the cinema, buy this Tesla, drink this 'Prime' drink. As Marcuse beautifully worded it, the disaffected millions, chewed out by capitalism, instead of rebelling against the system which exploited them, managed to 'find their soul in their automobile'. Capitalism, for Marcuse, served to rob people of their autonomy: the freedom to consume is no freedom if the object of your desire has been artificially induced. As such, Marcuse opened *One Dimensional Man* [1964] warning of the 'comfortable, smooth, democratic unfreedom' of the consumer society.

In similar vein, Erich Fromm also sought to fuse insights from Marx and Freud to advance Critical Theory. A central concept which Fromm developed was the idea of 'pathological normalcy'; that the existing status quo was fundamentally 'wrong', and 'irrational', but that it had become normalised and accepted in such a way that was itself 'pathological'. Fromm's dual diagnosis: of (1) an unhealthy society, and (2) an unhealthy acceptance of that society drew attention to the mechanism by which people came to accept the social world on its own terms. For Fromm, an important consideration was 'consensual validation': the more people that do something, however crazy it may be, the more likely we are to just go along with it. Indeed, the madman who shouts out 'this is stupid' is laughed at for his deviation from the masses. Yet, the 'madman' is increas-ingly not a lone individual shouting in the street. As Marcuse and Fromm identified, and what has become a pandemic in the past few decades, is the tidal wave of psychological disorders such as anxiety and depression.

For Fromm and Marcuse these are not symptoms of individuals who are 'broken'. Rather, society itself is 'pathological'; the individual who feels anxious in a world on fire, or on the brink of a nuclear holocaust, is perfectly normal. What needs to be reflected on, according to Freudo-Marxian Critical Theory, is the manners in which such natural healthy biological responses to the futility and desolation of capitalism are medicated and individualised. In contrast, Critical Theorists would suggest, socially induced neuroses call for a social transformation rather than the mass dependence of the general public on medicines to make the irrational social world seem rational. To be happy and sane in an insane world is in fact a sure sign of madness.

How Did These Concepts Shape Social Theory?

The Idea of 'Critical Theory'

The 'Critical Theory' envisaged by Horkheimer changed social theory forever. The particular concepts and ideas developed by the early Frankfurt School remain important to contemporary social research, which we discuss further below. Yet, the ideas of the early Frankfurt School matter for social theory at a 'higher level', impacting on what it means to do 'social theory' and 'social research' full stop. It is therefore important to reflect first on these 'macro' changes within social theory, and within scholarship at large, which the early Frankfurt School sparked.

Crucial to the impact of the Frankfurt School was the very concept of 'Critical Theory' itself; this awareness that knowledge and power are linked, and that this shapes how we should research and understand society. This has inspired thinkers across disciplines far beyond social theory. At a philosophical level, the idea of 'Critical Theory' challenged positivism (the 'scientific method') as an accepted 'pure' form of knowledge generation. As such, the Frankfurt School were responsible for a fundamental challenge to the dominant form of epistemology; to our understanding of how knowledge is formed. We could no longer simply believe in the objectivity of independently conducted scholarship. Rather, all thinking about society is now understood as being shaped by society (social epistemology). The entire progressive academy was never the same following this revelation. The breakthrough that the words we use, the framings we naturally turn to, even such common liberal ideas as progress, democracy and equality, reflect forms of power and ideology within society, had far-reaching repercussions. However social theorists view themselves, be it in terms of 'seeking truth', 'knowledge production', or simply 'research', all such activities are now held to require *reflexivity* and an awareness of one's *positionality* within complex structures of power.

Various schools of Critical Theory have emerged, drawing upon this insight, which sit far beyond the original ideas and politics of the Frankfurt School. While forms of Critical Theory remain which are invested in Marxism and which are primarily concerned with the relationship between capitalism, thought and desire, today there are various other forms of 'Critical Theory'. Perhaps the most famous 'Critical Theory' is 'Critical Race Theory'. Equally, much scholarship around gender, criminology, and disability is conscious of the relationship between power and knowledge, and explicitly presents itself as a 'Critical Theory'. You will therefore read about 'Critical Legal Theory', 'Critical Criminology', and you will find authors such as Judith Butler, Michel Foucault, and Gayatri Spivak referred to as Critical Theorists. This is because they share this interest in the relationship between power and knowledge.

As well as birthing this tradition of 'Critical Theory', the Frankfurt School expanded social research immeasurably. In place of siloed academics, each interested in their own subject area, Horkheimer's vision for Critical Theory saw a need to connect research on the economy with that on the psyche, with advertising, arts, literature. The entire social world needed to be studied in connection, rather than in isolation. This led to two key changes to sociology in particular. First, it led to a move to study more diverse areas within the auspices of 'social research'; academics sought to explore further than before within their fields, taking a sociological imagination to hitherto under-explored topics, be it accountancy or mythology. Second, because this naturally resulted in the collaboration of different specialists, it led to the move to a more *interdisciplinary* form of social research. Rather than social researchers focusing on either 'interview data' or 'statistical analysis', Critical Theorists worked to combine depth psychology with epistemology, political science with logic, aesthetics with economics. This fusion of methods of research has been embraced beyond Critical Theory, with 'interdisciplinarity' remaining a key feature of much subsequent research and an aspiration of many research programmes today.

As such, the ideas of the 'first-generation' Frankfurt School fundamentally changed social theory and social research. Their understanding of 'Critical Theory' challenged what people understood as knowledge, forced scholars to reflect on their own entanglement with social structural power, and exploded the tightly circumscribed concerns and methods of particular 'subjects'. With the birth of Critical Theory, progressive scholarship became interdisciplinary, and grew to appreciate reflexivity and positionality.

Contemporary Challenges: Gender, 'Race', and Teleology

As we have discussed throughout this book, much social theory is deeply problematic, reflecting racist, capitalist, misogynistic, anthropocentric, and ableist norms and values. The Frankfurt School famously teaches that all ideas are shaped by their society; however, the society of their day was racist and misogynistic, torn apart by fascism and war. It is thus worth reflecting on some of the recurring criticisms of the Frankfurt School, to determine whether the ideas the first generation left us with are laced with implicit problematic judgements. An important area where these concepts have recently been deployed to great effect is to explore the role of technology in contemporary society.

Teleology

One concern for people when they read first-generation Critical Theory is the relative absence of discussion of 'race' and colonialism within the early Frankfurt School's output. This is indeed odd when you consider that their crucial research question was 'how has capitalism survived?'. Surely capitalism's development of an underclass of 'gendered' and 'raced' labourers who are un/underpaid and exploited would need to be considered here. This absence of such enquiry is considered by some to be both poor scholarship and evidence of the normalisation of patriarchal, racial, and colonialist norms. At its core this criticism of the early Frankfurt School can be framed that it had an excessive focus on class and the economy, which led to the normalisation of exploitation in other social spheres. It could also be said that the School's view of the economy was too Eurocentric, failing to consider how European capitalism depended on the exploitation of resources from colonised states.

This claim is worth reflecting on and placing in the broader historical context. The early Frankfurt School was largely comprised of Jewish intellectuals whose lives were torn apart by the horrors of the Nazi period. Indeed, Walter Benjamin, an important name in Critical Theory, committed suicide while fleeing from the Nazis. True, there was not a substantial focus on the role of colonialism, or other forms of racism globally; however, in the historical context the *Shoah*, the choice to focus on anti-Semitic racism is historically entirely understandable. When viewed more historically, the particular focus on capitalism and anti-Semitism, in the context of the Wall Street Crash and the Holocaust, seems obvious.

However, the idea that the early Frankfurt School was blind to 'race' and colonialism has been taken further. In her book *The End of Progress*

[2016], Amy Allen has argued that some of the concepts and perspectives which Critical Theory has developed are infected by colonial and racist forms of reasoning. Central here is the idea of 'progress', which Allen studies in detail. It is undeniably true that there is a clear teleological story to much Critical Theory – a sense of societal progress as time passes. For Allen, we need to challenge such ideas, which she connects with false and highly problematic narratives. Instead, she calls for 'the end of progress' and the 'decolonisation' of the foundations of Frankfurt School thought.

Importantly, however, Allen then turns this criticism of Critical Theory on its head, arguing that Critical Theory *itself* has served to radically interrogate the notion of progress. In Adorno's *Negative Dialectics* [1966], the fundamental assumption that the working through of societal contradictions is inevitably taking society to a 'better place' is rejected. One could also respond that even if the early Frankfurt School held to a belief in the inevitability of communism, or that society would inevitably proceed in a more positive direction, this does not, in itself, invalidate the utility of concepts such as 'reification' and 'the Culture Industry'. This is, however, a complicated discussion and one which is ongoing.

Androcentrism

What is perhaps harder to dispute is the claim of the androcentrism of the early Frankfurt School. None of the key theorists were female, or indeed overly invested in discussions of feminism or gender. Worse, on the rare occasions women enter into the pages of classic Critical Theory texts they are fictional evil monsters: in the *Dialectic of Enlightenment* it is the Sirens facing Odysseus; later we encounter the murderous, amoral nymphomaniac Madame de Clairwil from the Marquis de Sade's *Juliette*. However, despite this broader trend, there were flashes of genius on the question of gender from Adorno as well as from Marcuse. In a key paragraph of *Minima Moralia* [1951], Adorno's analysis presaged much later feminist thought, arguing that the 'female character' is a damaging product of a masculine society. Further, it is worth noting that one of the most significant feminist and anti-racist activists and thinkers, Angela Yuval Davis (1944–), was taught by Herbert Marcuse, who credits the Frankfurt School for developing her work. While it is undeniable that the early Frankfurt School did not pay sufficient attention to concerns of gender, it was not entirely blind to the topic.

Upon reflection, it is worth noting that there are theorists who have challenged the early Frankfurt School's reluctance to engage with questions of 'race', coloniality, and gender. This has been taken further, with some scholars suggesting the concepts which the Frankfurt School leaves us with are laced with colonial and 'racist' norms, as its work is based on outmoded normative foundations. Such conversations are hotly contested, with much debate ongoing. The broad trend is to suggest that, in keeping with all scholarship, it must be 'kept alive' by adapting to the new insights of the day. In real terms, this means deploying first-generation Critical Theory concepts to help explore concerns of 'race', coloniality, and gender, in addition to class dynamics. Indeed, leading theorists of the Frankfurt School today, such as Nancy Fraser (1947–) and Rahel Jaeggi (1967–), do exactly this in their dialogue *Capitalism: A Conversation in Critical Theory* [2018]. In this book they draw upon key themes from first-generation Critical Theory to explore capitalism's relationship to 'race', gender, and anthropocentricism. Such an approach seems to show that the conceptual arsenal of the early Frankfurt School is not irreparably tainted by the blind spots in its research agenda or blighted by problematic philosophical commitments. Rather, while first-generation Critical Theory may reflect a focus of a narrower progressive scholarship, today's Critical Theorists deliberately seek to move beyond their 'male' and 'pale' ancestry.

How Are First-generation Frankfurt School Concepts Deployed Today?

As we discuss in Chapter 7, Critical Theory has changed markedly since the work of the 'first generation'. New ideas and concepts dominate in the work of Habermas and Honneth, with some of the ideas integral to first-generation Critical Theory no longer present. That said, the idea of reification and of competing forms of rationality remains across all 'generations' of Critical Theory. Axel Honneth produced an important study on *Reification* [2008], while Habermas's *Theory of Communicative Action* [1981/1991] suggests an important distinction between 'systemic' and 'communicative' forms of thought.

Science and Technology

However, it is worth noting that many of the concepts developed by the first generation of Critical Theory live on in cutting-edge social research outside the contemporary Frankfurt School. An important area where these concepts have recently been deployed to great effect is to explore the role of technology in today's society. This is particularly the case with attempts to understand how social media, and the digital world more broadly, shape our thoughts and feelings. A good example here is work by James Bridle, in particular *New Dark Age: Technology and the End of the Future* [2018]. Bridle is interested in the theme of knowledge itself being undercut by calculative logics and rationalities, corroding our capacity for critical thought. Here Bridle reconnects with ideas first expressed in Adorno and Horkheimer's *Dialectic of Enlightenment* to explore the impact of big data on our thinking today. The use of concepts from the first generation of the Frankfurt School is also central to Richard Seymour's study of Twitter, *The Twittering Machine: How Capitalism Stole Our Social Life* [2019]. Seymour's work shows the continuing use of concepts such as reification and instrumental rationality today.

Curiously, first-generation Frankfurt School ideas live on most pertinently outside both 'pure' Critical Theory and outside 'sociology', in the realm of Science and Technology Studies ('STS'). The prodigious work of Andrew Feenberg, such as *Technosystem: The Social Life of Reason* [2017] and *Critical Theory of Technology* [1991] are exemplar studies drawing on themes such as reification, instrumental rationality, and 'one dimensionality', which explore how our dependence on technology reshapes consciousness and behaviour in line with the functional requirements of our social world. In this regard, Science and Technology Studies has come to address many of the questions once central to the Institute of Social Research itself.

Conclusion

The ideas of the early Frankfurt School continue to inspire social research a century after the Institute for Social Research was founded. Critical Theory forces researchers to question the norms and values which lurk within their research; to challenge the hidden assumptions buried within our textbooks. 'Critical Theory' posed an existential challenge to 'traditional theory'; today, the idea that an independent, value-free form of research is possible is taken seriously by very few critical scholars.

While early Critical Theory has been subjected to criticism on the basis of its relative disinterest regarding gender and coloniality, the toolkit it leaves us with has subsequently been finessed and deployed to explore exactly such questions. As Allen shows, early Critical Theory can be used as a palliative to address the limitations of Critical Theory itself. In keeping with the key insights of Frankfurt School Critical Theory, I conclude by reflecting that all concepts and perspectives are indeed of their time and place, or, as Adorno and Horkheimer wrote, 'the core of truth is historical'. Indeed, the very idea of a concept, for Adorno, can have terrifying implications, capable of expunging the content of the particular being it refers to. What this means for us, as social theorists, is the need to constantly remind ourselves of the complications and complicities of each era, including our own, when we turn to, and deploy, key concepts and perspectives to help us make sense of our society. As per Max Horkheimer's advocation of a Critical Theory of Society, it is crucial to remember that power, knowledge, research, and social-structural power are always fundamentally connected.

Discussion Questions

1   How did the first generation of the Frankfurt School differ from earlier Marxist thought?

2   In which ways did the Frankfurt School fundamentally change social theory?

3   Was the early Frankfurt School too pessimistic in its approach to society?

4   How are key Frankfurt School concepts used to research society today?

5   In which ways does the approach of the early Frankfurt School differ from trends within contemporary social research?

Further Reading

Primary Texts

Theodor W. Adorno, *Minima Moralia: Reflections from Damaged Life* [1951]

This book consists of a series of fragments on a variety of subjects, ranging from literature to the emerging technology of the day. Throughout this text you can sense Adorno's profound dismay with the current social order. This is a difficult book to read which requires knowledge of many cultural references.

Theodor W. Adorno, *Negative Dialectics* [1966]

This incredibly complicated book represents Adorno's engagement with the philosopher Hegel. While Hegel viewed the dialectical development of ideas (through a synthesis of competing positions) to be positive and to lead to a social development, Adorno was less optimistic. In this text,

Adorno outlines a negative understanding of dialectics, in which dialectical conflict does not inevitably lead to a 'positive', constructive social outcome through determinate negation.

Theodor W. Adorno and Max Horkheimer, *Dialectic of Enlightenment* [1944/1947]

The co-authors identify a fundamental flaw in the dominant mode of reasoning. For Adorno and Horkheimer, a highly restrictive and dangerous instrumental attitude has taken hold of societies, which strips people and nature of their true value. This rise of this instrumental form of rationality is connected to both the rise of fascism and the emerging consumerist society.

Walter Benjamin, *Illuminations* [1968]

This book consists of a series of essays on topics ranging from literature to philosophy. The text is introduced by the philosopher Hannah Arendt who was given custody of Benjamin's papers. The most significant essays in the collection are 'Theses on the Philosophy of History' and 'The Work of Art in the Age of Mechanical Reproduction'.

Ernst Bloch, *The Principle of Hope* [1954/1955/1959]

The focus of this book is on utopianism and the belief in a better world. There is an important dialogue in this text between Marxist and Christian beliefs in hope for a better state to come. Bloch's work stands in clear contrast to Adorno's pessimism.

Erich Fromm, *The Sane Society* [1955]

In this highly readable book, Fromm argues that societies as a whole can become sick. Drawing upon the early Marx and Freud's psychoanalysis, the central argument here is that modern life is steeped in alienation and that the rise of neuroses and anxieties is a result of a flawed social order. Change is needed through social transformation to a social order which can enable human flourishing.

Erich Fromm, *The Pathology of Normalcy* [2010]

This book is based on a series of lectures and as such is very easy to read. Fromm's concept of 'pathological normalcy' is explained in detail, drawing upon themes across his work. Core here is the idea that the very normalcy of a bad situation is itself problematic and can induce logics of consensual validation.

Max Horkheimer, *'Traditional and Critical Theory'* [1937]

Based on Horkheimer's inaugural address to the Institute for Social Research, this essay is often referred to as being *the* founding text for Frankfurt School Critical Theory. This is a wide-ranging essay, with many editions having accompanying explanatory notes which will be of use to most readers. This is essential reading.

Herbert Marcuse, *One Dimensional Man* [1964]

In this book Marcuse outlines how new and restrictive forms of thought and experience have arisen with advanced industrial society. Like Fromm, Marcuse's work is based around a fusion of Marxian and Freudian insights. This text is highly readable and endlessly quotable.

Herbert Marcuse, *Reason and Revolution: Hegel and the Rise of Social Theory* [1941]

This text is a highly readable discussion of Hegel and Marx. This is essential reading for anyone struggling with the philosophical foundations of Critical Theory or who wishes to better understand the development of Marxist social theory more broadly.

Secondary Texts

Stephen Eric Bronner, *Critical Theory: A Very Short Introduction* [2011]

A very readable introduction to the Frankfurt School. As the name suggests, this is not a detailed study and could be read within a few hours. An excellent initial introduction to the topic for the uninitiated.

Phillip Felsch, *The Summer of Theory: History of a Rebellion, 1960–1990* [2021]

Felsch presents theory as a crucial part of the lives of a generation of young minds in Germany. Social theory is presented as having been part of a radical lifestyle, as the beating heart of a critical generation. This book locates the Frankfurt School within the context of theory more broadly, and is an important guide to understanding the significance of Critical Theory to a particular generation.

Rainer Funk, *Erich Fromm: His Life and Ideas: An Illustrated Biography* [2000]

Highly readable and succeeds in bringing Erich Fromm to life with an excellent collection of images. Particularly good at locating Fromm's work within the psychoanalytic tradition. Easy reading.

David Held, *Introduction to Critical Theory* [1980]

An extensive introductory text which goes into impressive detail. While positioned as an introduction, some sections may still take a little time to read through. This gives an excellent overview of the Frankfurt School; however, it is now a little dated.

Martin Jay, *The Dialectical Imagination: A History of the Frankfurt School and the Institute of Social Research, 1923–1950* [1973]

The authoritative history of the early Frankfurt School. This book was reviewed extremely positively by Herbert Marcuse, which, considering the subject matter, is some achievement.

Martin Jay, *Splinters in Your Eye: Frankfurt School Provocations: Essays on the Frankfurt School* [2020]

A selection of essays about the early Frankfurt School.

Stuart Jeffries, *Grand Hotel Abyss: The Lives of the Frankfurt School* [2016]

An extremely readable introduction to the lives and work of the Frankfurt School. Locates the thinkers within their broader historical moment and demonstrates the rich cultural tapestry in which they were located. Highly recommended reading.

Stefan Müller-Doohm, *Adorno: A Biography* [2008]

An extremely detailed, scholarly biography of Adorno.

Nick Thorkelson, *Herbert Marcuse, Philosopher of Utopia: A Graphic Biography* [2019]

Combines a brief biography with a summary of Marcuse's key ideas. Intersperses quotes with cultural references in a highly accessible and light-hearted manner. This graphic biography is produced by Nick Thorkelson, a cartoonist who was himself active in the protest movements of the 1960s, and who appears himself in places within the book. A quirky and enjoyable read.

Rolf Wiggerhaus, *The Frankfurt School: Its History, Theory and Political Significance* [1986]

A significant scholarly study of the early Frankfurt School. An excellent companion to Jay's *The Dialectical Imagination*.

Pierre Bourdieu: Class Meets Culture

Contents

DOI: 10.4324/9781003359555-6

'Kaz Smith' wears a Reebok tracksuit, her bleach-blonde hair squeezes into a tight ponytail. As she plays Katie Perry out of her phone and dances happily to herself, you notice a faded tattoo of a butterfly on her lower back. A friend calls and they speak loudly about plans to get a spray tan before a trip to Mykonos. Opposite her, sitting stiffly, is 'Kate Fortesque-Smythe'. As she brushes aside the folds of her calico dress, and rummages in her tote bag, you see a book on Bruckner's 8th Symphony and a tourist guide to Umbria. A friend messages and they text about a spelt loaf she discovered at an artisan café in Hampstead.

Based solely on this tiny sketch, you can have a good guess about these ladies' respective positions in society. You can predict which lady is most likely to be rich, or stopped and searched by the police, or refused entry into an exclusive yacht club, or who knows the rules of polo…. You can also guess whose child is more likely to grow up to have a successful high-profile career….

Pierre Bourdieu (1930–2002) showed that we make constant judgements about people based on their cultural performances, which impacts on the real-world opportunities people are offered. His work helps us understand how we read class from what people wear, what they listen to, what perfume they smell of, their accent, how loudly they talk, how they walk, what they laugh at, even their very names…. But more than this being of simple curiosity, his work focused on how such differences in 'cultural capital' play a role in how social hierarchies are reproduced and how inequalities are sustained.

In his most famous work, *Distinction: A Social Critique of the Judgment of Taste* [1979], Bourdieu discussed how there are cultural 'rules of the game' which people internalise that help the upper classes get ahead and which prevent working-class people from climbing the class ladder. These 'rules' aren't taught as part of an official school curriculum. If you come from an upper-class family you will just 'know' what to like, how to behave, what to say to fit into certain 'posher', privileged places. You will have a posh accent as you talk about your ski holiday, or your time at the opera. You will naturally enjoy museums, exhibitions, and make reference to classic works of art. You don't have to put any effort into this: it simply is how you live your life; you have internalised these classed markers, so it just your natural way of being. Bourdieu realised that sociologists needed to pay more attention to such embodied dispositions; to what he calls people's *habitus*.

Returning to the sketch above, Kate's middle-class habitus will get her accepted in certain exclusive places; her knowledge of 'high culture' affords her high 'cultural capital' which can open doors for her; get her bank loans, memberships, networking opportunities. Such opportunities may be much harder for Kaz on account of her lower-class habitus. Following Bourdieu's work, the significance of cultural factors in the maintenance of class hierarchies was acknowledged by most sociologists. As we shall see in this chapter, Bourdieu teaches us that culture and class work together in complex ways to reinforce social hierarchies.

Pierre Bourdieu: A Biographical Sketch

Pierre Bourdieu was born into a rural working-class family in Denguin, a small town in South Western France, near the Pyrenees Mountains. It was many miles both geographically and culturally from sophisticated Parisian life. His father was a postal worker who had not stayed in formal education. Yet, Pierre displayed true academic excellence, and his parents were both keen for him to be able to study. Following in the footsteps of Durkheim, he went to the École Normale Supérieure (ENS), that grandiose French equivalent of Oxbridge. Just like Durkheim, Bourdieu's work was to be forever shaped by his experiences at that university. At ENS, he experienced first-hand how economic hierarchies and cultural hierarchies interact, enabling certain students easier access to valuable opportunities. While the majority of the students at ENS were from ultra-rich, established families, well-versed in arts and culture, embodying upper-class French life, Bourdieu was not. He realised he was marked as different by his attire, his eating habits, how he spoke, what he aspired to. Even the way he walked made him look different.

Because people's educational experiences and the opportunities they can provide are so vital to social mobility, Bourdieu was fascinated by the processes of integration and exclusion he witnessed and experienced. He realised that there was a particular code, a set of accepted ways of thinking (or *doxa*) and a particular disposition (or *habitus*), which was privileged within the university space. This was not because it was most suitable for learning or was in any way objectively 'better'. Indeed, the knowledge, the dispositions, the interests which aided upward mobility were linked largely to forms of privilege and exclusion; they were actually markers which served to displace talent and effort and which privileged parental wealth. For example, your ability to confidently discuss your sailing holidays, or your time at the opera, or posh wine, does not prove how hard you work, or how much you know. However, it does mark you out as having particular kinds of 'capital'. This awareness that there was a particular logic, a set of rules of the game, in each particular space, inspired both Bourdieu's mature research programme and his political commitments to build a more inclusive educational system.

Bourdieu's life and work was marked by both his experience of the French class-cultural system, but also by his time in another country: Algeria. In 1955, three years after having completed his Ph.D., he was drafted into the French Army. This was a punishment for his anti-colonial politics. Unlike many of his upper-class contemporaries from ENS, who entered the Officers' College, Bourdieu chose instead to work with people from his own class background. As a result, he was dispatched to some tedious guard duties before being relocated to equally dull administrative tasks. However, he learned a lot from his life in Algeria, and he developed a real interest in the country's culture and customs. He went on to work at the University of Algiers for two years and he engaged in anthropological research and published *The Algerians* [1958] which brought him scholarly acclaim. His time in Algeria intensified his anti-imperialist politics which put him in great personal danger.

As such he returned to France, originally working as a teaching assistant to another acclaimed French intellectual, Raymond Aron (1905–83). Before long, Aron recognised Bourdieu's brilliance and had him running an entire centre focusing on Historical Sociology. This is where Bourdieu first began writing about the education system. However, before the decade was out Aron and Bourdieu broke company, the two disagreeing strongly about the protests which engulfed France in 1968. While Bourdieu was sympathetic to the student protesters, Aron strongly condemned their actions. Throughout the 1970 and 1980s Bourdieu developed the work which was to make him famous, focusing on the relationship between class inequalities and culture, combining insights from sociology and philosophy. From the 1990s be became a public intellectual, making frequent interventions in French public life. In particular, he campaigned against neoliberalism and marketisation, and he called explicitly for a greater distribution of economic resources throughout society. He was also a strident supporter of democracy and campaigned for greater public say over how key economic decisions were made. This more public-facing turn reflects the ideas and values of his academic life: he said he always viewed sociology as something of a 'combat sport', as a fight for a fairer, more just world. The sociologist was never neutral; just as with Karl Marx's sociology, and the Critical Theory tradition, Bourdieu's work reflects an interest in the relationship between theory and praxis, and a passion for theorising and researching as a way which could make the social world fairer.

Key Concepts

The concepts which Bourdieu developed help us understand how deep-rooted inequalities pass on from generation to generation. In particular, he does this by looking at the connections between class and culture in new and powerful ways. His understanding of class is as a grouping existing in social reality, rather than merely as something which exists due to academic, abstract stratifications. Classes may reflect economic differences but actually exist through real-world bonding and interaction, which occurs due to shared values and interests; through conversations about common culture. As such, his work looks at inequality as something deeply social and cultural rather than as solely an 'economic' question. The entire system which he presented is referred to as his *theory of social practice*, reflecting the interconnectedness of the cultural, institutional, and subjective realms. While he is best known for the terms 'habitus' and 'cultural capital', his work produced a wealth of concepts which continue to be deployed across social research and social theory today. Through his focus on class and culture, one can see obvious links with both the concerns of Karl Marx and the Frankfurt School. But the concepts he creates also have echoes with the work of both Durkheim and Weber. Following Durkheim, one can see how Bourdieu's concepts link to a concern with the role institutions play in stabilising society through reproducing norms and the collective consciousness. Following Weber, one can see an interest in social stratification and in the subjective worlds of social actors. But Bourdieu's concepts also point beyond sociology, drawing upon philosophy too, taking in insights from philosophers such as Maurice Merleau-Ponty (1908–61) and Alfred Schutz (1899–1959). These phenomenologist philosophers helped Bourdieu look at how class-cultural inequalities are *experienced*, by focusing on the different ways people perceive and live their social worlds.

Capital

Bourdieu's work is anchored in his insight that different forms of capital (or social resources) exist in society. From an economics perspective, your resources are primarily understood in terms of economic assets. You have your 'liquid assets' (e.g. cash or money in the bank) and your 'illiquid assets' (e.g. houses, offices, etc.). The wealth of a person or an organisation is understood as the combination of the two. For centuries, economists and sociologists had largely accepted this purely economic understanding of social resources. Bourdieu's primary intervention was to suggest that 'economic capital' was just one form of capital at work in society. He argued that inequalities in 'economic capital' need to be understood by looking at how multiple other forms of capital are traded and utilised by social actors. Bourdieu argued that just as people buy and sell things with and for money (economic capital), there are also forms of social, symbolic, and cultural capital in circulation. People are constantly drawing upon these different forms of capital, transforming one type into another, and using them to try and increase their social standing. In *Distinction* Bourdieu explained how these different capitals work as part of a single system. Let us look at each form of capital in turn.

Cultural capital is the most famous form of capital which Bourdieu discusses. He argues that it is partly through their possession and control of what indicates cultural capital that the upper classes maintain their standing in society. As such, the upper classes perpetuate a system in which one set of cultural products is held to be 'superior'; such as classical music, the 'classics' of Roman and Greek antiquity, or 'the Old Masters'. Bourdieu outlines three ways in which cultural capital is held: it is embodied, objectified, and institutionalised. Embodied capital refers to how people sit, behave, walk, talk. In the sketch above, Kate's stiff posture and sitting quietly marks her as middle/upper class, relative to the more relaxed, extrovert Kaz. Objectified capital refers to the possessions people own: for example, Kate's calico dress is an object which communicates and indicates cultural capital. It screams look at me, I am a sophisticated middle-class person. Finally, there is institutionalised capital. By this Bourdieu refers to the qualifications or accreditations a person has. Just as Kate is marked by her high cultural capital presentation, Kaz is equally marked by her relative lack of cultural capital. It is important to stress that for Bourdieu there is nothing objectively superior in upper-class culture. The cultural capital provided by knowing about opera, rather than rap, for example, is something that Bourdieu would argue needs to be challenged.

It is not merely the case that something has 'high cultural capital' simply because it is what 'upper-class' people like or do. For something to be 'consecrated' as being 'high culture' it requires constant institutional recognition. For example, students are taught about the great composers as part of the curriculum, there are prestigious awards ceremonies, and public festivals in high-status buildings, such as the BBC Proms at The Royal Albert Hall. As such, it is not simply enough for 'the upper class' to suddenly start engaging in a cultural practice for it to become 'high culture'. Rather, the recognition of something as 'high culture' is a slow and complicated process which will require constant re-legitimation. This is because there is no objective reason why Mahler should be seen as superior to Eminem. Therefore, it is not enough for there to have been a festival on the BBC *once* about classical music; rather, it needs to be constantly reinforced and re-legitimated to maintain the cultural hierarchy.

Social capital refers to your network: the people you know, that you can call on, can turn to for favours, knowledge, advice. Having extensive social capital will enable you to gain access to prestigious and exclusive opportunities: for instance, you could get your son or daughter an internship at an investment bank, or you could get expert accountancy advice, or front-row concert tickets. Social capital can help you gain cultural capital; if you know the right person you will know which author to talk about, which venue to go to, which opera troupe to follow. You can spend your economic capital attending venues where you can attempt to meet people with high social capital; for instance, by joining exclusive clubs. Likewise, by having friends with high social capital you may also be given opportunities to make lucrative investments, further expanding your economic capital. You may also be appointed to important roles or opportunities which may provide *symbolic capital*.

Symbolic capital refers to the power an individual holds on the basis of being recognised or esteemed by the social body. It refers to status and social standing and does not have to be connected at all to economic wealth. For instance, a recent example of where someone had symbolic capital may be the status attributed to nurses who were on the front line during the Covid pandemic. Symbolic capital is therefore connected to honour and social recognition. It could be drawn upon to gain social power or advantage: for instance, a nurse who worked through Covid, or a decorated war hero, could run for elected office, or may find it easier to get into a university course on the basis of having things to write about in their personal statements or to say in interviews. Another example of someone with symbolic capital would be an Olympic medallist. People with symbolic capital may also find it easier to build networks and gain powerful friends. Symbolic capital can therefore be transformed into social capital, cultural capital, or even into economic capital. Think of how Olympic medallists have gained money from advertising or have become politicians.

Throughout his work, Bourdieu demonstrated how all of these forms of capital interact in such a way as to sustain the privilege of the upper classes in society. As such, any attempt to understand how society reproduces itself and how inequalities are passed on must look beyond mere economic logics. Ingrained poverty and inherited wealth and privilege is something which needs to be studied at a socio-cultural register as much as at an economic one. Contacts matter, as do symbols and prestige. But so too does cultural capital: there is an unequal appreciation of upper-class culture over lower-class culture: and this serves to reproduce and maintain social inequalities.

Habitus

With his concept of *habitus*, Bourdieu gets into the head and the body of the social subject. He is interested in the embodied dispositions of social actors and how these reflect different class positions. One's habitus points to the naturalised desires, tastes, interests, knowledges of different people, which typically reflect their different class positions in society. The habitus is created as a result of the different forms of capital the subject has access to; it emerges out of their position within society. It is a result of both the forms of capital subjects have, but also the volume of each of them (how much cultural capital do they have?), and their direction of travel within society. For instance, upwardly mobile upper-class people have embodied desires for luxury over necessity, enabling them to fit more easily within 'upper-class' spaces. In contrast, working-class people are shown to have naturalised a different set of values and desires; they develop a habitus which values practicality, minimal pretension, maximum functionality. Through his concept of habitus, Bourdieu shows how we internalise the classed 'rules of the game' of our social settings.

This all sounds very abstract, so let us give it some context by returning to Kaz and Kate. Kaz and Kate will *naturally* want to wear different clothes, drink different drinks, eat different foods. Kate will naturally want to go to the opera, drink rare wines, eat organic, rustic foods. Kaz will naturally want to go anywhere but the opera! She will find it totally stuffy and boring, and would rather go to a club and dance. She cannot be doing with expensive wines, she would rather have a double vodka and coke. Likewise, she has no interest in poncy foods after her night out; she'd rather have a cheeky kebab and relax. We can see that her habitus shows her 'taste for necessity'; she is interested in function over form, which reflects the needs common to working-class communities. In contrast, the very idea of a kebab may make Kate's stomach turn. Kate is more invested in form over function; in quality over quantity. She can be seen to have a habitus which reflects 'a taste for distinction'. These differences are fundamentally naturalised and embodied: neither Kaz nor Kate are faking their desires. They have been thoroughly internalised within their minds and their bodies and they seem wholly authentic to each of them. They reflect how both have internalised the class-cultural norms of their position within society.

Habitus refers to the naturalisation of the class-cultural norms so that subjects authentically reproduce the values and attitudes of their social milieu. As such, it enables effortless cultural connection across class lines and serves to exclude and ostracise those who do not possess the naturalised desires for different tastes from entering different classed spaces.

Field

Bourdieu recognises that society is not one homogeneous whole; rather, he argues that it is made up of different 'fields' which have their own distinct 'rules of the game'. For instance, the way people gain power and prestige within the business world is very different to how standing is gained within academia or within the art world. While economic capital (financial success) and social capital (networks) are powerful influences within the business world, in academia and in the art world, cultural capital is often more highly prized. Academics are typically more interested in what people know and where their ideas have come from rather than how much money people have, for instance. There may be particular forms of capital within the field; for example, status may be linked to how many citations academics have for their research publications. Likewise, musicians may care about reviews in particular magazines and blogs. Bourdieu argues that individuals compete within each field and learn the rules of the game within each setting. There is a constant battle for standing and recognition within each field and people adjust to the metrics and variables through which success is perceived. The extent to which the individual's habitus is aligned to achieving the metrics of success in each field plays a substantial factor in the ease with which each actor can succeed in any given field.

Bourdieu believes that each field exists in relative autonomy from the rest of society. This is to say it has a set of norms and rules and procedures which are somewhat particular to it. As such, there are substantial differences in how capital operates in different social institutions: as we have discussed, lecturers are not the same as business executives or artists. Yet, while there is substantial 'field autonomy', fields are still shaped by broader social factors. For example, capitalism, racism, and patriarchy impacts on artists and educators alike. Fields thereby should be understood as having relative autonomy; they have their particular patterns and structures through which capital is achieved and exchanged, but they do not exist apart from the rest of society.

As these fields do not exist in perfect isolation, Bourdieu writes that there can be 'field effects'. This shows how fields are interconnected. For example, say a given artist had failed to fill a single tour date, and had their albums ridiculed in the media, they would naturally have low capital in their field. However, if suddenly their work earns them millions of pounds through a spike of downloads and streams, this 'economic' capital would surely change how they were viewed within the music world. The markers of success within the business field would also resonate into the music field. Likewise, if a hitherto unknown artist, with no economic capital, started receiving excellent critical reviews, their success in the artistic field may lead to lucrative contracts and success within the economic field. The similarity between the economic field and the artistic field is not simply incidental for Bourdieu, and it reflects his concept of *homology*, namely that there are structurally similar patterns, or resonances, across all of society, serving to enable its reproduction.

Homology and Structural Correspondence

Bourdieu's concepts of homology and structural correspondence work closely together and speak to the interconnected nature of society. The basic premise of these twin theses is that there are invisible shared patterns encoded across social domains, which serve to privilege the upper classes. Therefore, things may look radically different across different fields (law, education, music, business); but at a deeper level there are common structures which serve to facilitate the reproduction of the existing social system and maintain forms of privilege and inequality.

Homology refers to the strong tendency for an individual's habitus to reflect the class-cultural norms of their social world. There is a natural affinity between those who grow up within a very upper-class environment and the development of an upper-class habitus. The link which exists between their socialisation within the upper-class world and the development of their interests/norms/tastes for upper-class cultural artefacts is an indication of such structural homology. This is not to say that every person raised in an upper-class social world will develop an identical attitude or set of dispositions. However, the homology thesis suggests that there will be strong forces at work pushing many people in a similar direction on the basis of their class upbringing.

The structural correspondence thesis reflects how the various component parts of society operate together as a more or less coherent system. There are hidden structures and patterns which exist across seemingly different social institutions. For instance, the legal system and the sporting world can be seen to reflect particular hidden patterns, despite their outwardly facing divergences. This explains how and why access to both elite rugby, and to leading barristers' chambers, is both disproportionately controlled by upper-class, privately educated 'gate-keepers', who carry a particular set of class-cultural markers. The structural correspondence thesis suggests that the social world is marked by a particular set of logics or resonances, enabling its smooth reproduction, despite the irrationality and arbitrary nature of its inequalities.

When one takes the homology thesis and the structural correspondence thesis together, it becomes clear that Bourdieu sees the social world as functioning to perpetuate a particular set of privileges. The way people think and act and feel, at the level of the habitus, is predisposed to mirror their class position through the homology thesis. Likewise, the structural correspondence thesis suggests that particular habitus and class-cultural performances are likely to be privileged across all social domains, as the entire social world has a shared resonance with particular codes and values. As such, the dominance of particular codes and cultures serves to be constantly reinscribed to the advantage of a particular social milieu: those with higher capital, in all its forms.

Symbolic Violence

Throughout his work on class, culture, and inequality, Bourdieu was clear about the irrationality of the status quo: there is no reason why things have to be the way they are! The value attributed to upper-class culture does not derive from some greater intrinsic merit or some aesthetic/cultural superiority. There is nothing objectively superior to snowboarding over skateboarding, or to Debussy over Drill. Just because something is considered 'high culture' does not mean that it should be viewed as 'better'. Yet, the markers of cultural capital with which different cultural artefacts and performances are imbued is shown to be central to maintaining social inequalities. How then is this artificial and irrational hierarchy sustained? This is where Bourdieu's concept of *symbolic violence* enters the picture.

Symbolic violence is the concept Bourdieu used to explain how the unequal and irrational social system is maintained. Crucially, it is through a system where people consent to their inferior role within society. Examples of symbolic violence occurring could be the policing of people's grammar, suggesting that there is only one 'correct' form of speaking and that other forms of expression are somehow 'wrong', 'inferior', and 'unacceptable' in the public sphere. By belittling the way working-class people speak and by naturalising the 'correct' form of formal upper-class English, the socio-cultural hierarchy is maintained. Crucially, this process occurs peacefully: nobody from Eton or Oxford has a gun to the head of people from inner cities, forcing the letter 'h' to be pronounced by those with a South London accent. Yet, the idea that there is a 'correct' form of speech and a 'proper' accent is a powerful exclusionary and disciplining force. This is perhaps most extremely presented by the use of

Pierre Bourdieu

derogatory classed language, such as 'chavs' or 'plebs', to reflect class-cultural demarcations. The word 'pleb' was part of a national scandal in the UK back in 2012, when an upper-class Conservative Party politician, Andrew Mitchell, allegedly swore at police officers and called them 'plebs' when he was trying to assert his authority.

Another example of symbolic violence is through the policing of dress codes. Comments, snide looks, offhand jokes can be made if somebody went to a particular upper-class space wearing 'inappropriate' clothing. The definition of 'appropriate' here is crucial; the idea of symbolic violence is the process of inscribing what is and is not 'appropriate'; of naturalising an arbitrary class-cultural order. The particular logics and impacts of such symbolic violence can be to cause shame or embarrassment in the 'transgressing' social actor, making them feel 'out of place'. It is as much the threat of the shame of being a victim of symbolic violence, of being publicly embarrassed, as the actual reality of symbolic violence, which functions to maintain socio-cultural codes.

How Did These Concepts Shape Social Theory?

Bourdieu's work has had a profound impact on sociology and social theory. A legion of cultural sociologists emerged, inspired by his research programme, exploring culture as a field intimately connected to inequality and social reproduction.

Inequality and Cultural Sociology

Bourdieu's work served to reshape how inequality was studied, placing culture at the centre of a new generation of debates around social hierarchies. Before Bourdieu, culture was not viewed as a prime mover in conversations surrounding inequality. In fact, for the Frankfurt School, the cultural realm was seen as 'epiphenomenal' to the economic domain. What that meant was that for Critical Theorists all cultural products reflected the essence of the market system. As such, for thinkers such as Adorno and Horkheimer, the 'Culture Industry' served to prevent social change and induced artificial desires. There was no scope for the cultural realm to bring about social change. In contrast, for Bourdieu, disparities in cultural capital drive social reproduction; cultural capital is co-eval with economic capital. As such, culture became something worthy of investigating for a new generational of scholars; it was not merely a ripple from the economic base, but a vital area of the social world requiring sociological investigation.

Since Bourdieu, the question of cultural class has echoed throughout social theory and social research, with various concepts emerging. A key area of research has been to discuss whether there are still 'high' and 'low' cultural rungs within society. When Bourdieu was writing it was certainly the case that graffiti was seen as an inferior, 'lower' form of culture to appreciating 'the Old Masters', for example. But the cultural-classed dimensions are ever changing, both in their content and in the extent to which the divisions are clean-cut. For example, the celebrity figures of Silicon Valley are today famous for wearing simple T-shirts; once the domain of rebels played by Marlon Brando and James Dean, now it is Mark Zuckerberg's preferred attire. There has been extensive debate following Bourdieu as to whether there remains a single repertoire of class distinction.

One alternative to the idea of a fixed class-cultural hierarchy has been the idea of the 'cultural omnivore'. This stems from the work of Peterson and Kern who argued that with the rise of modern technologies it was easier for people to consume from a variety of cultural domains. For Peterson and Kern, the rise of the cultural omnivore suggested that there was no longer a single marker of distinction. This suggested that Bourdieu's theory of social inequality being reproduced through cultural markers of class privilege was less relevant. However, today sociologists increasingly agree that cultural omnivorousness itself is a reflection of a new repertoire of distinction: that to be able to impress and gain admittance to the most esteemed spaces you are now required to be literate about *both* high and low culture. The suggestion is that the cultural omnivore is not a position which is held equally across society; rather, there exists an inverted pyramid, with the upper classes increasingly expected to consume all culture, while the working classes engage with a slimmer mix of the most popular, accessible cultural products.

The question(s) of whether there are indeed new repertoires of distinction, and what form they might take, rumbles on. What remains the case today is an interest in identifying class-cultural hierarchies and connecting these to broader patterns of social reproduction.

Sociology as a Combat Sport

One of Bourdieu's lasting legacies was his view of sociology as being 'a combat sport'. This approach to sociology reflects his Marxian heritage. Marx famously argued that thinkers had only interpreted the world; the point, for Marxists, is always to change society, to make it fairer and less irrational. Bourdieu fully embraced this view and he inspired a new generation of social researchers to reflect on the relationship between social research and social transformation. While the Frankfurt School had already long argued that independent social research was impossible and that 'critical' ('political') rather than 'traditional' ('objective') theory was the solution, the School's approach was embedded within abstract philosophical and depth-psychological ideas. Adorno and Marcuse, for example, wanted to challenge forms of 'repressive desublimation' and 'instrumental rationality'. For many sociologists, such an approach was held to be inaccessible and hard to operationalise, leading to an 'ivory tower' abstraction from the social world. In direct contrast with the Frankfurt School, Bourdieu sought to elevate the status of working-class and mass popular cultural artefacts. For Bourdieu, the real-world political and economic impacts of exploring the denigration of working-class culture can be exposed by social research. This process of disclosing the contradictions and injustices of the social world was part of a process of changing the social system itself. As such, social research is part of a political process, challenging embedded privilege and exposing injustices. With Bourdieu's work, more 'mainstream' sociological domains (such as the study of culture) became increasingly critical and the idea of a 'critical sociologist' itself became more mainstream, rather than the preserve solely of radical Marxists.

The idea that sociology could serve to challenge social injustices and disturb the mechanisms of inherited privilege led to sociologists reflecting on their own role in society. Following Bourdieu's work, we can see a rise in sociologists practising 'critical reflexivity'. This is where sociologists reflect on their own values and position within society relative to the research process. This requires researchers to challenge their own biases and to consider whether their beliefs and actions are themselves leading to the reproduction of social hierarchies. For example, it would require scholars who focus on classical music to consider why they turn to this topic rather than rap, and to see whether their research serves to normalise and naturalise its 'high-cultural' value and implicit aesthetic superiority. Such questions are now a central tenet of sociological research and interact with ideas from both critical theory and feminist epistemology. These traditions combine to reflect the idea of sociology as a 'combat sport', requiring sociologists to battle their own prejudices and biases, and taking an active and critical approach to their work. Excellence in social research today is now typified by researchers being aware of their positionality and demonstrating critical reflexivity.

Bourdieu also inspired a new generation of 'activist' sociologists, with social researchers using their disciplinary training to explicitly rally for social change. Bourdieu himself became a noted public intellectual, allying himself with various causes, such as campaigns for more accessible education and for greater public say over economic decision making. Today, it is common for sociologists to campaign on a range of issues; especially on topics of 'race', gender, and poverty. As such, Bourdieu's legacy has been not merely to centre culture within research into social injustice but to create a new generation of activist sociologists who view sociology as a means of both better understanding the social world, but also of creating a fairer and more rational place to live.

Problems for Use in Contemporary Social Theory

Bourdieu's work has shown how important it is to link class and culture when studying inequality. Yet, his approach has been criticised for promoting an excessively cultural understanding of class, which can inadvertently reproduce a 'post-materialist' narrative. As such, his concepts, if not deployed critically, can serve to obscure the economic exploitation upon which class differences are based. Equally, Bourdieu's focus on 'culture' and 'class' can be criticised for failing to focus on how multiple identities interconnect in the reproduction of social inequalities. It is not solely 'class', but also 'race', gender, and sexuality which require theorisation in any attempt to understand the reproduction of cultural hierarchies and the persistence of social inequalities more broadly. As such, despite the critical edge which Bourdieu brought to recent sociology, his work risks simultaneously reinforcing a post-material paradigm and neglecting intersectional experiences of symbolic violence. These would both be entirely at odds with Bourdieu's own views: he was passionately opposed to colonialism and campaigned against neoliberalism. Yet, the concepts he bequeathed to social theory, if not critically deployed, can risk furthering a social research agenda which focuses too narrowly on a cultural conception of class as the primary factor in exploring inequalities.

Forgetting the Mute Compulsion of Capital

Since the 1990s, the social sciences have experienced a 'post-material' turn, focusing less on economic divisions and redistribution and more on questions of culture, recognition, and identity. Bourdieu's concepts have fed into this transition, connecting class and culture in new and powerful ways. The problem, however, is that this occurred at a moment when various supporters of the free market were trying to normalise neoliberalism and suggesting that we are living in a 'post-class' world typified by increasingly equal opportunities. Throughout the late 1990s, political parties of left and right were embracing the market as an ideal arbiter of resource allocation. The fundamental class conflict rooted in the economic exploitation of the labouring class by the business-owner class was being rapidly, and conveniently, obscured, which served the

Pierre Bourdieu

interests of big business. The normalisation of the free market and its embrace by once left-leaning actors was complemented by a cultural notion of class, disconnected from a foundation in economic, material exploitation. This was problematic politically and it was also bad for social research. As Nancy Fraser (1947–) has argued, so much of the social world is directly connected to economic class logics, and cannot be studied through the post-material, post-class framings of recognition, culture, and identity alone. Adopting a too culturalist conception of class, and forgetting its economic foundations, has been criticised by various sociologists, such as Rosemary Crompton (1942–2011), for 'throwing the baby out with the bathwater'.

The epitome of this 'post-class' framework is in the comedy presentation of class differences being fundamentally cultural, rather than economic. A notable example is the British comedian Rob Beckett, who has a standup routine based around the idea that 'you know you are working class rather than middle class when your TV screen is larger than your bookshelf'. While this loosely reflects (some) class-cultural entertainment preferences, it reflects a fundamental displacement of the antagonistic and exploitative basis of the class relation, which was once central to how class was understood. This is also interesting as a change in comedy at a cultural level. Previously there was a range of radical comedians, such as Frankie Boyle, Rory Bremner, and Mark Steel, who focused more on satirising the economic and political landscape. Today, comedy reflects this post-class environment, furthering the neoliberal myth that we are all in it together, as equal consumers in the marketplace. The erasure of the fundamental class exploitation which follows such an exclusively culturalist understanding of class should give sociologists pause for thought.

This matters for two reasons. The first is that there is a tremendous source of social power rooted within the economic class system. Recently, Søren Mau has written of this as the 'mute compulsion' of capital; as the power which emerges from within the capitalist system itself. Sociologists need to be able to explore how market mechanisms impact on societies and shape subjects to act in the ways they do. Second, Marxists have long looked at class antagonisms as a source for potential social change. For Marxists the conflict between economic classes would inevitably lead to revolutionary social transformation.

The Marxist view is that the social world is based on the exploitation of the mass of labourers by the bourgeoisie, and that, as such, capitalist societies are inevitably irrational and unjust.

This focus on class conflict as a contradiction at the heart of the capitalist social world served as a fulcrum for leveraging demands for emancipatory structural changes. As such, the displacement of the conflict between the proletariat and the bourgeoisie, as exploited and exploiting economic classes, for a new framing, disconnected from the means of production, to 'lower class' and 'upper class', obscures the revolutionary emancipatory potential which Marxists see as pregnant within the class contradictions of social reality.

While a class-cultural analysis can complement an economically anchored critique of the social world, it also risks displacing the economic core of social life. Now, for Bourdieu, this cultural component to class reproduction was intended as a complement to existing economic understandings of class; he did not want us to forget about capitalism and its laws and logics. However, both within sociology and across society more broadly, there is an increasing movement away from understanding class as something anchored in one's relationship to the means of production. Such an overinflated cultural understanding of class ignores the deep economic conflict which exists between the bourgeoisie and the proletariat linked to their fundamentally opposing class positions within capitalism.

Lacking Intersectionality

Another important criticism of Bourdieu's approach is that he is overly focused on class and does not consider the importance of other registers such as 'race' and gender in his understanding of the reproduction of social injustice. Today, theorists are increasingly aware that class, 'race', and gender intersect (see Chapter 8 on gender). As such, a repeated contemporary criticism of Bourdieu's approach is that he fails to offer a sufficiently multidimensional analysis of how social privilege is reproduced. In short, the criticism is that he is too concerned with class and does not engage sufficiently with 'race' and gender. This is not, in itself, a criticism of his broader approach to theorising, connecting class, culture, and power. Rather, intersectional theorists want to see the substantive components of Bourdieu's theory embellished with additional insights. What this means is that his theory needs to be adapted to show how the value placed on 'high culture' reflects both the classed, but also the 'raced' and 'gendered' striations of society.

For Bourdieu's understanding of cultural class to be most effective today it needs to be combined with insights from gender and critical race theory; seeing how class interweaves with 'race' and gender. After all, it is typically the forms of culture associated with upper-class white men that are most valued; while it is the forms of culture associated with lower-class women of colour which possess the least cultural capital. As such, attempts have been made to connect Bourdieu's insights with those from gender by a range of thinkers, such as Bev Skeggs, Lois McNay, and

Bridget Fowler (1943–). Similarly, attempts have been made to bring Bourdieu's concepts into dialogue with 'race' and 'nation' in the work of scholars such as Ghassan Hage (1957–). These authors would all agree that to optimally understand how inequalities are reproduced within society, and to understand particular cultural hierarchies, Bourdieu's theory needs to be brought into dialogue with insights from complementary theories of 'race' and gender.

How Do Bourdieu's Ideas Impact on Social Theory Today?

Bourdieu's concepts continue to be drawn upon by sociologists today. With the changing social landscape (for example, with digitisation and increased cultural sensitivity to gender discrimination), his concepts have been developed to explore different forms of privilege and distinction. As such, new forms of 'capital' have been theorised, which we discuss below. His broader framework for understanding society, his 'theory of practice', has been developed by various theorists offering variations on his original model. We briefly introduce the theory of practice developed by Theodore Schatzki.

Capital

One of Bourdieu's central insights which continues to resonate throughout contemporary social research is the idea that there are multiple forms of capital at work in society. Sociologists draw upon concepts such as 'cultural capital' and 'social capital' routinely across cultural sociology, the sociology of education, and within consumption studies. One important complementary development has been the creation of new concepts to support such analyses, in the form of new kinds of capital being theorised. These are presented as being additional and distinct forms of capital which cannot be reduced into those originally outlined by Bourdieu. This has happened quite prolifically, with lots of new kinds of capital being presented. Indeed, this has happened to such an extent that Geoffrey Hodgson (1946–) has argued that the concept of 'capital' is becoming overly stretched because 'everything has become capital'.

One example of a new form of capital is the idea of 'digital capital', a concept discussed by Massimo Ragnedda (1976–). By 'digital capital' Ragnedda refers to the 'accumulation of digital competences' and 'digital technologies'. In essence, this means having the knowledge to use digital tools to get information, to solve problems, to create content; and to do so safely and efficiently. He also stresses that having access to the digital technologies themselves matters: you need to have access to the software and the hardware to gain or deploy digital capital. Ragnedda's core idea is that the accumulated 'digital capital' which such skills and tools offer should be theorised as a new form of 'capital' in its own right, and should not be subsumed within 'cultural' or 'social' capital. Ragnedda argues that this is because 'digital capital' speaks to a different social skillset; the ability to 'bridge' between the online and offline worlds. As such, Ragnedda has argued that 'digital capital' needs to be understood as a unique form of 'bridging capital' which should be valued as a distinct social resource.

In her book *Honey Money: The Power of Erotic Capital* [2011], Catherine Hakim (1948–) controversially argued that attractiveness should be considered as a form of capital. She argues that your erotic capital can be drawn upon for social advantage and can be transformed into other forms of capital. For example, you can leverage your erotic capital to gain admittance to certain exclusive networks (gaining social capital), or you can even use it to gain economic money, by finding a richer partner or by charming your way into higher paying employment. Hakim writes that 'erotic capital' consists of multiple components, such as charm and social skills, as well as physical attractiveness. Hakim argues that erotic capital is deployed differently along gender lines, with men and women utilising it in different ways to achieve different ends. While 'digital capital' has been increasingly accepted as a useful term by social researchers, there is more resistance to the term 'erotic capital' as a sociological concept. Hakim has herself made some controversial statements, writing in *The Evening Standard* that 'the returns of attractiveness equal the returns of qualifications. Many young women now think beauty is just as important as education'. Her work has been turned to by some readers as a guide to 'empower' women to develop and deploy 'erotic capital'. For some feminists this is itself highly problematic, and may serve to reproduce problematic gender roles and stereotypes.

Practice Theory

Bourdieu's work helps explain the reproduction of social hierarchies through an approach to society which connects culture, institutions, embodied dispositions, and the practices which people take part in. This focus on social practices can easily be seen from the titles of his books, such as *Outline of a Theory of Practice* [1972] and *The Logic of Practice* [1992]. The conversions of different forms of capital, and the attendant privileges they enable, are of course a crucial part of this framework.

The theory Bourdieu presents links cultural values, social structures, and individual tastes, actions, to help explore and explain these practices. As such, it provides a sophisticated map for understanding how and why people behave as they do. While in Bourdieu's account the material actions and behaviours of people were significant, they were not given overall primacy. Yet, over the past three decades, we have seen a rise of new theories of practice which draw upon Bourdieu, but which diverge from him, focusing more on the materiality of social life and social practice, and less on the noumenal or the social-structural. This new focus on practices, less anchored to social structures, has been referred to as 'the practice turn'.

One particularly influential practice theory is that developed by Theodore Schatzki in his books *Social Practices* [1996] and *The Site of the Social* [2002]. Schatzki's approach typifies this privileging of the embodied actions and behaviours people take part in. There is a focus on the material, on the tools, spaces, places, and movements which reproduce social life. Space and materiality are foregrounded in Schatzki's work in a manner that is less central to Bourdieu, who is equally concerned with the cultural and symbolic hierarchies in society. Yet, for Schatzki, prioritising material practices can help understand much of the social world, including the subjective dimension. This is because for Schatzki it is through *doing*, through taking part in shared cultural practices, that people come to know their society. Linking with ideas deriving from the philosophers Ludwig Wittgenstein [1889–1951] and Martin Heidegger [1889–1976], Schatzki argued that people act in a manner that makes sense to them. Understanding develops out of practical behaviours. This is also seen as crucial to how identities are created; people develop their sense of self through the practices they take part in. Today, it is increasingly Schatzki's approach, which foregrounds material practices, that is turned to by social researchers, especially within the fields of consumption studies and organisational studies. This is an important way in which Bourdieu's ideas resonate throughout contemporary social research, but have also been adapted by subsequent thinkers.

Conclusion

Bourdieu remains a towering presence in social theory; all social science undergraduates will inevitably encounter his concepts and an army of Bourdieusian sociologists continue to deploy them, aspiring to work within the auspices of his critical, reflexive research programme. Bourdieu's idea of sociology as a combat sport typifies his approach to social research and served to radicalise some of the more moderate wings of the discipline. There was even a feature film, *La Sociologie est un sport de combat*, released in 2001, which sought to capture Bourdieu's work and to show him through his day-to-day life as a prominent, activist sociologist. His analysis of inequalities, which located both education and culture firmly within such conversations, continues to inspire research today.

Yet, as with all the theorists we have discussed, his work is far from free of controversy. For more orthodox Marxists, the cultural conception of class which his work has served to promote can be seen to have obscured the economic dimension of class at exactly such a historical moment when third-way parties globally were trying to advance a 'post-class', 'post-material' agenda. Such an argument would suggest that Bourdieu, who was passionately concerned with material economic inequality, may have accidentally released concepts and theories which served to unintentionally reinforce and obscure structural exploitation. At the same time his work has been criticised for the perceived primacy it affords to class as a vector of social privilege. He certainly did not engage extensively with the intersectional insights which are centred in much contemporary social theory. As such, Bourdieu has been criticised for both failing to engage sufficiently with an economic analysis of class; but equally he has been criticised for failing to engage with non-class axes of social injustice. However, both criticisms are perhaps a disservice to Bourdieu's life and work: he cared passionately about economic inequality and was a vocal advocate for the rights of people who suffered injustice on various grounds, not merely class.

Questions for Discussion

1   Is Bourdieu's theory deterministic? Does he leave space for people to resist and challenge the forms of social reproduction which he outlines?

2   Do you think fields have autonomy? What does this look like in practice?

3   In which ways is Bourdieu similar to Marx?

4   Is Bourdieu's work overly concerned with class at the expense of other logics of social exclusion?

5   Is the cultural conception of class Bourdieu's work accentuates serving to hide fundamental logics of economic exploitation?

Further Reading

Primary Texts

Outline of a Theory of Practice [1972]

This was Bourdieu's first major work in the field where he would become famous, linking individual behaviours and social structures. This book is best understood as a conversation with the French structuralist tradition, with Bourdieu seeking to add more agency and primacy to the agentival actions of individual actors than the structuralist tradition permitted. Many of the themes which Bourdieu developed throughout his ideas can be seen here.

Distinction: A Social Critique of the Judgement of Taste [1979]

This is Bourdieu's most famous work, where many of the ideas and concepts developed in *Outline of a Theory of Practice* are applied to the topic of cultural consumption. As such, it can help to think of *Distinction* as a continuing theoretical development and empirical application of the ideas presented in *Outline of a Theory of Practice*.

The Logic of Practice [1980]

This book is a development of both *Outline of a Theory of Practice* and *Distinction*. Many of the key themes from both are further expanded upon and refined here; for example, ideas such as 'field' and 'habitus' are both returned to. A theme which is new to this book is the 'practical' nature of practice. It is this 'practical sense' which guides individual behaviours.

Homo Academicus [1984]

A detailed study of the French academic world. Bourdieu directs many of his key concepts to the study of university life and discusses 'academic habitus', 'academic field', and 'academic capital'.

In Other Words: Essays Towards a Reflexive Sociology [1990]

A collection of essays focusing on the idea of 'reflexive sociology'. By 'reflexive sociology' Bourdieu is concerned with self-critical social research, with the sociologist constantly conscious of their positionality and the nature of their own conceptual toolkit and how it may impact on their findings. Taken together, the essays collected here point towards the need for a reflexive sociological community, with Bourdieu offering up his own work and methods for critique as part of this broader challenge.

Language and Symbolic Power [1991]

Bourdieu argues here that language is not neutral, functioning merely to enable efficient communication. Rather, language is shown to be inflected with, and enables the manifestation of, power relationships and social hierarchies.

On Television [1996]

In keeping with his broader project, this selection of essays and interviews shows how television serves to reproduce cultural hierarchies and thereby reinforce broader power relationships.

Acts of Resistance: Against the new Myths of Our Time [1998]

This book marks Bourdieu's move to provide a more explicit critique of neoliberalism. The focus here is on the increasing levels of social injustice, the damage done by unchecked globalisation, and the harms of deregulation. The book is deeply political, trying to encourage both academic and political resistance to 'the tyranny' of the market.

Firing Back: Against the Tyranny of the Market [2003]

A continuation of the themes in *Acts of Resistance*. Here, Bourdieu calls for a more international coalition to fight back against neoliberalism.

Secondary Texts

Fiona Devine, Mike Savage, John Scott and Rosemary Crompton, Eds., *Rethinking Class: Cultures, Identities and Lifestyles* [2004]

An edited volume bringing together leading social researchers writing about themes of class and culture. This volume will help contextualise Bourdieu's work relative to other developments in the social sciences and humanities, such as post-modernity and the cultural turn.

Michael Grenfell, *Pierre Bourdieu: Agent Provocateur* [2004]

An intellectual biography exploring Bourdieu's life and ideas. Engages in detail with many of his key concepts.

Michael Grenfell, Ed., *Pierre Bourdieu: Key Concepts* [2012]

An excellent and accessible guide to Bourdieu's thought. Each chapter is focused on a particular concept. A great resource for a first-year undergraduate.

R. Petersen and R. Kern, 'Changing Highbrow Taste: from Snob to Omnivore' [1996]

An important article originally published in *American Sociological Review* suggesting that upper-class Americans are now far less selective in their cultural consumption. While this group retains a disproportionate engagement with 'high culture', Petersen and Kern's work shows that they increasingly engaged with 'low culture' too. As such, Petersen and Kern challenge the idea that there is a simplistic cultural repertoire of distinction, suggesting instead that upper-class social actors are now best framed as 'cultural omnivores'.

Dylan Riley, 'Bourdieu's Class Theory: The Academic as Revolutionary' [2017]

This article, published in *Catalyst*, provides a searing critique of Bourdieu, arguing that his work offers no understanding of social change and that it ultimately appeals to elite sociologists, as it gives them a sense of purpose and meaning and resonates with their lived experiences. Riley suggests that Bourdieu's work ultimately provides no real explanations and generates no real problems or solutions.

K. Robson and C. Sanders, *Quantifying Theory: Pierre Bourdieu* [2009]

Shows how Bourdieu's ideas and concepts can be operationalised for dealing with big datasets.

David Swartz, *Culture and Power: The Sociology of Pierre Bourdieu* [1998]

Focuses on the key theme in Bourdieu's work: the relationship between culture and power. This book not merely introduces Bourdieu's key concepts, but it also explains ways in which they have been misinterpreted by Bourdieu's critics and shows areas where the concepts themselves need further development. This is a useful critical introduction.

J. Thatcher, N. Ingram, C. Burke and J. Abrahams, Eds, *Bourdieu: The Next Generation: The Development of Bourdieu's Intellectual Heritage in Contemporary UK Sociology* [2018]

In each chapter, different sociologists explain how they use Bourdieu's concepts in their research. This book is not merely a good introduction to Bourdieu; it also shows how social theory and concepts can be deployed to support empirical research.

Jen Webb, Tony Schirato and Geoff Danaher, *Understanding Bourdieu* [2002]

An accessible introduction to Bourdieu's work organised into thematic chapters. An ideal text for a student new to Bourdieu's work.

chapter 7

The Frankfurt School Today: Modernity, Communication, and Recognition

Contents

DOI: 10.4324/9781003359555-7

The Institute for Social Research, home of the 'Frankfurt School', was founded in 1923. Both the wider world and academia have changed considerably in the past century. Today's Frankfurt School thinkers reflect these changes and are markedly different from their 'first-generation' forefathers. While in Chapter 5 we discussed the anti-capitalist, interdisciplinary Critical Theory of 'first-generation' thinkers such as Theodor W. Adorno and Herbert Marcuse, this chapter focuses on the newer, intersubjective theories of Jürgen Habermas (1929–) and Axel Honneth (1949–). *Intersubjectivity* is the key concept for understanding contemporary Critical Theory, which is focused largely on the processes enabling shared experiences and understandings about the world to emerge through productive interactions.

Today, according to Mark Fisher and the 'Capitalist Realist' tradition, it is 'easier to imagine the end of the world, than the end of capitalism'. This was not the case when Adorno and Marcuse were at the height of their fame, with radical anti-colonial movements and self-styled 'communist' states always in the public eye. When Adorno and Horkheimer were writing, the idea that a more rational, more socialistic society could exist felt realistic, even inevitable. Yet, with the symbolic fall of the Berlin Wall, and the embrace of free-market norms by once left-wing parties, the dominance and resilience of capitalism seemed unwavering. As Francis Fukuyama (1992) worded it in a famous book, it seemed that, with liberal capitalism, we had reached 'the end of history'. For many centrist and left-liberal scholars, it indeed felt as though liberal and pluralist democracy, based on a free-market vision of the economy, was the final destination of humankind's social and political journey. Such sentiments are writ large in contemporary Frankfurt School Critical Theory, which distinguishes it from its radical forebears. While the fundamental questions driving first-generation Frankfurt School research were 'where was the revolution Marx had predicted? and 'how can we bring it about?', today's Frankfurt School theorists have a more ambivalent relationship with capitalism. As we discuss below, unlike Marcuse and Adorno, Habermas and Honneth are not Marxists striving for the fall of the free-market system.

As discussed in Chapter 5, it is convention to speak of various 'generations' of Critical Theory, reflecting shifting political and theoretical commitments. The first generation of the Frankfurt School reached something of a political and theoretical dead-end in the late 1960s. While radical activist students sought revolutionary conflict with the capitalist, repressive state, Adorno was adamant that the preconditions for such a conflict were not met. In short, Adorno argued against taking revolutionary action; the forms of consciousness and social norms in place remained fundamentally capitalist. Adorno argued that to attempt revolutionary transformation at that time would be unwise and would fail, risking descent into the 'state-capitalist' authoritarianism of the Soviet Union. For students and activists to agitate now would simply be a case of prioritising doing something (anything!), regardless of whether it made sense to do so (Adorno's 'actionist critique'). While Adorno called for calm and further social critique, his more radical students were infuriated. A popular chant rang out on left-wing campuses: 'If Adorno is left in peace, capitalism will never cease!'.

Adorno's work, as well as his politics, seemed increasingly out of step with the times. He invested increasingly in the power of transcendent art, and these ideas were later published posthumously in *Aesthetic Theory* [1970]. While students were fighting pitched battles against the police over the war in Vietnam, Adorno was sedately listening to new kinds of 'liberating' music. Critical Theory was clearly struggling to connect with the mass base of students who looked up to the tradition for ideas and leadership. The injunction to philosophise distortions of rationality as a weapon against a world of napalm and starvation was simply too much for radical students to accept.

In place of Adorno's focus on deformed rationality, which for many came to be the primary association of the Frankfurt School towards the end of the 1960s, a new voice emerged within the Frankfurt School: Jürgen Habermas. Habermas quickly made a name for himself with his proposed re-grounding of the Critical Theory tradition and for engaging in some (heated) public debates. With time, Habermas guided Critical Theory away from Adorno's philosophy, which he held to be overly reliant on metaphysics (to abstract claims about reason and being). Habermas was still invested in the notion of 'reason'; however, he sought to connect his work much more explicitly with individual subjects and with studies of social institutions. Where Adorno spoke of forms of reified consciousness in rather abstract, unfalsifiable ways, Habermas focused instead on public opinion creation, the public sphere, and communicative reason. Key interventions in this regard are Habermas's *Post-Metaphysical Thinking I/II* [1988 and 2017] and *Theory of Communicative Action Vol. 1 & 2* [1981/1991]. In both studies Habermas sought to provide greater specificity when discussing 'reason' and to connect with the natural sciences to provide an empirical anchor for his claims. Habermas's work marked a substantial change in style and direction within Critical Theory and is thus referred to as representing a 'second generation' of the Frankfurt School. Many of the values of Habermas's work continue to dominate in the 'third-generation' approach today, whose principal exponent is Habermas's former student, Axel Honneth.

Second- and third-generation Critical Theory have much in common, both reflecting this transition away from metaphysics and away from the Marxian concerns of Critical Theory's birth. Tellingly, both Habermas and Honneth adopted a new approach to modernity itself, holding the unfolding of history to show a range of 'societal learning processes' which ushered in the possibilities for greater individual autonomy. Such possibilities were held to be visible through a focus on intersubjective relationships, such as the way in which people communicate with each other, or *recognise* each other. In places within Honneth's more recent work, such as *Freedom's Right* [2014], the focus has shifted to identifying moments where subjects fail to appreciate the freedom which modern institutions enable, such as the 'Western' legal system. This clearly demonstrates a very different worldview to early Frankfurt School thinkers.

For Habermas, the key intersubjective domain for analysis is the world of language. Through communication, subjects were held to share a common interest in being understood, and there existed a social space unencumbered by the logics of capitalism, or 'the system' at large. There was held to exist a species of 'communicative rationality' which could be explored through a range of traditions such as linguistic philosophy, pragmatics, developmental psychology, and neo-Kantianism. In Habermas's work, language offers the possibility of a normative foundation for social research: the just, ideal world could be theorised as a place in which each subject has an equal ability to speak and to make themselves understood (the 'Ideal Speech Situation'). Honneth's Critical Theory develops many of these themes; however, he moves from language acts to a focus on subjects' ability to 'recognise' each other. Honneth's Critical Theory of society remains intersubjective, like Habermas's. While Habermas focuses on the role of language, Honneth focuses on recognition. Honneth's Critical Theory is based on the idea that through a sufficiently detailed and sophisticated analysis of recognition relationships we can understand and critique the entirety of the social world. The focus remains on empirically grounded intersubjective relationships; in this regard he views his work as building upon Habermas's rejection of metaphysics.

Habermas and Honneth reoriented the social theoretical commitments and political aspirations of the Frankfurt School. As we shall discuss in this chapter, while second- and third-generation Critical Theory was able to connect with a new activist movement seeking greater recognition and inclusion within the social world, their Critical Theories fail to adequately interrogate how social-structural logics of race, class, and neo-coloniality impact on the lived realities of citizens in our interconnected world. In this chapter we draw out how, in its current form, contemporary Frankfurt School Critical Theory may indeed be 'too male, too pale, and too frail', presenting a very narrow, limited set of concepts which fail to capture the experiences of many people. As such, the latest developments with the Frankfurt School tradition have been controversial, with authors such as Michael J. Thompson arguing that in recent years, we have seen *The Domestication of Critical Theory* [2016].

Key Concepts

While Habermas and Honneth developed distinctive Critical Theories, their work shares an investment in intersubjectivity. What should be clear from the discussion below is the real differences that exist between early and later Frankfurt School Critical Theory. Over the years the Frankfurt School's political commitments, social-theoretical concepts, and philosophical foundations shifted considerably. Few of the concepts or principles which Adorno, Marcuse, and Fromm operated with remain in today's 'third-generation' Frankfurt School texts.

Modernity and 'Social Learning Processes'

Recall from Chapter 5 that Adorno and Horkheimer held a very negative view of modernity. In *Dialectic of Enlightenment* [1944/1947] they argued that the basis of modern thought, 'identity-thinking', was deeply problematic, destroying individuality. 'Enlightenment' forms of cognition were held to lead inexorably to the Holocaust and to totalitarian societies. Likewise, Herbert Marcuse identified the rise of a 'One Dimensionality' of social experience with the rise of the 'advanced industrial society'. Capitalism, science, and technology were held to exist in a complex relationship which served to perpetuate a repressive social order. For the early Frankfurt School, the progression of the decades did not necessitate progress towards a more rational and humane social order.

In contrast, Habermas and Honneth both identify positive, emancipatory features of modernity. Societies, like organisms, were held to be capable of learning and of evolution. For Habermas, a key positive development with modernity was the 'bourgeois public sphere', encapsulated by the rise of 'coffee houses' where people would meet to discuss the topics of the day. Such spaces encouraged a form of social interaction in which the strength of argument held sway, rather than simple economic might or feudal obligation. The development and fate of such modern public space, and of public debate more broadly, has been an enduring feature across Habermas's work, starting with *The Structural Transformation of the Public Sphere* [1962] and leading into his more mature work such as *The Theory of Communicative Action* [1981]. While Habermas ultimately concluded that the bourgeois public sphere, and the open debate it once encouraged, had been increasingly colonised by market forces, he retained an investment in the possibilities for the meaningful democratic dialogue which modern institutions can enable. In his later work and in recent public interventions he explicitly supported the European Union, which he argues holds the possibilities for enabling complex forms of sovereignty and retaining space for deliberative discussions.

Likewise, in Honneth's breakthrough text, *The Struggle for Recognition*, he identified how intersubjective struggles had paved the way for greater societal inclusion and have led to greater appreciation of different cultures. His later work *Freedom's Right* provided an extensive discussion of how the entire modern state served to represent possibilities for such positive, liberating, recognition relationships. Honneth argues that specific forms of freedom ('legal', 'moral', and 'social' freedom) are enshrined within the modern (European) social formation. Honneth's text is itself a rewriting of Hegel's earlier work, *Philosophy of Right*, which outlines how the social world had reached a state of fine-tuned perfection during the Prussian autocracy. While Hegel presented nineteenth-century Prussian autocracy as the manifestation of ultimate freedom through his concept of the working through of *Geist*, Honneth follows the post-metaphysical approach of Habermas, and seeks to anchor his claims in how modern institutions facilitate healthy recognition relationships. In Honneth's work it is clear that modernity is held in a positive light. Public sphere institutions, the liberal democratic state, even the free market, are viewed as enabling freedom and supporting a healthy self-relation. Such a view of modernity as enabling social and self-development is clearly very different to the commitments evinced by first-generation scholarship.

Post-Marxism

Frankfurt School Critical Theory can be understood as a development of the 'Western Marxist' tradition. This approach to understanding society places capitalism and class relations at the heart of any socio-political analysis; however, it is not based on a dogmatic reading of Marx's economic analysis. For the founders of the Western Marxist approach, such as György Lukács, there is indeed held to be a primacy to the logics of exploitation embedded in the economic domain. Crucially, however, this insight inspires further philosophical and sociological investigation. The way the economy works is held to substantially determine other social spheres, yet these social spheres are also crucial areas of analysis. The central stratification analysed by such theorists tends to be class and class relationships and how the nature of class conflict is obscured by ideology. In this regard Lukács famously argued that there was an emancipatory historical destiny to the proletariat, who he regarded as being both the 'subject' and the 'object' of history. They needed to gain class-consciousness and realise their world-historical calling. By this, Lukács meant that history worked through their struggles, and they represented the historical agency capable of driving forward social progress. Class was afforded an unshakeable primacy in Lukács's analysis. As discussed in Chapter 5, the early Frankfurt School was far from 'blind' to other structures such as race, providing famous studies on the rise of fascism and the Holocaust in particular. However, crucially, this rise of the far right was held to be causally connected to social-structural logics, which were fundamentally anchored in economic and class-based relationships.

In contrast, Habermas and Honneth adopt a different approach to Marxism which can be called 'post-Marxist'. Indeed, one can view the development of the Critical Theory tradition as a gradual movement away from Marxism. In today's Frankfurt School theory, the focus is no longer on market relationships. Class and market imperatives are no longer viewed as being the prime movers of social action, social conflict, and identity formation. That said, both Habermas and Honneth continue to operate with some important Marxist concepts and differentiations while believing that they hold less utility in changing social and academic worlds. In a speech in 1989, Habermas famously said that 'I mostly feel that I am the last Marxist'. Therefore, it is perhaps best to think of the concepts central to the contemporary Frankfurt School as being *influenced* by Marxism, rather than fundamentally Marxist in nature.

Recall that for classical Marxists, there exists a divide between an economic 'base' and a socio-cultural 'superstructure'. The logics of the economic base substantially control what happens in all the other non-economic domains which are simply lumped together as 'the superstructure'. Habermas reformulated this binary division while retaining aspects of Marx's insights. In his *Theory of Communicative Action* [1981] Habermas proposed a theory of society which was divided between 'systems' and 'lifeworlds', rather than base and superstructure. The 'system' was no longer simply 'capitalism' and the 'lifeworld' was now not merely some incidental domain, of limited concern to 'proper' Marxist scholarship. In Habermas's vision, 'lifeworlds' refer to the everyday, the community experiences, social interactions, and quotidian affairs. In contrast, the 'system' contains not merely the economy, but also all bureaucratic and legalistic dynamics. Each domain was held to be the natural home of a different kind of rationality. The system was the domain of instrumental action, where strategic calculation was the norm. In contrast, the lifeworld was a domain where communication was supposed to be the main objective. Habermas argued that in recent years we were witnessing the colonisation of the lifeworld by the logics of the system; of instrumental rationality creeping into and shaping our everyday life in a manner opposed to the interests of the demos. This approach has clear echoes of Marxist theory, but it is also substantially more expansive and shows more of an interest in the lifeworld as a site of independent action.

Honneth has moved further beyond Marx; however, like Habermas, he also still operates with some nominally Marxist concepts, such as reification. Importantly, in *The Struggle for Recognition*, Honneth argued that we need to move beyond the Marxist obsession with productivism and class. In place of focusing on an analysis of the market, Honneth has argued that we should view the entire socio-economic world through the lens of 'recognition', of intersubjective relationships between people (see below). This has been controversial in that some theorists have argued that this actually makes it harder to analyse important aspects of the social world. This was the focus of a key debate with Nancy Fraser which was published in a book, *Redistribution or Recognition: a Political-Philosophical Exchange* [2003]. With Honneth's move to a Critical Theory of recognition, the focus on the proletariat as the 'subject-object' of history has been entirely displaced in favour of appealing to, and anchoring his research within, struggles for identity and inclusion within the social world. This is also a source of controversy, with authors such as Michael J. Thompson and Stathis Kouvélakis (1965–) viewing this as a betrayal of Critical Theory's emancipatory aims.

Post-Metaphysics

First-generation Critical Theory drew heavily upon Hegelian-Marxism. This approach to theory holds that societies instantiate different forms of rationality. In simple terms, this means that *how* people think (not just their opinions) is impacted on by social institutions. Habermas's early work retained this vision. This was clear in his book *Knowledge and Human Interests* [1968] where he reflected on the aims of various forms of scholarship and criticism. One theme in this book is that through critical reflection people can become better connected to the macro-changes in social thought which are embedded in different institutions. Crucially, this understanding of 'rationality' is metaphysical; it cannot be subject to immediate empirical analysis. This area of scholarship has been historically connected to the German philosopher Immanuel Kant's thought on rationality and consciousness, seeking the development of a 'first philosophy' or a 'philosophy of consciousness'. Such rationalist philosophy was typically disconnected from empirical social science. Inspired by conversations with his friend the philosopher Karl-Otto Apel [1922–2017], Habermas's work firmly moved away from such meta-physical commitments. His mature, nuanced position was presented in two books, *Post-Metaphysical Thinking Vols I and II* [1988/2017]. This turn to post-metaphysics is important for contemporary Critical Theory.

In contrast to the metaphysical idea that there are substantive values embedded within the fabric of the social order which shape *how* people think, Habermas based his later work on observable social-scientific insights. In particular, Habermas moved to engage with empirically grounded traditions which focused on empirical, person-to-person ('intersubjective') interactions. In this regard, Habermas's substantive Critical Theory depended less on Hegelian and Kantian abstract philos-ophy and drew upon new traditions, previously outside the scope of Critical Theory. In particular, Habermas incorporated insights from American scholarship, such as pragmatics and symbolic interactionism. These traditions feature prominently in Habermas's work on language and communication (see below).

Similarly, Axel Honneth's work is grounded upon the idea that any Critical Theory of society today must not be based on abstract metaphysi-cal commitments. Rather, Honneth's work is reliant on insights from Donald Winnicott's object-relations theory. His work also retains Habermas's interests in Symbolic Interactionism and American social the-ory in general. Indeed, Honneth's work can be viewed in part as offering a recasting of central ideas and works of classical social-political thought through a strictly non-metaphysical lens. For example, Honneth's book *Reification: A New Look at an Old Idea* [2007] recasts the Marxist idea of reification through a new intersubjective viewpoint. Similarly, Honneth's *Freedom's Right* [2014] offers an extended discussion of the relationship between social institutions, norms, and individual freedom, in a manner that reconstructs Hegel's *Philosophy of Right* [1820], however without any reliance on the metaphysics which undergirded Hegel's project.

In short, the key concepts utilised in contemporary Frankfurt School theory are intended to be 'post-metaphysical'. Whether or not this goal is always achieved has been a source of debate. What is clear, however, is a stated commitment to a 'post-metaphysics'.

Communicative Action

While Habermas has written prolifically on a vast range of subjects, he is best known for his work on communication. In his two-volume work, *Theory of Communicative Action* [1981], Habermas provided social theory with a range of concepts that have sparked research far beyond the confines of the Frankfurt School itself.

While Adorno and Horkheimer viewed the Enlightenment project as eroding the possibility for unalienated interaction, Habermas's mature Critical Theory is based on the possibility for productive, equitable, and rational intersubjective exchanges. Habermas's project sought to explore rationality not as some metaphysical essence which could never be empirically analysed but as something grounded within the way people spoke to each other. Within conversations, particularly legitimately conducted arguments, Habermas saw a form of rationality at work which had not been deformed by capitalism and modernity. For Habermas, this linking of reason and language offered an empirical route into analysing rationality and society; one which had normative content and which could identify possibilities for social progress. This idea of reason embedded in the structures of language is what 'communicative action' refers to.

At the core of Habermas's work on communicative action is his idea of a 'universal pragmatics' (UP). Like 'Critical Theory' itself, UP refers to both an area of study and a quasi-political commitment. The basis of universal pragmatics is the belief that people want to understand each other and that many of the conflicts which exist in the world arise out of failures to appreciate what other people are thinking. Scholars of UP consider there to be the possibility for reaching peaceable and fair agreements through intersubjective dialogue. The goal of universal pragmatics is to theorise and facilitate processes of reaching mutual understanding through exchanges between people. This 'understanding' can be viewed at two levels. First, at the most basic level of grasping the content of the proposition presented – consider the utterance 'I feel hungry'. One must grasp the meaning of the words ('I', 'feel', and 'hungry') and the impact of their particular word order and emphasis. But crucially, such an understanding occurs at a deeper, second level, reflecting a shared awareness of the possibility of communication and understanding between each party. Social coordination becomes possible through such mutual recognition. UP is particularly invested in the rational reconstruction of the foundational possibilities for mutual understanding which arise through intersubjective dialogue.

Habermas's work seeks to focus on the emancipatory and peaceable possibilities inherent in attaining a state of mutual understanding through communicative action. The project of universal pragmatics is interdisciplinary, drawing upon linguistics, the philosophy of language, symbolic interactionism, epistemology, philosophy of mind, and a range of social theoretical traditions. The ultimate objective of the project of UP, and of Habermas's Critical Theory of Communication, is the development of a world in which all subjects have the capacity to be equally understood, where all claims and statements are treated on their merits. This is the 'ideal speech situation' described above.

Recognition

A key term for second- and especially third-generation Frankfurt School Critical Theory is 'recognition' [*Anerkennung*]. The concept derives from the philosophies of Johann Gottlieb Fichte (1762–1814) and especially of G. W. F. Hegel (1770–1831). For Hegel, recognition refers not merely to the basic epistemic capacity for identification (for instance, I may recognise your phone as a Google Pixel). It also refers to the deeper sense of appreciation of the worth, merit, or status of the Other. Think of the more formal and legal occasions where we use the word 'recognition' today, such as 'recognising a court' or 'recognising someone's humanity'. This deeper concept of recognition is crucial to much of Hegel's work and is described at length in his *Phenomenology of Spirit* [1807]. For Hegel, a crucial part of human psychological development is moving from a unitary, solipsistic being to a socially conscious being who engages with Others. This process is described at length in one of the most famous passages of Western social and political philosophy, the so-called 'Master and Slave' or 'Lord and Bondsman' parable. In this abstract tale, Hegel describes the process by which people come to appreciate the social nature of existence. This process is traumatic and deeply conflictual. It is also highly abstract and is difficult for all readers to immediately comprehend.

Hegel tells of how a basic form of subjecthood (X), who thinks they are the only thinking agentival being in the world, comes to encounter another subject, capable of agency, who also considers themselves to be the unique master of their universe (Y). This is an almighty shock and blow to the egos of both X and Y. A battle ensues between the two subjects, each seeking to force the other to accept the role of 'object', to reinforce their own unique status and superiority. This becomes a struggle for existence, a desperate fight to protect one's self-understanding as uniquely superior. Eventually, X dominates Y and achieves superiority, forcing Y back into a state of objecthood, to do X's bidding as a slave. However, this is now no longer satisfactory for X who has been forced by their interaction to acknowledge at some deep level a fundamental change in their status. To retain their title as a true, agentival subject, they realise that they need not merely the obedience of Y but Y's acknowledgement of their status as an agent. However, such an acknowledgement cannot be meaningful if it comes from a slave, forced into the role of object. Such status acknowledgement could only come from another volitional subject. As such, X and Y are required to meet as equals. It is only through the mutual recognition of a subject by another subject in conditions of parity that true subject status can be bestowed. Hegel's parable continues, but this part of the story is the key to understanding much of the 'recognition' turn in critical social theory over the past 40 years.

Axel Honneth was inspired by Hegel's writings on recognition and came to build an entire Critical Theory focused on such recognition struggles. Honneth's work can be understood as a development of Habermas's interests in intersubjectivity and post-metaphysics with a focus on recognition rather than on linguistic communication. Like Habermas, Honneth was keen to root his theory within empirical evidence and not merely within metaphysical abstraction. As such, his *Struggle for Recognition* [1992], where he presents his substantive Critical Theory, draws on object-relations theory and a range of other psychological studies. Honneth identifies three particular types of recognition which he argues we can empirically prove are essential to enjoying a meaningful and happy life. These are love (recognition from your family), esteem (recognition from your work), and rights (legal recognition). If any of these three are missing, an injustice is held to occur and society requires critique and transformation so as to remedy the unacceptable withholding of recognition. For Honneth, the development of societies can be seen as the continual attempts to create a fairer, more modern world, in which each of these species of recognition is offered. The modern world, for Honneth, in his book *Freedom's Right* [2014], serves to facilitate recognition through its various institutions. All social problems, in Honneth's Critical Theory, can be understood as failures of healthy recognition relationships to be facilitated, as 'pathologies of recognition'.

How Has This Shaped Social Theory?

Habermas's work in particular has had a massive influence on social theory. He has reshaped the field in a way that no other theorist has in the past half-century, with the exception of Michel Foucault (see Chapter 9). While today Honneth's approach to Critical Theory is increasingly influential, many of his conceptual innovations have their origins in Habermas's earlier reformulation of the Frankfurt School project. In some regards these impacts are obvious, such as the *intersubjective turn* in social theory and across the humanities and social sciences. Yet, other important developments are subtler, such as an increased willingness among theoreticians post-Habermas to engage with a range of divergent theoretical traditions to develop concepts and perspectives for social research.

The Intersubjective Turn

Following Habermas, the social sciences have taken an *intersubjective turn*. This means that the focus of much social theorising and social research has been on exploring the constitutive relationships which exist between subjects. While this is evidently the case in the work of subsequent Frankfurt School theorists such as Axel Honneth and Rainer Forst [1964–], the intersubjective turn has been impactful far beyond the confines of Critical Theory.

This *intersubjective turn* is based on a widespread embrace of many of the foundations of Habermas's own work. For example, among sociologists of health and illness, of youth, and of 'race' and migration, there is an appreciation of the need to pay close attention to the emerging empirical data on the importance of interpersonal relationships. This is seen as offering an important evidential foundation for social research rather than relying on the metaphysical assumptions of earlier eras. In this regard the intersubjective turn can be understood as part of a broader movement away from metaphysics, which Habermas's work helped inspire.

Importantly, there is a sense of intersubjective experiences possessing an important critical capacity. This can be identified when subjects engage with each other, be it in how they communicate (as in Habermas's own work), how they recognise each other (in Honneth's account), or in how they attempt to justify their claims (in the more recent work of Forst). This valuable intersubjective capacity (for recognition, etc.) is presented as offering a reservoir of critical consciousness, some fundamental, foundationally human basis for understanding and criticising flawed relationships and social structures. While with the rise of both post-modernism and post-structuralism (see Chapter 9), it is philosophically difficult to make a grand claim that position X is universally right, we can instead base our normative claims in the experiences of suffering, of disrespect, etc. As such, the focus on intersubjective experience has become a perspective through which to explore larger social structures and patterns of exclusion and discrimination. The sense that this can provide a foundation for social critique which is both philosophically justifiable and empirically verifiable has led to the uptake of an intersubjective approach across many areas of study.

The intersubjective turn has fundamentally displaced key ideas of earlier critical social theory. For example, the idea that there are innate and inviolable human capabilities for recognition, for peaceful communication, and for justification, which can offer a critical entry point to social interactions, is seen as an absurd claim by Marxist scholars. The fundamental Marxist insight that our consciousness and critical capabilities are shaped by our economic and material lives has been replaced by this new focus on the alleged emancipatory potential of our inviolable intersubjective capabilities. We discuss this further below.

Fusing Theoretical Traditions

Frankfurt School Critical Theory had always sought to combine insights from different traditions and to engage in interdisciplinary research. In practice, this meant the bringing together of insights from Marx, Weber, and Freud, resulting in a unique fusion of political economy, interpretive sociology, philosophy, and psychoanalysis. This was always remarkable in comparison to other traditions (such as structural functionalism), which operate with a much narrower set of thinkers and concepts. However, Habermas served to drastically expand the range of traditions within which Frankfurt School Critical Theory operated further still, drawing upon insights from linguistics, pragmatics, empirical psychology, symbolic interactionism, and the philosophy of law. This open-mindedness to embrace a range of divergent traditions and disciplines has had an undeniably revitalising impact on social theory and has stimulated a range of new concepts and approaches. Again, while this can be seen very clearly within subsequent Critical Theorists, such as Honneth's interest in object-relations theories, an openness to a fusion of a broader range of ideas and traditions has impacted on social theory more broadly. A famous example here would be Judith Butler, who, like Honneth, draws upon many different schools of thought. Butler has written that it has been 'an honour' to engage with Honneth's thought and writes approvingly of 'the complexity of [his] theory'.

The relationship which exists between social theory and philosophy in particular has been altered by second- and third-generation Critical Theory. Today, a far more expansive range of philosophical ideas are engaged with by social theorists. While there have always been overlaps between the goals and interests of philosophy and social theory, this had previously occurred within informally circumscribed limits. Recall how for Durkheim sociology was explicitly presented as a science, with a clear sociological method: ventures into the abstraction and conjecture of philosophy were to be avoided, as they risked discrediting sociology's 'scientific' status. Partially as a result of this conscious attempt at distanciation, and also due to other socio-cultural factors, social theory had largely limited its engagement to the critical 'continental' tradition of philosophy, working through ideas which had a heritage in a school of thought known as German idealism. We can place Karl Marx's thinking, for example, firmly in this category. In contrast, the 'analytic' canon of philosophers, typically based in American and English universities, was largely excluded from social theory, and often considered too abstract to be of use for applied social research. Habermas's work made a fundamental bridge with these analytic traditions, building concepts and theories which drew equally upon established social theoretical concepts and both continental and analytic philosophy. In particular, Habermas and subsequent social theorists have turned to analytic philosophy to explore how to theorise society in a way that reflects the many different attitudes and values which exist in a multicultural society.

Modernity and Modernities

Habermas's work on modernity and on social learning processes is radically different to that of the early Frankfurt School. While Adorno and Horkheimer, for example, viewed modernity as connected with the growth of 'barbarism' and reductive, destructive modes of thought, Habermas sees modernity as a fundamentally positive and emancipatory project; an attitude echoed by Axel Honneth. In contemporary Critical Theory, modernity is held to enable a diversity of expression, a freedom of communication, and the capacity for expedited social learning. The problems with our social world can be viewed as a fact that modernity is an unfinished project, that we are not modern enough. Again, this is directly opposed to the view of modernity presented by Adorno and Horkheimer in *Dialectic of Enlightenment*. This new, unabashedly positive view of modernity catalysed extended discussion on both modernity and on Habermas and Honneth's theories thereof.

The works of Anthony Giddens (1938–), Peter Wagner (1956–), Gerard Delanty (1960–), Hartmut Rosa (1965–), and Bruno Latour (1947–2022) demonstrate just some of the breadth of scholarship which has contemplated modernity over the past 30 years. Yet, while these very different thinkers have all provided interesting engagements with modernity, with greater or lesser degrees of direct engagement with contemporary Critical Theory, perhaps the most striking conceptual response has been to suggest that there may exist 'multiple modernities'.

The theory of multiple modernities emerges from the work of Schmuel Eisenstadt (1923–2010), Jóhann P. Árnason (1940–), and Bjorn Wittrock (1945–), and can be viewed as a direct rejoinder to Habermas. For advocates of a 'multiple modernities' approach, there is such remarkable historical, economic, and cultural divergence in how modernity is experienced that it is necessary to speak of 'modernities' in the plural. This is presented as an important corrective to the Habermasian understanding of a singular modernity which brings with it unifying, universal social-learning processes. The idea that it is worth speaking of multiple modernities is supported by empirical evidence that modernity has always presented itself differently. Even within geographically delimited spaces such as Europe, there exists remarkable variation. This remains the case today, with markedly varying degrees of secularisation, state control, and individual autonomy existing across continental Europe.

What Are the Limitations of Second- and Third-generation Critical Theory?

Frankfurt School Critical Theory now sits closer to liberal democratic theory than to the Marxist scholarship of its heritage. This has been highly divisive. For some, this has enabled insights from Critical Theory to be liberated from outdated Marxist ideas and to be applicable to real-world challenges, such as how to better provide care for those in retirement, or how to best integrate a more diverse workforce. Yet, as we discuss below, these changes have been highly controversial, with scholars such as Michael J. Thompson arguing that they constitute nothing less than *The Domestication of Critical Theory* [2016].

Forgetting Capitalism

For Thompson, contemporary Critical Theory is a pale imitation of its earlier self. The work of Habermas and Honneth has served to displace the critique of capitalism from the centre stage of analysis. This is a real problem: capitalist logics remain the dominant force shaping people's lives and are a serious factor in the existential threat of global warming. Now is not a good time to decentre the critique of capitalism from our Critical

Theory of society. This change in focus, while starting with Habermas, has expedited with the Critical Theory of Axel Honneth. Indeed, Honneth is not critical of capitalism in important passages of his work. In Honneth's *Freedom's Right*, the market is presented as offering possibilities for healthy forms of recognition, suggesting that there is nothing inherently wrong with the market system. Thompson reminds us that the critique of capitalism as a fundamentally irrational and destructive system, based on the exploitation of the labour of the vast majority of society, is at the heart of earlier Critical Theory. Arguably the Frankfurt School's move away from a hostile engagement with capitalism is a betrayal of the very idea of critical social theory.

For Nancy Fraser, another strident critic of mainstream contemporary Critical Theory, the problem is not simply the sidelining of the critique of capitalism. Rather, as she draws out in an important exchange with Honneth, *Redistribution or Recognition* [2003], contemporary Critical Theory is structurally incapable of engaging with many of the central problems of the capitalist economy. In Honneth's Critical Theory, all that is required to conduct social theory is a sufficiently developed analysis of how intersubjective recognition relationships are operating within society. Yet, Fraser reminds us that many of the crucial features of capitalism, which control the lives of billions of people, operate on a level removed from intersubjective exchanges. She encourages her reader to consider the:

> supply and demand for different types of labor; the balance of power between labor and capital; the stringency of social regulations, including the minimum wage; the availability and cost of productivity enhancing technologies; the ease with which firms can shift their operations to location where wage rates are lower; the cost of credit; the terms of trade; and international currency exchange rates.

Clearly, these crucial features of capitalism and of society require a theory which does not look just at social status and intersubjective recognition. Sadly, Honneth's theory leaves social theorists blindsided, unable to explore these adequately through the framing of recognition alone. This is a serious and unresolved problem for the many scholars that seek to develop and refine a Critical Theory of Recognition.

Blind to Power

For Thompson and Lois McNay, contemporary Critical Theory is also blind to how power truly operates within societies. The intersubjective turn, as discussed above, is based on the belief that all social actors have deep-seated intersubjective capacities (to recognise, to communicate, etc.) which cannot be touched by outside forces. People are held to have an inalienable capacity for meaningful, status-attributing recognition relations, or to engage in open and transparent dialogue to achieve a meaningful understanding of the other's position. For both Thompson and McNay this is simply unrealistic. People are thrown into a world strewn with power relations. How we come to learn to recognise and communicate with each other is evidently shaped by the complex forms of structural power which exist across all social domains. For Thompson, the belief that people have these pure incorruptible intersubjective skills is naive and represents a form of 'neo-Idealism': an investment in subjects' capabilities which cannot possibly exist. Rather, as Marx wrote in his *A Contribution to the Critique of Hegel's Philosophy of Right* [1843–4], our ideas and our cognitive capabilities are shaped by our material worlds.

A good example of how this operates in action can be seen by looking at how people engage with social media. In Habermas's theory of Universal Pragmatics, there is a deep-seated capacity for meaningful understanding, compromise, and agreement in communicative exchanges. Yet, a brief glance at Twitter or YouTube comments demonstrates how the social media age has transformed and denatured our capacities for communication. The aim of intersubjective exchange is no longer to attain mutual understanding, or to demonstrate the superior coherence of a particular proposition. Rather, the objective is to shock, to grab attention, to steal headlines. It seems hard to marry Habermas's belief in progress, modernity, and communicative action with a world in which a serving President of the United States, Donald Trump, encourages Covid-19 sufferers to drink bleach. Clearly all communicative exchange is impacted by material circumstances, and today these are often structurally rigged towards an attention-based economy. Our capacity to develop intersubjective exchange and compromise can be structurally undercut by market logics.

There is also a danger to this false belief that people's ability to form meaningful, healthy recognition relationships is not tarnished by sociostructural power. Many feminist social researchers have studied how victims of domestic abuse have come to find meaning and even selfworth in the abusive situations they are in. The all-too-familiar claim that 'he only hits me because he cares about me' demonstrates how people's sense of recognition, and of meaningful interpersonal relations, can be pathologically deformed by coercion and by the normalised abuse of power asymmetries. This is particularly problematic theoretically, as the move to intersubjective social theory has typically been supported by social researchers who wanted to move beyond the perceived obsessive focus on market forces and logics. However, it seems that the intersubjective turn is not merely incapable of engaging with key aspects of capitalist society; it also fails to provide a satisfactory normative anchor for theorists invested in identity politics, and gender and racial justice.

Eurocentrism

A further limitation of contemporary Critical Theory is the Eurocentric understanding of modernity at the heart of both Habermas's and Honneth's theoretical imagination. While the ascent of modernity may have increased average life-expectancy and opportunities in the Global North, this story is not the case globally; far from it. The trajectory of modernity needs to include the story of slavery, of empire, of (neo-) coloniality, concerns which are never central to Habermas's or Honneth's work. This Eurocentric notion of modernity is problematic both as it is historically inaccurate in its implicit universalisation of European 'modernity', but it is also politically problematic in that it serves to obscure and naturalise the logics of extraction and environmental destruction which continue today. Honneth's *Freedom's Right* offers an extensive discussion of an ideal-typical Western nation-state and demonstrates how its institutional spheres facilitate healthy recognition relationships. However, he fails to acknowledge how the development of these institutions is fundamentally predicated on the mass murder and enslavement of millions of people. This is a crucial and highly problematic exclusion. Further, the central productive logic of capitalism upon which the entire edifice is built, of infinite growth, is already producing terrifying environmental crises. Modernity exists as much in the legacy of slavery in colonies, of predicted catastrophic floods in the Asian subcontinent, of 'scientific' racism, and of nuclear testing in French Polynesia.

While contemporary Critical Theory can rightly be criticised for having a naively optimistic and Eurocentric view of modernity, there is a more pressing concern for many activist groups beyond the Global North. In *Red Skin, White Masks: Rejecting the Colonial Politics of Recognition* [2014], Glen Coulthard demonstrates how abstract sentiments such as 'rights' and 'communication' are useless substitutes for the material suffering which exploited and abused nations have faced. What is required is not a focus on abstract intersubjective capacities, to recognise the truth claims of groups, or to offer apologies recognising past wrongs. What is required is *immediate* transfer of native lands, and the termination of extractive mining programmes. Increasingly, activists and decolonial scholars are calling for financial reparations for past and ongoing colonial exploitation. In short, recognition and a politics of dialogue and 'mutual respect' can serve as a smokescreen to justify holding off on genuine, material change.

Contemporary Frankfurt School Critical Theory is highly controversial, and is passionately rejected by those loyal to first-generation insights. This has led to a splintering of Frankfurt School scholarship.

How Are Third-generation Concepts Deployed Today?

Despite being somewhat unpalatable to more Marxian members of the Frankfurt School, Habermas and Honneth have both been remarkably successful in achieving an impact with their Critical Theories across the social sciences. As we discuss below, their concepts have been deployed to explore everything from 'fake news' to the Eurozone crisis, from migration to social care. Whatever philosophical and political limitations can be identified in their reformulation of Critical Theory it is undeniable that their work has brought Frankfurt School ideas into dialogue with a range of new fields of study.

Communication and the Public Sphere

Many of Habermas's concepts have found their way across the social sciences and humanities. Perhaps the two most impactful have been his notions of the 'public sphere' and 'communicative reason'. These have both been deployed regularly across social research over the past few decades, and since 2016 in particular. While Habermas inflected these concepts with a progressive, optimistic faith in modernity, the rise of authoritarian populism and 'fake news' have led to these concepts being deployed more critically. Some scholars, such as Bosco and Ribeiro, have demonstrated how Habermasian themes can be used in their original form to explore the rise of populism, with their work focusing on the ascent of Jair Bolsonaro in Brazil as a result of social media manipulation. However, there have also been numerous studies which have recast Habermas's concepts as foils in the current socio-political era. There is an extensive literature on how the attention economy has supplanted the democratic and emancipatory ideals associated with earlier manifestations of the internet. Habermas's concepts are often deployed here to largely show how the possibility for communicative action has been undercut by the marriage of affective politics, nationalist populism, and the instrumental-rational core of social media. In this regard, Christian Fuchs, in *Digital Demagogue* [2018] and *Critical Theory of Communication* [2016], shows both the merits and the limitations of Habermasian concepts today.

Habermas's notions of the 'public sphere' and of communicative rationality also found favour among many theorists of deliberative democracy. Consider, for example, the work of Jane J. Mansbridge (1939–). These concepts also entered the mainstream of much international political theory. Habermas is still writing public commentaries, drawing upon many of his concepts when discussing crises of the Eurozone.

Recognition

Similarly, Honneth's account of recognition has been highly popular for a range of social researchers, many of whom work far beyond the confines of the Frankfurt School. An important area where recognition has taken hold has been in the study of social work. A key figure here is Stan Houston, who has drawn upon Honneth's work while providing an important critical commentary. The recognition framework has also been deployed in migration studies, with Gottfried Schwieger's collection, *Migration, Recognition, and Critical Theory* [2021], indicative of trends in the field. These are just two of the most obvious examples, with Honneth's approach also featuring within contemporary studies in pedagogy, critical criminology, and social movement studies.

Honneth's recognition approach, however, has probably made its biggest impact within social theory itself, serving to radically reframe a whole host of social problems through the recognition paradigm. His work has seen a remarkable uptake, especially considering the manifold limitations outlined by critical scholars, as discussed above. However, efforts have been made by a range of critical social theorists to explore problems from economic poverty to cognitive sociology through Honneth's paradigm. In sum, the concept of 'recognition', like that of the 'public sphere' and of 'communicative reason', will today be found right across the humanities and social sciences.

Conclusion

The Critical Theories of Habermas and Honneth have reoriented the Frankfurt School from Hegelian-Marxism and metaphysical abstraction into the world of mundane, applied social research. György Lukács once criticised the research institute for residing in 'the grand hotel Abyss', of watching the world burn with a detached indifference. Today, contemporary Critical Theory has a far more direct relationship with orthodox social research, connecting with studies of migration, the Eurozone, and care labour, for example. Yet, Lukács, a committed Marxist, would likely have found the writings of Honneth and Habermas far more distasteful than the 'Ivory Tower' dialectical theory of Adorno. For while Lukács could fairly criticise (some) first-generation Frankfurt School theorists for their failure to get their hands dirty by avoiding the rough and tumble of the political fray, he did not consider their work to be explicitly supportive of the capitalist system. This is the charge laid at the door of Honneth and Habermas by many of their contemporary critics, such as Michael J. Thompson. Once, the Frankfurt School provided a cadre of dialectically minded scholars who sought to identify and expose the contradictions at the heart of capitalism. Today, capitalism is no longer at the centre of the Frankfurt School's political project. Thompson (2016) is not alone in suggesting that when capitalism is discussed by contemporary Critical Theory, a far more ambivalent and at times positive framing is adopted.

In light of the myriad limitations of contemporary Critical Theory, especially its failure to enable an interrogation of core dynamics at the heart of capitalism, it appears indicative of the worst failures of contemporary social thought. Where one may intuitively consider that 'newer' social theory would be more attuned to the logics of class, race, and gender, it proves to be far from the case. As discussed above, the understanding of power upon which the intersubjective turn is predicated has failed to heed crucial insights on false consciousness and ideology, hard-earned lessons which spring from critical race and gender theory as much as from Marxist thought. In conclusion, contemporary Critical Theory has succeeded in making an academic impact in an increasingly domesticated social science. What is perhaps most depressing about the 'male, pale, and frail' second and third generations of Critical Theory is not their substantive limitations; rather, it is the ease with which these limited concepts have served to ingratiate themselves within mainstream social research.

Discussion Questions

1   How does contemporary Frankfurt School Critical Theory differ from first-generation Frankfurt School Critical Theory?

2   Why do some scholars consider Critical Theory to have been 'domesticated?'

3   Differentiate between the Critical Theory of Jürgen Habermas and Axel Honneth.

4   Does the world need more modernity?

5   Is social theory better off without metaphysics?

Further Reading

Primary Texts

N. Fraser and A. Honneth, *Redistribution or Recognition: A Political–Philosophical Exchange* [2003]

An accessible dialogue between two leading critical theorists, Nancy Fraser and Axel Honneth. Honneth famously proposed that a 'monistic' recognition perspective for social research can capture all social reality. In contrast, Fraser argues that a 'perspectival dualist' approach is needed, so that the researcher can capture both recognitional and distributional injustices. This debate occurs in different theoretical registers throughout the book.

J. Habermas, *The Structural Transformation of the Public Sphere* [1962]

In this book Habermas charts the development, evolution, and decline of the public sphere. Emerging with coffee house and salon culture in the 1700s as a counterweight to aristocratic and state power, the public sphere was presented as originally a bourgeois phenomenon. Rational and critical discourse dominated and the better argument held sway. Yet, over time, critical-rational discourses were swept aside as commercial interests came to dominate the public sphere. In time, powerful elites squashed the emancipatory potential of these islands of critical discussion. Yet, the ideal of a public sphere and communicative and critical rationality lives on as a guide for how to structure democratic societies.

J. Habermas, *Legitimation Crisis* [1973]

Like Marx, Habermas argues that capitalism is prone to crisis. Habermas identifies three particular kinds of crisis which occur: economic, cognitive-institutional, and legitimacy. The book focuses mainly on legitimacy crises, where there is increasing lack of support from the public for the dominant social institutions. Habermas's solution to the legitimacy crisis he diagnoses is for greater transparency and increased public democratic engagement.

J. Habermas, *Theory of Communicative Action: Vol. 1 Reason and the Rationalization of Society* [1981] and *Vol. 2 Critique of Functionalist Reason* [1991]

This is arguably Habermas's most famous work, where he introduces many of his key concepts. It is a complicated text and not an easy read for an undergraduate new to social theory or philosophy. Habermas's argument is that communication is crucial to the 'lifeworld' of society. A good society is one where people can communicate freely with each other and be listened to, where 'communicative rationality' holds sway. In contrast, another form of rationality, 'instrumental rationality', emerges from the social 'system' (i.e. capitalism). Communicative and instrumental rationality thus exist in tension, reflecting this battle from the demands of the system and the demands of the lifeworld.

J. Habermas, *Post-metaphysical Thinking I and II* [1988/2017]

Because of the plurality of worldviews in modern societies, Habermas argues for a more modest, procedural, and inclusive approach to theorising. In contrast to grandiose narratives linked to unfalsifiable metaphysical claims, Habermas seeks to ground social critique and social theory in the normative value of open discourse. The idea of an ultimate superior teleology is rejected; instead, what is promoted is the processual: the dialogue itself. This book is part of a broader move away from Hegel and the German Idealist legacy and connects with a broad embrace of pragmatist philosophy.

J. Habermas, *Between Facts and Norms* [1992]

An important work of legal and democratic theory. Habermas argues that laws and moral values should be established through inclusive, fair, and respectful dialogue between subjects. Laws are just when they are created and updated through communicative action processes rather than merely because they are created by democratically elected sovereign bodies.

A. Honneth, *The Struggle for Recognition* [1992]

Honneth argues that a Critical Theory of society with normative content can be constructed based on subjects' experiences of misrecognition. Honneth builds upon the philosophy of the young Hegel, which he brings into discussion with a range of other thinkers and traditions. This is a crucial book for understanding contemporary Frankfurt School Critical Theory.

A. Honneth, *Reification* [2007]

Based on his Tanner Lectures, this short book reframes reification through Honneth's recognition perspective.

A. Honneth, *Disrespect: The Normative Foundations of Critical Theory* [2007]

A wide-ranging selection of essays on topics from recognition and social pathology to human rights and cultural belonging. Suitable for advanced undergraduate students or postgraduate students.

A. Honneth, *Freedom's Right* [2014]

Honneth's reworking of Hegel's *Philosophy of Right* without a metaphysical foundation in *Geist*. A complex book which has proved controversial. This text moves substantially beyond the conceptual arsenal and political commitments of first-generation Critical Theory.

Secondary Texts

Kenneth Baynes, *Habermas* [2015]

A clear introduction to Habermas's work. A good companion to Outhwaite's *Habermas: A Critical Introduction*.

James Gordon Finlayson, *Habermas: A Very Short Introduction* [2005]

A brief and accessible introduction to Habermas. The Outhwaite introduction is preferable if you have time. If time is against you, this is a fair substitute.

Lois McNay, *Against Recognition* [2008]

McNay offers a detailed critique of the recognition paradigm. This is a philosophically rigorous and wide-ranging text, engaging with the recognition turn beyond Critical Theory itself. More suited for postgraduate students.

William Outhwaite, *Habermas: A Critical Introduction* [1994]

An incredibly clear overview of Habermas's wide-ranging work. Outhwaite explains complex concepts with real mastery.

Danielle Petherbridge, *The Critical Theory of Axel Honneth* [2013]

A critical, but ultimately supportive, engagement with Honneth's social theory. Petherbridge starts by praising Honneth's early work, suggesting that it can provide important normative foundations for Critical Theory today. She then argues that Honneth's mature scholarship does not fully live up to this potential; however, the possibilities for doing so are there, within his work. What is required is largely a matter of tweaking: with sufficient edits Petherbridge argues that you can build a Critical Theory of society upon Honneth's understanding of intersubjectivity.

Michael J. Thompson, *The Domestication of Critical Theory* [2016]

Thompson offers a scathing critique of second- and third-generation Critical Theory, arguing that it is politically compromised and philosophically untenable. A crucial text critical of recent developments within Frankfurt School scholarship. Most suited to a postgraduate readership.

Christopher F. Zurn, *Axel Honneth: A Critical Theory of the Social* [2015]

A clearly written introduction to Honneth's Critical Theory. While there are some moments of critical engagement, Zurn is largely supportive of Honneth's project. As such, this book would be well paired with Thompson's *The Domestication of Critical Theory* to see the variety of perspectives in circulation.

Gender: Theorising Patriarchy

Contents

DOI: 10.4324/9781003359555-8

It is only within the past few decades that gender has been embraced as a central concern for social theory and social research. Indeed, it is only within the past few decades that the term 'gender' has been used to refer to an area of study at all. In the 1960s, the term used would have been 'feminism' instead. Back then, the word 'feminism' pointed to both an area of academic study ('feminist theory') and to political campaigning against *patriarchy*. Today, it is more common to speak of 'gender theory' or 'gender studies' as a discipline and to use the word 'feminism' to refer to political commitments against patriarchy. That said, the words used in this area are particularly important. The terms 'gender' and 'feminism' are freighted with particular political and philosophical inflections; the reasons someone may choose one word over the other are varied and complex. As we shall see in this chapter, words and 'discourses' are central to gender theory. As such, perhaps more than in any other chapter in this book, conceptual precision is crucial when it comes to understanding and researching this topic.

There has long been a peripheral literature in the social sciences and humanities exploring the gendered nature of social reproduction. A key figure here is Mary Wollstonecraft (1759–97), whose *Vindication of the Rights of Woman* [1792] recast the revolutionary liberal spirit of her era with a focus on gender. Similarly, Olympe de Gouges' (1748–93) *Declaration of the Rights of Woman and the Female Citizen* [1791] challenged the 'natural order' of male authority, an act of rebellion which contributed to her execution by guillotine in 1793. Arguably the most significant classical author on the topic was Karl Marx's long-time collaborator, Friedrich Engels (1820–95). Building partially on Marx's unpublished notes, Engels wrote a pioneering study, *The Origin of the Family, Private Property and the State* [1884]. This has since become an undisputed classic of social and political thought and continues to influence feminist scholarship today.

Engels noted the remarkable changing view on female sexuality across society: from a reverential pagan wonder of 'Mother nature', worshipping women for being capable of the miracle of birth, to the unspeakable Victorian shame of the very thought of a sexually liberated woman. The transition could not be starker. For Engels, this change was linked with the rise of private property and marked 'the world historical defeat of the female sex'. The increased concern with alienable property led to an obsession with inheritance and having a 'true' heir. This introduced a stronger policing of female sexuality, which became rigorously controlled and the subject of surveillance and moral condemnation. As Engels wrote, with these changes 'the woman was degraded and reduced to servitude; she became the slave of his lust and a mere instrument for the production of children'. Over time, this critique expanded and grew into a more developed Marxist feminism. Another important early voice here is Eleanor Marx (1855–98), Karl Marx's daughter. She co-authored *The Women Question* [1886] with Edward Aveling (1849–98), in which they argued that female oppression was so closely intertwined with capitalism that women's emancipation necessitated a socialist revolution. Yet, such revolutionary ideas from classical social theorists are not at the heart of today's 'mainstream feminism' which has a more liberal flavour.

Historically, feminist scholarship and activism has been placed into various 'waves', reflecting changing social, political, and scholarly concerns. While the dominant ideas guiding Gender scholarship up until the present have been constantly evolving, the values of 'first-wave' feminists, seeking inclusion and equality within the broader socio-economic system, remain central to much mainstream feminism today.

First-wave feminism (c. 1870–1930) was primarily associated with liberalism and with campaigns for female suffrage. The central principle was that women should be treated equally to men, that they were of equal moral standing, were equally rational, and should have access to the same legal rights. The core objective politically was the active inclusion on equal terms for women and men within the existing social order. The Suffragists, for example, did not seek the radical overthrow of the capitalist, racist, patriarchal system. They did not seek to reorganise how children were raised, or seek to revolutionise gender identities. It is worth noting that at the time the right to vote was limited in many ways; for example, only *property-owning* men could vote. The ambition of first-wave feminism was the expansion of fundamental legal rights to the female property-owning class, to ensure equal participation and inclusion within the existing social order. First-wave feminism was thus largely a campaign led by rich, white, liberal women, to enable their equal participation within the public sphere, on a par with rich, white men. As we shall see, such an approach to gender remains dominant today, with Equality, Diversity, and Inclusion (EDI) policies being the main entry point for much contemporary feminist politics.

Second-wave feminism emerged in the 1960s and was invested in a wholly different set of political objectives and its scholars developed a new set of concepts and perspectives. While first-wave feminists sought public-sphere legal rights to aid female emancipation, second-wave feminists realised that the legal right to own property, or to vote, had not led to the emancipation of women from a life of drudgery and domestic labour. Betty Friedan (1921–2006) famously wrote of *The Problem That Has No Name* [1963], the silent depression faced by American housewives as they complete their tedious, soul-destroying tasks. The right to vote had not brought women into a world of adventure, of equality, of liberating opportunities. For Simone de Beauvoir (1908–86), women remained trapped in the role of *The Second Sex* [1949], defined by their persistent inferiority to the 'male'. While some men were capable of experiencing 'transcendence' in their working lives, the vast majority of women remained anchored to the everyday, the 'immanent', the tedious. For second-wave feminists this required a radical new politics built upon challenging the socialised role of 'women' in society. Rather than campaigning solely for further public sphere rights, second-wave theorists constructed a new understanding of social power, arguing that 'the personal is the political', bringing renewed attention to the domestic sphere. Where first-wave feminists wanted inclusion within the social world through legal rights in the public sphere, second-wave feminists wanted emancipation from oppressive social relations, public and private, which required a retheorisation of female socialisation and a new concept of politics.

Third-wave feminism emerged towards the end of the 1980s and brought a focus on identity, 'race', and sexual positivity. Where second-wave feminists had focused on the problematic differences in socialisation between 'men' and 'women', third-wave feminists challenged the existence of any meaningful biological binary at the level of sex. Judith Butler's (1956–) work, such as *Gender Trouble* [1990] and *Bodies that Matter* [1996], broke down neat binary identities into more complex socialised categories. The 'objective reality' of 'straight' and 'gay', or of 'men' and 'women', was questioned by both new scientific knowledge and the rise of post-structuralist philosophy. Identity categories were further nuanced by the third wave's embrace of the voices of scholars mindful of how 'race' intersects with gender; voices which had been somewhat excluded from the second wave. Insights from authors such as bell hooks (1952–2021), Audre Lorde (1934–92), and Kimberlé Crenshaw (1959–) were incorporated, providing the third wave with a rich, conceptual toolkit. While third-wave feminism offers the possibilities for a transformative, radical research agenda, mainstream feminism today focuses on more narrow legalistic concerns, echoing first-wave campaigns. Key liberal feminist demands today are for further public sphere rights, recognition, and inclusive working policies. There is also a growing, but limited, discussion of a possible emerging 'fourth wave' of feminism; however, its precise coordinates remain uncertain.

As we discuss in this chapter, concepts from the study of Gender have invigorated much contemporary social research. Yet, as we draw out, there exists a gulf between the sophistication and concerns of the latest insights from gender theory and the political motivations and reality of how such concepts and knowledges come to life across the socio-economic worlds.

Key Concepts

The study of the gendered divisions within society has changed dramatically over the years. Indeed, the term 'gender' itself is new to denote the object of study itself, reflecting theoretical and political changes. Previously, the dominant term was 'women's studies'. 'Gender' is today preferred by many theorists, as it is a more expansive term which does not implicitly support a gender binary, nor denote a singular focus on the 'female' experience. As our exploration of the key concepts from gender theory below demonstrates, the field is far from solely concerned with 'women', with non-binary gender expressions and the normative male role both important sites of analysis.

Patriarchy

A common mistake is to assume that the study of gender is all about criticising 'men' to emancipate 'women'. This is an oft-repeated slander faced by feminists. Gender is concerned instead with a social structure called *patriarchy*. Patriarchy is a system comprised of multiple connected logics, much like capitalism. Central to patriarchy is a normative order, a set of assumptions or values. For example, in a patriarchal society there are clear attitudes held towards certain subjects: that women 'ought' to be caring, homely, and maternal, or that men 'ought' to be unemotional and brave. The set of values naturalised by patriarchy is referred to as *heteronormativity*.

Like any social system, those who follow its expectations, and fit neatly into its logics, experience forms of societal privilege, while those who exist outside its preferred identities and who challenge its norms experience additional obstacles and hardships. For instance, a boy who wishes to challenge heteronormative logics by wearing a dress may find himself bullied at school for embodying typically 'feminine' tastes. Hence, while women are intuitively more disadvantaged than men by the patriarchal order – and to a great extent this remains the case – the situation is significantly more nuanced.

Patriarchy is predicated on the existence of a gender binary, of there being 'men' and 'women', both with associated expectations and characteristics. Those who express a non-binary identity are anathema to the patriarchal order and as such are the subject of heteronormative condemnation. As a result, trans individuals suffer the highest rate of suicide and have a global life-expectancy significantly below that of cis-gender individuals. There is growing awareness of this reality, with trans-rights movements growing globally. Further, both men and women are disadvantaged when they do not reproduce patriarchal norms. The leading cause of death of men under the age of 30 in the United Kingdom is suicide; this is in part a result of the heteronormative ideal that men 'do not talk about their feelings'. Therefore, while women are principally structurally oppressed by patriarchy through their heteronormative association with the limited roles of carer, wife, mother, the patriarchal system limits the life choices of all people, not just women.

Patriarchy also has a corresponding set of assumptions about sexual attraction, reinforcing a normative heterosexuality; the idea that men 'ought' to be sexually attracted to women and vice versa. Those who do not reflect these norms, be it those who are asexual, bisexual, queer, or gay, are societally disadvantaged. Consider the legacy of homophobia taught from the pulpit by the Christian church and the crusade against 'LGBTQ ideology' in parts of Europe today. Likewise, consider the 'single-person premium' suffered by adults who choose to live alone, often being forced to pay considerably more for choosing to live a single life rather than being in a married couple, as heteronormativity dictates.

Patriarchy, like capitalism, is a concept; it is a theoretical device to help researchers comprehend and analyse their worlds. Like capitalism, the term 'patriarchy' reflects a critical attitude. As such, the term is overwhelmingly used by feminist scholars. Patriarchy, then, refers to a societal order in which heteronormative conduct is elevated and where various layers of societal coercion exist which encourage people to behave in line with gendered expectations. The study of this patriarchal system is the concern of gender studies. The deconstruction and overthrow of this patriarchal system is the goal of most feminists. Importantly, patriarchy is usually understood as being interconnected with other social structures, such as capitalism and imperialism. It may help to consider patriarchy as being the master concept of gender theory, towards which all other concepts and ideas coalesce.

A key conceptual demarcation provided by second-wave feminism was to distinguish 'sex' from 'gender'. It is important to preface the following discussion by stating that the move beyond the 'sex–gender' distinction, and the incorporation of the non-binary experience, is an essential part of 'third-wave' scholarship.

The second-wave 'sex–gender' distinction was presented with great clarity by Simone de Beauvoir (1908–86) in *The Second Sex* [1949]. 'Sex' was held to refer to the biological category of 'male' or 'female'; in contrast, 'gender' referred to the socialised behaviours deemed either 'masculine' or 'feminine'. The idea that 'sex' and 'gender' referred to different things was important. It suggested that while 'sex' was a fixed biological given ('male' or 'female'), gender was socialised, with 'masculinity' and 'femininity' being shaped by society, rather than inevitably following on from one's sex. From this perspective, biology did not determine one's destiny. In simple terms, that one has a penis does not necessarily mean one will grow up to enjoy football and lager. Likewise, that one has a vagina does not necessitate an inevitable preference for fashion and white wine. Gender was now understood as a socialised set of norms. Those who had a male 'sex' were expected to grow up in accord with certain gendered expectations; those who had a female sex had a different set of expectations placed upon them. These expectations were not a product of nature and biology but of society.

The conceptual distinction between sex and gender is significant for two different reasons. First, it suggests that there is no inevitable, eternal link between biology and tastes and character. Rather, society inscribes values which change with time and place. For example, Viking warriors, who embodied masculinity in tenth-century Scandinavia, would have long, flowing hair. Such an aesthetic would not be associated with masculinity in twenty-first-century Surrey. The awareness that gender was socialised enabled an appreciation of the social specificity of gender norms and enabled a theorisation of their transition and variability. Crucially, it also enabled a critique of existing gender expectations. As the work of Friedan and de Beauvoir made clear, gender norms served to facilitate a patriarchal society in which a sub-group of men were supported to flourish in the public sphere, while women were structurally restricted to the 'immanence' of their domestic objecthood: baby-maker, cook, cleaner. For de Beauvoir, this gendered socialisation was crucial to understanding and criticising society. Of particular importance to de Beauvoir was the gendered nature of the great myth of romantic love and monogamy through which the free woman 'chooses to desire her enslavement'. In moulding their self-image around the gendered notion of romantic love, of accompanying one man for life, women were seeking satisfaction solely through their role as supporting object to a man. It was a trap which women needed to escape from. For de Beauvoir, this gendered nature of social aspirations needed to be realised and combated; to 'emancipate woman is to refuse to confine her to the relations she bears to man'.

The idea that gender was not determined by a binary sexual identity (man or woman) opened up a world of possibilities. As second-wave feminism transformed into the third wave, gender theorists began to embrace the reality that if gender was not simply an extension of the male/female binary, why would it need to have only two manifestations? The possibilities for non-binary gender expression, and of more complex identity categories, suddenly became limitless.

Queer Theory

Queer theory refers to a body of scholarship that emerged in the 1990s which challenged the idea of a fixed 'normal' form of social behaviour. To do so, queer theorists drew upon ideas from a range of subjects, including social constructivism and post-structuralism, often bringing these into dialogue with insights from the natural sciences. Judith Butler's *Gender Trouble* [1990] is perhaps the most famous text which emerged from the queer theory tradition, in which post-structural thought was united with cutting-edge research from human biology. Butler's work served to destabilise the idea that there is a natural binary order within society, be it of 'male' or 'female', or 'gay' or 'straight'. In contrast, queer theory conceptualises a world beyond such binaries in which identity categories are constantly shifting. Butler thus calls upon her readers to perform 'gender trouble', to think beyond binary gender identities.

In contrast to de Beauvoir's distinction between a biologically fixed binary between 'men' and 'women' and a socialised gender identity, Butler's work argued that the fixity of the sexual binary must also be challenged. This idea came from two directions. First, from the biological sciences. Butler argued that at a fundamental level there are no meaningful binary divergences between biological 'men' and 'women'. There are often 'cases in which the component parts of sex do not add up to the recognizable coherence or unity that is usually designated by the category of sex'. Bodies, say the science, do not actually fit neatly into two genders.

Butler works through the obvious responses. The idea that biological men have X amount more testosterone is simply unviable as a determinant of a clear sexual binary; there are simply too many exceptions. Even the most basic distinction, of chromosomal divergence, was held to be false, as differing chromosomal presentations exist. Even at the most obvious, anatomical level, that of penises and vaginas, the biological binary is held to fail. This is because the clitoris and the penis are fundamentally made of the same tissue; the development of a penis, rather than a clitoris, is a matter of the extent of development. The difference is not qualitative and binary but, rather, like gender and sexuality, it is best understood as existing on a spectrum. Butler further supported her argument as to the scientific non-existence of a sexual binary through reference to the full array of identities which exist beyond male and female.

Butler united her scientific criticism of the sexual binary with a rigorous post-structuralist assault on fixed identity categories. For post-structuralists, the relationship which exists between 'signs' (i.e. words) and what they refer to ('the signified') is constantly changing. Consider the idea of 'work', for instance. While 50 years ago few people would consider care work done by family to be 'work', following decades of recent scholarship, such crucial care provision is increasingly understood as 'work'. As such, the understanding of all terms is held to be socially variable and exists within a world shaped by changing power relations.

Third-wave feminists afford more attention to non-normative gender identities: be it the experiences of those who are transgender; those who live their lives outside the European context in a third gender, such as the experiences of the Hijra community in South Asia, or the two-spirit community in North America. For Butler, terms such as 'men' and 'women' are reflective of structural patterns, and the social embrace of a sexual and gender binary should be linked to broader socio-cultural forms of power.

For Butler, the dissolution of the biological category of sex is crucial. Sexual identity is not fixed, static, unyielding. Rather, both sex and gender were now understood as socially and culturally contingent, a result of the words and norms of the given society. In contrast to a world in which there existed a fixed biological sex and socially contingent (and deeply patriarchal and problematic) gender relations, Butler spoke of the primacy of gender. In this regard, the category of 'sex' was somewhat dispensed with. In its place was the *performativity* of gender. One's gender identity was not fixed, determined by sexual identity. Neither was it static and merely socially imprinted. Rather, for Butler, gender identity was constantly enacted through the behaviour of the social subject; through 'a sustained set of acts, posted through the gendered stylization of the body'. One lives out one's gender identity through every action, every choice, every discourse; how one holds oneself, what one eats, drinks, believes. This notion of performativity links to older ideas associated with the philosophy of language. At its core, Butler's notion of performativity of gender suggests that gender identity is an act; it is lived and presented; it is a belief which is inscribed through one's conduct. This is not to suggest that the body is any less important than in earlier theory. Rather, bodies are held to be read socially, instead of existing in an isolated, pre-social binary presentation. The concept of gender performativity and Butler's dissolution of the fixed biological category of sex in favour of socially variable gender identities has had remarkable reach across social theory and social research.

Care Labour and Feminist Political Economy

An important area of Gender scholarship is Feminist Political Economy (FPE). Research in this field looks at how social resources (including labour power) are allocated along gender lines. An important insight provided by Gender theory, drawing upon FPE, is the realisation that for centuries a restrictive understanding of 'labour' had dominated. For years, research about 'work' focused on labour as a public-sphere activity, work that was done to earn money. Raising children and looking after the home, in contrast, was perceived as 'what God intended women to do'. To consider it 'labour', on a par with men's paid employment, was unthinkable, even blasphemous. Gender theory has served to challenge these ideas and presents researchers with a useful conceptual toolkit for a more expansive notion of work.

A crucial concept which emerged in this regard is 'care labour', which refers to the unpaid work put into raising children, caring for older relatives, cooking for one's partner, maintaining a home. While such activities had historically been dismissed as insignificant, gender theorists argued that this was a substantial burden and should be considered a form of labour as deserving of respect and remuneration as any other. For Angela Y. Davis, writing in *Women, Race and Class* [1981], this burden amounted to a form of 'domestic slavery'. Such 'care labour' is now considered a serious expenditure of time and energy and the concept plays an important role in gender research. Importantly, care labour is today not simply utilised to refer to 'women's work'; rather, in an increasingly heterogenous social world, men are now often also engaging with both elder and childcare as never seen before, especially members of the so-called 'sandwich generation'.

The significance of 'care labour' has grown in tandem with the rise of women's entry into the paid workforce. During the first half of the twentieth century trade unions had fought for the importance of 'the family wage', the idea that a single income should be sufficient to support a family. This had traditionally occurred along gendered lines, with men viewed as the natural singular family earner. In tandem with the rise of campaigns for female entry into the workforce, the power of labour was waning relative to the power of big business. As such, the progressive campaign for women to also enter the workforce as equals, should they wish to do, became transformed into a normalisation of families requiring two wages to afford the basics of existence; a place to live, food, etc. This transformation has been discussed at length by Nancy Fraser in her book *Fortunes of Feminism* [2013].

With families now requiring two incomes, a challenge exists; where once the mother 'naturally' looked after the children and the home, her time has now been allocated to also earning a market wage. As such, this poses a challenge: where is this 'care labour' going to come from? We have a clear 'crisis of care'. In reality, as per the research of Arlie Hochschild in *The Second Shift* [1989], women overwhelmingly take on *both* roles: now taking both paid work *and* continuing to do a disproportionate amount of care labour. This additional strain has been referred to as 'the double burden' or the 'second shift'. While men are increasingly also taking part in care labour, the strain disproportionately falls on women, and especially working-class women, who are unable to afford market-provided childcare and household help.

Contemporary gender theorists have conceptualised an additional 'third shift'. This additional burden refers to the 'affective labour' which is overwhelmingly committed by women rather than by men. This exists in a variety of forms which, as with care labour, has previously long been overlooked and naturalised as simply 'what women do'. Affective labour refers to the work and time put into delicate emotional work, be it calming a partner down after a stressful day at work, facilitating conversations with the wider family, or maintaining a general 'upbeat' vibe throughout the household. There is a gendered expectation that women are just better at 'soft skills' in all their forms; but, when both men and women are working in a stressful neoliberal environment, returning to a home and being the constant 'calming' influence is far from easy and the necessary repression can be unhealthy. The concept of 'affective labour' has also come to incorporate power asymmetries, norms, and gendered expectations related to a range of sexual interactions. As per the work of Fahs and Swank [2016], this incorporates, but is not restricted to, accepting limited sexual pleasure, tolerating sexual pain, and conceptualising sexual satisfaction relative to the partner's experience. Heteronormative expectations of women as mother, nurse, cleaner, sexual satisfier are now merged with the market requirement of co-wage owner. This can be conceptualised as the existence of three different but demanding 'shifts'.

Intersectionality

A key ingredient in third-wave feminism was the incorporation of insights from Black Feminist scholarship. One of the most impactful concepts which this introduced to the gender studies lexicon was *inter-sectionality*. This theory is associated with the work of lawyer and civil rights advocate Kimberlé Crenshaw, who popularised the term in 1989 in a paper in a law journal. Crenshaw noted that while there were slowly increasing legal protections on the grounds of gender discrimination and on the grounds of race, these left intersectional gaps: for instance, they failed to address the needs of black women. Legal protections on the grounds of gender were overwhelmingly aimed at supporting the needs of white women, while the protections on the grounds of race were targeted at supporting black men. Crenshaw thus identified the need for an intersectional analysis.

Third-wave feminism was interested in a broader range of identity categories and sought to better comprehend the complexity of patriarchal discrimination. In this regard, Crenshaw's work identified how the experience of various disadvantaged social groups are not merely additive. To be an old, black, disabled women looking for work is not merely a matter of suffering from multiple distinct subspecies of discrimination. Rather, the identity of 'old, black, disabled woman' is a particular intersectional category, with each identity marker connecting with each other in a synthetic and not merely additive manner. The experience of being an old, black woman is not a case of being 'old' + 'black' + 'woman'. Rather, the identity 'old, black woman' represents an intersectional manifold of multiple axes of oppression.

Much contemporary intersectional theory is utilised to support the contemporary EDI agenda. This seeks to combat discrimination, seeking to create a more equal and inclusive society, which has a greater appreciation for diversity. Intersectional thought often also connects with 'standpoint' theory, associated with Patricia Hill Collins' notion of the 'outsider within'. In *Black Feminist Thought* [1990], Hill Collins contends that there are reserves of knowledge which exist within under-privileged communities. The life experiences of a gay, disabled, black woman, for instance, offer a critical potential to articulate forms of discrimination in a manner inaccessible to those who did not have such an embodied experience. For Hill Collins, this needs to be appreciated by both activists and academics. Hill Collins' work is controversial, however, as it risks simplifying identity categories in a manner which suggests a false homogeneity of experience. Not all black, gay women have the same thoughts and experiences, for example. Indeed, there have long been passionate disagreements between many people who share overlapping forms of oppression. Further, as per much of the gender theory presented above, our ideas, desires, and forms of thinking can be shaped by problematic socio-political structures, suggesting that all testimony needs to be critically interrogated. That said, the focus on the intersectional experience as an important resource for scholarship is a defining characteristic of third-wave feminism and has had an impact across the academy.

How Did These Concepts Shape Social Theory?

Gender theory has had a substantial impact across the academy and within social theory in particular. It has transformed what is deemed worthy of theorising and of researching. In particular, concepts from gender theory have served to problematise identity categories, they have provided tools to explore gendered norms and expectations, and have enabled the interrogation of different forms of labour.

Fluid Identities

The primary virtue of the new conceptualisations of 'gender' does not lie simply in having an increasingly accurate 'identification' toolkit. It is not simply a matter of possessing more accurate labels to categorise individuals. Rather, the fundamental nature of static, binary, identity thinking has been challenged. Queer theory brings with it a new appreciation of the importance of thinking of identities as existing on a shifting spectrum, as being constantly in flux and always socially mediated. In place of a fixed identity, gender scholarship holds that people occupy various changing 'subject' positions, be it of 'father' or 'daughter', 'mother' or 'carer'. Subjects find themselves entering and exiting various subject positions through their changing life circumstances, while, simultaneously, the discursive construction of each subject position is also forever in flux. Masculinity, for example, is constantly being reworked, the norms of which are forever being recast. A professor's cropped hair may one day be the epitome of feminine fashion, the next month it would seem unequivocally masculine, or non-binary. Equally, as the months pass, the professor may grow their hair longer. People's bodies and performances of gender change, however, so does the social understanding of gender categories and gendered subject positions.

Following insights from gender theory, social theory increasingly engages with a range of identity categories relative to shifting subject positions; as dynamic, socially and historically variable, and nuanced by the particularity of individual experiences. Such insights have enabled the development of targeted concepts which have facilitated research into the minutiae of gender norms. In this regard, two concepts come to the fore: 'hegemonic masculinity' and 'emphasised femininity', both of which have been deployed to further contemporary social research on a range of topics.

Hegemonic Masculinity

The concept 'hegemonic masculinity' derives from the work of R. W. Connell (1944–) and synthesises insights from Marxist and gender theory. The term 'hegemonic' harks back to the work of Antonio Gramsci (1891–1937), who wrote at length about the socio-cultural processes through which certain groups achieve and maintain dominance. While Gramsci's focus was the dynamics which enables the bourgeois to retain their hegemonic position within society, Connell's framing enables an exploration of the ways through which particular masculine norms retain dominance within the gender hierarchy. Connell's concept of 'hegemonic masculinity' refers to an ideal-type reflecting an imagined presentation of ultimate 'manliness'. For example, the ideal of contemporary Western masculinity may be best encapsulated through a fictional character, such as Jason Bourne, or James Bond. However, as with the character James Bond himself, such masculinity is constantly changing (Phoebe Waller-Bridge, writer and star of *Fleabag*, is now advising on the Bond scripts). The hegemonic form of masculinity reflects the idealised notion of the masculine in any given time; however, it is not static but socio-culturally variable. It is also always aspirational, never fully attainable. It serves as a guiding horizon of the desirable form of male behaviour, and as such has a strong socialising influence. As James Messerschmidt's *Hegemonic Masculinity: Formulation, Reformulation, and Amplification* [2018] demonstrates, in the decades since Connell first outlined the concept, it has had remarkable reach and undergone considered theoretical development.

Emphasised Femininity

Connell's feminine counterpart of hegemonic masculinity is 'emphasised femininity'. This concept exists in response to hegemonic masculinity as it is always shaped by societal valuation of the masculine. Emphasised femininity refers to a construction of the idealised femininity which seeks to satisfy the male. As such, like hegemonic masculinity, it reflects *normative values*; how women are *expected* to behave. Such expectations change with time and with shifting socio-economic demands. The expectations of the emphasised femininity of the 1950s would see a housewife content to be confined to the private sphere; to find joy in cooking her husband's food and satisfying him sexually. Girls are socialised from a young age to adhere to the expectations of emphasised femininity; with an appreciation for care labour and passivity inculcated through their gendered selection of toys and circumscribed play activities. While the politico-economic changes caused by the necessity for multiple household incomes has led to the entry of most women into the public sphere, the values of the normative emphasised femininity of the 1950s have not fully dissipated. Studies show that even in professional settings, women are overwhelmingly viewed as inferior, as sexual objects, who ought to be naturally predisposed to ensuring male attainment and satisfaction. The changing nature of both hegemonic masculinity and emphasised femininity has offered rich areas for contemporary social research.

A significant social change that has occurred over the past 50 years has been the normalisation of middle-class white female public-sphere employment. For millennia, the heteronormative ideal was for a woman to be solely a mother and housewife. The transitions which have occurred within the realms of labour have been a subject of extensive sociological study. The concepts discussed above, such as the double burden, affective labour, care labour, and the third shift, have facilitated much contemporary social research. This has focused on attempts to deconstruct gender stereotypes and to promote more equitable inclusion of women within the workforce.

Gender theory has made a clear impact on social theory and social research. Key concepts from gender theory are undeniably pertinent to the struggles of the day and to ongoing societal transitions. For example, the retheorisation of labour, through the categories of gender studies, proved of real utility during the Covid-19 pandemic. The conceptual arsenal discussed above has been deployed by numerous scholars, across subjects, to demonstrate how heteronormative ideals had been quickly re-inscribed through lock-down. Care labour was significantly re-feminised, with men's careers being facilitated at the cost of women's.

Problems for Use in Contemporary Social Theory

The study of gender has clearly provided social theory with a vast array of concepts. Yet, while the rich conceptual arsenal detailed above can be used to facilitate a critical interrogation of patriarchal structures and norms, the dominant approach today, 'liberal feminism', reflects the interests of a limited, rich elite in the Global North. Too often concepts from the gender arsenal are deployed to support campaigns for better *inclusion* within irredeemably exploitative social structures to further the sectional interests of a tiny few. This is despite much progressive feminist scholarship existing which draws out exactly why such an approach will fail to challenge patriarchy, and may even serve to reinforce heteronormative values. There are thus growing calls from activists for both the study of gender, and the dominant form of feminist politics, to be 'decolonised' and to reconnect with a more revolutionary, transformative politics. There is also increasing awareness that much nominally feminist scholarship can be used to ironically entrench colonial hierarchies and actually silence, rather than empower, women. As the postcolonial feminist Chandra Talpade Mohanty (1955–) writes in 'Under Western Eyes', there is a risk that liberal feminist discourses offer merely essentialising and ethnocentric perspectives on 'helpless' 'third world women' which unintentionally serves to deny their agency and reinforce neocolonial ways of thinking.

Equality, Diversity, Inclusion

Unfortunately, the dominant manifestation of feminist concepts today lies in Equality, Diversity, and Inclusion (EDI) initiatives. In keeping with first-wave feminism, such campaigns seek a more equitable incorporation of people into the existing social system. From an EDI perspective, sustained attention needs to be placed on the entry of members of disadvantaged communities into senior positions across the public sphere. The challenge is to break through the glass ceiling, to have more 'different faces in high places'. Ultimately, such a politics is invested in creating a more diverse workforce where there are fewer barriers to employment and promotion based on arbitrary personal characteristics.

Such an approach is deeply flawed and serves to obscure many of the key feminist insights detailed above. Principally, an EDI approach suggests that what is needed is more equitable inclusion within the existing system. In reality, feminist scholarship points to the need for the *transformation of* rather than better *inclusion within* the racist, neo-colonialist, capitalist, patriarchal society. The fundamental structures which re-inscribe patriarchy are not engaged with through EDI approaches. For example, the reality that capitalism relies upon unpaid care labour and the exploitation of female labour in the third world are essential feminist insights. Consider the conditions of sweat-shop workers across South East Asia. The discussion of the links between capitalism, racism, and patriarchy is key to much leading critical feminist theory. Important here is Social Reproduction Theory, which is today associated with Tithi Bhattacharya, as explored in *Social Reproduction Theory: Remapping Class, Recentering Oppression* [2017]. Earlier versions of Social Reproduction Theory began this concern with the links between reproduced patterns of poverty, gender, race, and class back in the 1980s; a good example being the work of Lise Vogel, such as *Marxism and the Oppression of Women* [1983]. Similarly, feminist Critical Theorists, like Nancy Fraser and Rahel Jaeggi also show in work such as *Capitalism: A Conversation in Critical Theory* [2018] how patriarchy is fundamentally connected to capitalism and to racism.

The complex structural latticework of oppression must be challenged as a whole. EDI approaches seek inclusion within this deeply patriarchal, racist, capitalist structure; such an approach serves merely to legitimate the deeply irrational patriarchal-capitalist system, and serves to restrict the possibility of real change. The limitations of the EDI approach are best characterised through two examples which have been at the fore of socialist and decolonial feminist campaigning.

Consider first the example of the 2017 Cleaners' Strike at the London School of Economics (LSE). The University was founded by Fabian thinkers who were deeply concerned with inequalities; hence the case study is particularly troubling and demonstrates how universities can also be the site of extreme exploitation. While the University had an extensive campaign to support more representative inclusion of workers at higher levels (through EDI policies), the key workers who actually clean the offices, clean the toilets, wipe the floors, were outsourced; their labour became the responsibility of a highly capitalistically minded, for-profit company. While the EDI policies of the University were esteemed for taking steps towards a fairer, more inclusive university, the women upon whose work the university depended were no longer a key concern of the institution.

While paid staff of LSE had 41 days' paid leave and six months' fully funded sick pay, the outsourced cleaners, who were overwhelmingly women of colour, were paid nothing for the first three days of sick leave and then following that just £17.87 per entire day. They were paid under £10 per hour while living in London, where rent is extortionately expensive. As Mildred Simpson, a cleaner whose family moved from Jamaica to London, is reported as saying in a *Guardian* column: 'We're doing all the dirty work while they're drinking their champagne'. This example shows how patriarchy operates in reality: through the intersection of gender, race, and class. Working-class black women are *increasingly* exploited as a result of outsourcing and privatisation, while a small group of the most privileged women have additional opportunities available to them. Even here, it is typically only the most privileged women, those who are able to escape the heteronormative role expectations of mother, carer, and housewife. EDI does nothing to shift the real structural problems, while it can serve to entrench the capitalist system, which is deeply intertwined with patriarchal forms of extraction.

A second case study shows the limitations of EDI through a decolonial lens. While campaigns for better inclusion within the workplace in the UK are championed by institutions here, the approach is blind to the inequalities occurring overseas and where the company's profits substantially come from: through exploitation of women of colour in the developing world. A famous example is the horrific case of the Rana Plaza factory, which occurred in 2013 in Dhaka, Bangladesh. A structural failure of a building led to its total collapse and the death of over 1100 people. The building hosted numerous garment factories, including for brands such as Benetton, Mango, Prada, Versace, and Gucci. The building itself was simply unsafe, with multiple floors built without the necessary permits. While EDI initiatives in the UK may enable a black, gay woman to become CEO of a fashion house in London, the basic reality is that the wealth which that company gathers comes from the exploitation of the women who died in factories such as Rana Plaza. Neo-colonial exploitation and the structural exploitation of capitalism is hidden behind the veil of EDI policies. The sweat-shop labour of millions is hidden behind the façade of a CEO who is a woman of colour. The need for a decolonial feminist scholarship has thus been championed by a range of feminist voices. Françoise Vergès' *A Decolonial Feminism* [2021] teaches us to be mindful of how feminist demands have been coopted by countervailing interests, to obscure the structural realities of exploitation.

The Decay of Intersectionality

The key insights which today are associated with intersectionality actually have their origin in a radical group called the Combahee River Collective (CRC), who are most famous for their *Combahee River Collective Statement* [1977]. This text is often presented as offering the first exposition of 'identity politics' and provides the theoretical groundwork for the theory of overlapping forms of oppression, upon which Crenshaw's work elaborates. While intersectionality is now championed in hiring practices in most employment sectors and can sit comfortably alongside the broader EDI agenda, the Combahee River Collective were explicitly committed to the destruction of capitalism and imperialism, which they viewed as fundamental prerequisites for the liberation of marginalised and oppressed people.

The first paragraph on the CRC statement includes the line,

> The most general statement of our politics at the present time would be that we are actively committed to struggling against racial, sexual, heterosexual, and class oppression, and see as our particular task the development of integrated analysis and practice based upon the fact that the major systems of oppression are interlocking.

This statement echoes many of the claims of today's feminist groups who are not liberal in their ideological outlook, such as Social Reproduction Theorists and Critical Theorists. The key claim is that the dominant modes of oppression intersect and as such need to be deconstructed and transformed. As a result, such insights call for a politics of transformation, acknowledging the intrinsic and overlapping forms of exploitation which exist. There are thus no calls for policy provision to enable inclusion within the fundamentally exploitative system. The system itself needs to be challenged.

It is important to note that much contemporary 'intersectionality' politics is aimed at combating discrimination to enable better inclusion within the system, typically by understanding where legal lacunae exist where multiple marginalised subjects are excluded from legal rights. This is very much at odds with the insights and politics of the CRC, who were not invested in legal theory. Rather, their politics was fundamentally revolutionary and radical. Their statement continues, 'We realize that the liberation of all oppressed peoples necessitates the destruction of the political-economic systems of capitalism and imperialism as well as patriarchy'. As such, the members of the Combahee River Collective saw the systems of oppression as connected; it would be nonsensical to think of making capitalism more amenable to feminist demands. Rather, radical societal change was necessary.

The degradation of the revolutionary CRC statement opposing intersecting *structures of oppression* into the current liberal and legal form of 'intersectionality' represents a remarkable taming and co-optation of Black feminist insights. While intersectionality can be utilised to further greater *inclusion* within the international market order, the CRC are explicit about the objectives of their Black Feminism: radical social-structural change. The CRC could not have been clearer that they sought revolutionary social transformation. In contrast, through their rebirth in liberal texts, their insights re-emerge in a manner substantially more conducive and palatable to the interests of capitalism and patriarchy. Yet again, the story is of a theoretical vision from feminist scholars being coopted and degraded so as to function as a medium for a greater politics of inclusion, with their transformative revolutionary component lost.

How Do These Ideas Impact on Social Theory Today?

Gender studies has provided a powerful conceptual toolkit which enables the interrogation of pressing social problems. That there is a history of key insights from gender theory being coopted by opposing interests does not invalidate the fundamental value of the concepts which gender theory provides.

Political Transformation

There remains a crucial political necessity for research around divergent gendered experiences. This can be seen through simple statistical analysis of the incidence of gender-based violence, which tragically increased during the COVID-19 pandemic. This has occurred within the domestic setting with terrifying consequences. Equally, there is renewed attention on the complicity of police forces in misogynistic violence. The horrific case of the murder of Sarah Everard by a serving police officer in South London in 2021 serves to underscore both the urgency of the feminist project, but also the limitations of investing within a solely legal register. Abolitionist feminist groups have indeed sought to combat gendered and raced police brutality through calls to defund the police, recently expressed in *Abolition. Feminism. Now.* [2022] by Angela Y. Davis, Gina Dent, Erica R. Meiners, and Beth E. Richie. Such radical calls are based on the awareness that internal inquiries and calls for better inclusion within a fundamentally patriarchal and racist system will never succeed in changing the cultures of violence, misogyny, and impunity. The pandemic of gender-based violence is held by such authors to require not mere legal protections and better inclusion within the exploitative patriarchal institutions of the public sphere. Clearly the necessity exists for a sophisticated and revolutionary gender politics which requires the deployment of many of the concepts discussed above: hegemonic masculinity, gender performativity, and an awareness of the interconnections between multiple structures of exploitation.

While such horrific stories rightly feature more prominently in the media and in the public's consideration of gender differences in society, there remains an important necessity to challenge the everyday inequities of the gendered divisions of labour. The evolution of the conceptual apparatus capable of determining the 'affective' third shift, in addition to the more transparent 'second shift' of obvious care work, needs to be a catalyst for political change and further developed social research underscoring the irrationality and inequity of much domestic labour allocation. This requires the continued development of critical social theoretical concepts because the liberal feminist calls for better inclusion within the dominant systems of oppression entirely sidelined the foundational inequality caused by the naturalisation of gendered care labour. Women may be paid less per hour than men in their waged labour and liberal feminists rightly consider that this needs to be challenged. However, what such liberal politics is systematically blind to is the reality that women are socialised to also complete *an additional* number of hours of unpaid labour each day and that this is also central to the way labour is allocated in the capitalist system. Rather than focusing myopically on the paid labour domain, further critical social research is required to disclose and challenge the systemic inequities and irrationalities at the core of the capitalist–patriarchal nexus. Such a radical political project cannot be built on a liberal feminist politics, and as such there remains a crucial demand for the further construction and deployment of feminist critical social theory today.

Conclusion

Insights from the study of gender have clearly substantially shaped contemporary social theory. Yet, while the concepts provided by the rich theoretical tradition can enable a critical engagement with the structures which naturalise and perpetuate exploitation, the dominant form of liberal scholarship fails to provide a vehicle for critical social theory. The investment in equality, diversity, and inclusion serves to promote a politics of optimal inclusion within the fundamentally exploitative social system. What is needed, as Social Reproduction Theorists, Critical Theorists, Black Feminists, and Marxist feminists argue, is a transformation of the system itself. While liberal feminism continues to restrict research into the gendered divisions of society, the tools for a critical interrogation of patriarchy are present within the arsenal of critical social theorists. The challenge is to overcome the immense power of capitalist logics to coopt critical voices and to enable gender theorists to mount a truly systemic critique of the social world, which underscores the interconnections between patriarchy, capitalism, racism and neo-coloniality, and anthropocentrism.

Discussion Questions

1 What is the sex/gender distinction in second-wave feminism and how has this been challenged by third-wave scholarship?

2 To what extent have critical feminist insights and concepts been coopted by liberalism?

3 In what contexts is it useful to deploy Dorothy E. Smith's 'standpoint epistemology'?

4 Distinguish between the theoretical and political commitments of Crenshaw's intersectionality and those of the Combahee River Collective.

5 What does hegemonic masculinity look like today?

Further Reading

Primary Texts

Judith Butler, *Gender Trouble* [1990]

The 'bible' of third-wave feminism. In this book Butler demonstrates how 'sex' as well as 'gender' is socially constructed. While the text is not designed for an entry-level reader it is not inaccessible and, because of its importance to contemporary gender theory, it is definitely worth persevering with.

Combahee River Collective Statement [1977]

A classic statement of intersectional Black Feminism. Demonstrates the revolutionary, transformative agenda presented by the CRC and shows the more radical roots of today's more mainstream 'intersectionality'.

Angela Y. Davis, *Women, Race and Class* [1981]

A key Marxist feminist work. Combines 13 essays on topics ranging from slavery to criticism of (then) contemporary feminist politics.

Simone De Beauvoir, *The Second Sex* [1949]

A landmark text of second-wave feminism. This is a long and at times complicated work; however, by reading sections such as 'Early Tillers of the Soil' one can gain a clear insight into de Beauvoir's style and argument.

Nancy Fraser, *Fortunes of Feminism: From State-managed Capitalism to Neoliberal Crisis* [2013]

Combines a highly readable account of the limitations of liberal third-wave feminism with a clear vision for future feminist scholarship and activism.

Betty Friedan, *The Feminine Mystique* [1963]

Alongside *The Second Sex* this book was a core text for second-wave feminism. An international bestseller, Friedan writes in an accessible and engaging style.

Patricia Hill Collins, *Black Feminist Thought: Knowledge, Consciousness, and the Politics of Empowerment* [1990]

An excellent introduction to Black Feminism engaging with both academic and non-academic works.

Arlie Hochschild, *The Second Shift: Working Families and the Revolution at Home* [1989]

Based on extensive interviews, this landmark text was reissued in 2012 with updated data.

bell hooks, *Feminism is for Everybody: Passionate Politics* [2000]

An accessible text, suitable for someone entirely new to the field. hooks' book is argumentative and informative, making the case for the importance of feminism today.

Mary Wollstonecraft, *A Vindication of the Rights of Woman* [1792]

A classic text of Enlightenment thought. Wollstonecraft provides a classical liberal argument for the inclusion of women within the public sphere.

Secondary Texts

Breanne Fahs and Eric Swank, 'The Other Third Shift? Women's Emotional Work in Their Sexual Relationships' [2016]

An important journal article which discusses the gendered elements of sexual satisfaction.

Lorna Finlayson, *An Introduction to Feminism* [2016]

An accessible introductory text with a political inflection.

Mary Holmes, *Gender and Everyday Life* [2008]

An accessible introductory text.

Stevi Jackson and Sue Scott, *Gender: A Sociological Reader* [2001]

Focuses on contemporary themes such as gendered embodiment and paid and unpaid work. This reader is a valuable resource for students looking to explore more contemporary issues within the field of gender.

Yvonne Kapp, *Eleanor Marx: A Biography* [2018]

A richly detailed biography of one of the most remarkable feminist scholars and activists.

Michael Kaufman and Michael Kimmel, *The Guy's Guide to Feminism* [2011]

A light-hearted and highly accessible introduction with some cartoons and a few jokes thrown in. Substantively, this is a more mainstream take on contemporary feminism, but worth engaging with. This won't lead people to a socialist-feminist revolution, but it may persuade some reluctant male students that feminism is worth engaging with.

Diane Richardson and Victoria Robinson, *Introducing Gender and Women's Studies* [2020]

Contains 15 essays by different authors on themes of contemporary relevance. Strong on areas of gender and race and gender and sexuality.

Sara Salih, *Judith Butler* [2002]

Discusses the impact of Butler's work across a range of subjects. While aspects of the book move beyond social theory, this text is well worth engaging with to fully grasp the breadth and significance of Butler's thought. The book ends with a useful annotated bibliography.

Jennifer Mather Saul, *Feminism: Issues and Arguments* [2003]

Structured around key feminist issues such as pornography and abortion, this text gets straight to the debates at the heart of much feminist thought.

Nikki Sullivan, *A Critical Introduction to Queer Theory* [2003]

An excellent introduction to queer theory which beautifully elucidates key concepts through cultural references. While some younger undergraduates may find some of the cinematic references slightly dated, the book is still an excellent guide to the subject.

Margaret Walters, *Feminism: A Very Short Introduction* [2005]

Accessible to someone entirely new to the subject. As the name suggests, this text offers a whistlestop tour through feminism.

chapter 9

Post-structuralism and Post-modernism: 'It's All So Much More Complicated Than That!'

Contents

DOI: 10.4324/9781003359555-9

In the late 1960s, an intellectual movement emerged in France and swept across academia which rejected established ways of thinking. It introduced a new set of concepts such as 'discourse' and 'deconstruction' which challenged Enlightenment beliefs in objective ways of knowing the world. In place of fixed 'modern' forms of thought, a group of theorists gained fame who embraced ambiguity, fluidity, and complexity. While generations of 'modern' scholars (i.e. Marxists, liberals, functionalists, etc.) embellished grand stories of how societies changed, these French scholars rejected neat categories and certainties, arguing instead that the social world was far too complicated for any 'modern' system to handle. One important characteristic of this wave of thinking was its rejection of fixed identities. This included refusing to accept a name for their own school(s) of thought. Today, we think of this movement as being a combination of a 'post-modern' approach to culture and art and a 'post-structuralist' approach to language and philosophy. Key thinkers of the period were Michel Foucault [1926–84], Jacques Derrida [1930–2004], Jean-François Lyotard [1924–98], and Jean Baudrillard [1929–2007]. Ironically, perhaps the idea the four scholars agreed on most was that labels such as 'post-modernism' and 'post-structuralism' were limited and unhelpful. Nevertheless, today they are held as the principal architects of such traditions.

This movement was a rejection of a way of thinking called 'structuralism' which had gained popularity in the 1950s. French anthropologist Claude Lévi-Strauss [1908–2009] took the idea of structuralism out of linguistics and applied it to society and culture more broadly, suggesting that, just as with language, we need to view the social world as being fundamentally interconnected and having an overarching structure. For structuralist thinkers, through a careful examination of the relationships among its component parts, theorists could come to understand the rules of the entire social system. There were held to be fundamental patterns imprinted throughout the social world which shaped all social action. Throughout the late 1950s and early 1960s, this became the inspiration for scholars across many fields, with sociologists, psychologists, linguists, and anthropologists seeking to discover these deep 'social structures'.

Post-modernism and post-structuralism emerged as a rejection of the core ideas of structuralism. In particular, the belief that there are universal laws hardwired into all societies became seen as deeply misguided. Indeed, even the idea that there is a stable order in each individual society was rejected, let alone some stable order common to all social systems. Everything is held to be in flux, with ambiguity and dynamism the only certainties. For post-modern and post-structural thinkers, even if there were some deep-rooted laws written into a particular society, there is no guarantee that theorists would be able to access or understand them. Instead, these thinkers point to the context-dependent nature of knowledge and to the fluidity and plurality of meanings, relationships, and identities. Most significantly, these thinkers argued that social power impacts on how we perceive all relationships, reshaping our views of 'truth', 'knowledge', and 'progress'.

While post-modernism and post-structuralism have much in common, they also have important differences. Those who identify as post-structuralists may actively dislike the tradition's association with 'post-modernism' in this chapter. These differences are important to understand as well as the similarities. Post-structuralism focuses more on questions of meaning and discourse, originating within linguistics and philosophy; in contrast, post-modernism is more cultural and artistic in origin and focus. As we discuss in this chapter, the central insight which post-structuralism provides is that language, power, and knowledge are constantly interconnected and are forever being reshaped. In contrast, post-modernism focuses on the existence of plurality; of multiple stories, identities, and possibilities, and criticises the naivety of attempting to present a singular narrative of the social world. Beyond differences in focus, post-structuralists typically see their perspective as more philosophically rigorous, more politically engaged and theoretically developed than post-modernism, which they hold to be 'broad-brush' and 'playful'.

Key Concepts

The concepts discussed below all share an insight with the Critical Theory tradition: that the way we know and study the world is shaped by social power. As such, there is no such thing as 'value-free' research or 'neutral' knowledge. Academia is not objective and independent of society; rather, it serves to reinforce or to challenge dominant ways of thinking. These particular ways of thinking are all held to support and stabilise different forms of society (i.e. capitalist, patriarchal, racist). As a result of this shared insight, many of the concepts of this period are also associated with 'critical theory'. Some people therefore consider the key figures of this movement, such as Michel Foucault, to also be 'critical theorists'. This can be confusing and is possibly misguided because there are fundamental and irresolvable differences in methodology and focus between 'critical theory' and post-modernism and post-structuralism. This is because the Frankfurt School's critical theory was firmly anchored in a dialectical approach to social research, which this new wave of theorists rejected on principle. Dialectical methods focus on the instability of contradictions in ways of thinking and acting, contradictions which are inevitably resolved. In contrast, this new wave of theorists embraced open-ended contradictions and the permanent instability of thought.

Post-modernism

While 'post-modernism' refers to an artistic and cultural movement, it is also anchored in a specific theoretical commitment. This is best expressed in Jean-François Lyotard's book *The Postmodern Condition* [1979], where he described post-modernism as the rejection of the 'grand narratives' of modernity. By 'grand narratives' Lyotard refers to the all-encompassing stories of human progress and development; philosophical/economic such as Marxism, religious/cultural such as Christianity, or technical such as the belief in scientific progress. Lyotard argues that 'post-modernism' refers to the period where *all* grand narratives (also known as 'meta-narratives') have lost their appeal and are subject to widespread cynicism and fragmentation. People no longer believe in these grand explanations for social life, or they just follow small parts of them. There are no longer any stories which can be told with total confidence about how the whole social world works. There are two related concerns here: people no longer believe in any of the past grand narratives; but also, they no longer believe that any universal grand narrative could exist. People have simply rejected this way of thinking.

This reflects a broader rejection of universalism: the idea that there are values or dynamics which are valid in all places and at all times.

Consider Marxism: *The Communist Manifesto* [1848] famously begins with the line, 'the history of all hitherto existing society is the history of class struggles'. This claim speaks to *all* human societies, *all* having a particular shared pattern and history. This is a universal claim. In contrast, in the post-modern world there is no confidence in such universal laws. Post-modernists would instead identify multiple context-dependent interpretations and stress the complexity of all past societies and the irreducible variety of the conflicts which developed within them. In post-modernity, people simply do not believe in the truth of universal, grandiose narratives. As a result, any attempt to suggest there is a story which can capture the direction of human societies, from past to present, which can tell us where we are going, how we will 'progress', is rejected and derided. Indeed, the very notion of 'progress' comes under increased scrutiny, even mockery.

This environment fed into a broader rejection of macro-sociology and led to a fear of writing with any certainty about the future. The grand stories of humanity were no longer the topic of debate for professional, serious social researchers. In a world where there is no certain knowledge, sociologists increasingly look at targeted, particular stories. They move to undertake more micro-sociological research and offer guarded, tentative interpretations. Marx and Engels tried to identify the history of all existing societies, pointing in the direction of an inevitable revolution, an 'eschatology', or ultimate 'end' of human development. Instead, today, micro-sociologists research precise areas in intense detail; for example, 'identity formation through haircuts in 18- to 30-year-old Chinese diaspora communities in Oxford from 2022 to 2023'. This is a much tighter focus than 'the history of human societies'! This is not to say that such research is less valid on account of its smaller size or ambition. Rather, it reflects a more conservative approach, seeking to avoid making unchecked universal claims which do not stand up to scrutiny, or which risk reproducing unjustifiable narratives.

Deconstructionism

Deconstruction has much in common with post-modernism, rejecting meta-narratives and the possibility of universally valid knowledge. Yet, deconstruction differs in focus, being philosophical and literary in orientation. While Lyotard is the key figure associated with post-modernism, it is Jacques Derrida, and in particular his book *Of Grammatology* [1967], which is linked with deconstructionism. While post-modernism focused on the rejection of the grand narratives of the past and with simple binary identities, deconstructionism looks in more detail at language and provides a method for exploring the ambiguities and fluidities of meaning and interpretation. In keeping with all the concepts of this period, deconstructionism privileges complexity, plurality, and contingency over certainty or universality. The focus of this approach is more on interpretation and on reading texts, rather than on grand stories of human history or progress. Deconstructionism speaks to a particular methodology for interpreting texts, by focusing on and analysing unstable binaries. Where post-modernism rejects the possibility of a singular narrative of universal validity, deconstructionism is more circumscribed, rejecting the idea of fixed narratives within particular texts.

Deconstructionism has parallels with the work of the semiotician Roland Barthes [1915–80]. In *The Death of the Author* [1967], Barthes argued that we should not read books seeking to find some 'true' meaning which the author intended. Rather, Barthes argued that what matters is how the text is interpreted. This links with Derrida's concept of '*differance*' which captures his idea that meaning is always in flux and can never be truly contained by language. As such, meaning, including meanings that are written down in texts, are open to a multiplicity of changing interpretations. Accordingly, there is no right or wrong way of understanding a book or an essay. There are multiple, ever-changing interpretations which can legitimately be derived. In contrast to the appreciation for certainty, and the fixed, objective knowledge of the Enlightenment, deconstructionism points to the objective instability of knowledge derived from texts, showing how interpretation is always dynamic and volatile and riddled with ambiguity.

Deconstructionism entered social theory carrying its rejection of stable binary concepts, be it male/female, or sex/gender. It brought a new concern with breaking down established hierarchies and structures, both within texts but also within conceptual maps and epistemologies. It also furthered the challenge to grand narratives alongside post-modernism. Taken together, deconstructionism and post-modernism leave the social theorist in an uncertain world, where ambiguity and complexity are the new certainties.

Discourse and Power/Knowledge

The next two concepts derive from the work of Michel Foucault and are associated with post-structuralist theory. Foucault held that power and knowledge were fundamentally inseparable and he united them in a singular concept: 'power/knowledge'. This captures the complicated and fluid understanding of power which is a central tenet of post-structuralist thought. In contrast to structuralism, which views power as running through semi-predictable patterns and according to particular rules (such as the market or patriarchy), post-structuralism views power as flowing through ever-changing 'discourses'. 'Discourse' is a crucial concept for post-structuralists and it is how 'power/knowledge' travels throughout society.

Discourse is one of the most complex concepts you will come across in social theory. It can sound very abstract and intimidating at first encounter. The idea that power is tied to knowledge is itself at odds with more traditional understandings of power, which are connected more simplistically to coercion and control. While Chairman Mao famously said, 'power flows from the barrel of a gun', post-structuralists would suggest that needing to hold a gun to somebody is a marker of weakness rather than power. Only a weak actor needs a gun to get people to do something; post-structuralists argue that you have real power when you can get people to *want* to do things, when you can reshape their lives in line with goals and values you have implanted. From such a perspective, power operates *discursively* (i.e. through discourses), shaping the values embedded in society. Power is connected to remoulding how we know what counts as success, shame, health, and deviance. Power/knowledge flows through many different discourses to shape these values.

Foucault gives examples of discourse in action in his four-book series *History of Sexuality* [1976/1984/1984/2018]. He argues that the very notion of 'sexuality' is itself something that is socially constructed through discourse(s). While 'sexuality' is understood colloquially as an objective measure of sexual preferences, Foucault showed how it is actually a deeply social concept which is socio-culturally embedded, emerging in a particular place and time. The very ideas of 'heterosexuality' or 'homosexuality' are shown to be recent inventions and do not connect to some underlying biological essence. The idea of 'sexuality' and of different 'sexualities' is created through discourse; they are social inventions, constructed and maintained socially, through power/knowledge. In Foucault's work, discourses are shown to naturalise particular ways of thinking as 'scientific' and 'objective', but also to shape particular forms of subjecthood. By way of an example, in *History of Sexuality* Foucault shows how those who take part in certain non-normative sexual practices were historically presented as 'deviant', 'perverted', or 'ill'.

As such, it is not merely 'homosexuality' that is discursively constructed but also the very ideas of 'illness' or 'patients', or 'hospital' or 'perversion'. Foucault's concepts of discourse and power/knowledge break down the idea that there is something objective about how we view and position different people or institutions. His work makes the reader continually aware of the relationship between knowledge, power, language, and discourse. The categories, or 'subject positions', into which we place people or organisations are held to be discursively shaped and are a result of power/knowledge flowing throughout society. How we come to understand ideas, such as 'terrorists' or 'freedom fighters', 'victims' or 'murderers', is thus shaped by social power and is constantly changing.

Power/knowledge flows through all layers of society, shaping understandings of different subject positions and institutions. This is not to say that post-structuralists reject the material world or are not invested in studying social practices. Rather, it is to say that all social interactions are themselves understood and situated by and through discourse(s). As such, 'going to the doctor' or 'celebrating a wedding' are viewed as deeply ingrained within, and only comprehensible through, discourse(s). In this regard, when it comes to how we know the social world, it is 'discourse all the way down'. There is thus a complex, power-strewn social world, which social researchers need new tools and concepts to explore. As a result of Foucault's work, and the popularisation of 'discourse', new methodologies emerged enabling 'discourse analysis' (see below).

Biopolitics

Foucault argued that discourses operate so as to control how populations behave; they serve to 'discipline' subjects, encouraging groups of people to conduct themselves in particular ways. In *Discipline and Punish* [1975], Foucault described how such 'disciplinary power' enabled a new form of social control to develop in modernity. While in earlier societies the sovereign had power over life and death, most visibly through torturing and executing enemies, today, power operates to shape how people behave when they are alive and nominally 'free'. From Foucault's perspective we exist in a world of 'biopolitics' and 'biopower', where what matters is the ability to shape people's lived behaviours. This is enabled by institutions and mechanisms which monitor and police people's conduct. The result is the normalisation of certain forms of behaviour and the regulation of populations, often through discourses around health, which tell subjects how to live. 'Biopolitics' refers to the shaping of people's conduct through the institutional normalisation of practices and their monitoring through surveillance technologies. 'Biopower' refers to the operationalisation of biopolitical infrastructures; it is through biopower that institutions exert their influence and shape conduct.

To help explain the rise of biopower in modern societies, Foucault uses the Panopticon as a metaphor. The Panopticon was a practical idea for a particular design for a prison suggested by the English utilitarian philosopher Jeremy Bentham [1748–1832]. Bentham proposed that instead of requiring hundreds of guards to police the inmates, if a single tower was placed in the very centre of the prison and all cells had a transparent door or window, one single guard would be able to view all the prisoners, turning their gaze to view different cells in turn. Bentham proposed that the watchtower's structure was such that the prisoners could not tell if they were being monitored in particular at any given point. As such, every prisoner would feel, and act, as if they were constantly being monitored, even when they weren't. Bentham proposed this method to enable efficient and unobtrusive surveillance. For Foucault, the Panopticon is a metaphor for how disciplinary power operates throughout modern societies. We internalise the rules of institutions and come to relate to their norms and values. We self-police and monitor our own conduct, without being forced to act in a certain way by evident coercive powers. Foucault extends the metaphor of the Panopticon to explain how institutional power operates across society, not just in prisons but in schools, factories, the armed forces, even pubs.

We live in a world where our conduct is constantly policed and under surveillance. This can be through the assessment of our work progress through targets and grades or through calorie counting or alcohol unit monitoring. What Foucault's turn to the idea of the Panopticon carries is the fact that we increasingly do the policing of our conduct ourselves. We *choose* to check our step counts, to go on a detox diet, to set a goal for how much work we want to do. We *choose* to buy technologies that enable us to self-police and self-discipline, such as smart watches or sleep-tracker apps. Through the exercise of biopower, institutions mould our behaviours and set new norms and standards, whether it be for more steps to be walked or fewer calories to be consumed.

Hyperreality

Jean Baudrillard developed ideas from post-modernism and post-structuralism in light of the development of new media technologies. His key concept was hyperreality, which he outlined in his book *Simulacra and Simulation* [1981]. Hyperreality refers to a condition where it is increasingly difficult to distinguish between reality and simulation. In hyperreality, social actors find it hard to grasp what is real and what is simulated when they are confronted with a barrage of signs, advertisements, rolling news, augmented reality systems, and post-modern culture. Everything blends into a neon, digital, cinematic haze.

Baudrillard drew upon semiotics and argued that 'signs' were taking on a new and far greater role in societies. In the past, signs had a clear function: they acted as a referent to something precise and concrete in the world. The 'signifier' is the technical term for the physical form of a sign. A signifier serves to refer to some actual thing, for example, a hospital, which is called the 'signified'. Signs previously had a clear role of referring to a 'real' signified and it was therefore easy to distinguish between the two. It is not difficult to grasp the difference between the word 'hospital' or the letter 'H' on a road sign and the actual huge building full of doctors, nurses, and patients! Baudrillard argues that a key feature of hyperreality is that the role of signs and their connection to a material reality was changing. He said that signs are becoming 'self-referential', referring to yet more signs or to simulations rather than to signifieds.

There are also simply ever more signs and simulated realities in existence, be it the famous golden arches of McDonald's or Disney Land resorts. This is as a result of the revolution in digital advertising, the proliferation of consumer culture, and the ascendancy of 24-hour news media. Today, decades after Baudrillard first came up with the concept, we live so much of our lives through our computers and our smart phones, and are inundated with news alerts through push notifications. We stare at screens saturated with links and adverts to intangible commodities. Many of these promoted services are turned to by people to anchor the social narratives of their existence, such as Facebook, Instagram, or TikTok. We increasingly live in virtual and augmented realities, we play immersive games and take part in interactive televisual media, reality shows, phone-in voting, or Black Mirror's *Bandersnatch*. We buy tokens or credits for online platforms which can themselves feature forms of native advertising. In a world of self-referential signs, people lose track of reality and struggle to find true meaning. As a result, we live in a social world adrift from reality, lost in a maze of signs: in Baudrillard's expressive phrase, we live 'in the desert of the real'. We spend more time looking at visualisations of events, such as photo streams of friends' parties, than we spend at the parties themselves. Hyperreality spins the subject dizzily between representations and simulations, lost in virtual reality and self-referential signs, unanchored from the concrete realities of social life.

Baudrillard applied this concept in his polemical analysis of Operation Desert Storm. In *The Gulf War Did Not Take Place* [1991], Baudrillard argued that media representations of the Gulf War were so divergent from the actual reality that it had become a simulation. The 'smart weapons' and clean narratives broadcast to Western primetime TV audiences failed to capture the brutality and complexity of the material or political situation. What was presented through rolling news media as a sophisticated 'war' was in fact a superpower with vastly superior firepower demolishing an enemy which could barely even engage it in combat. Because the only knowledge of the war for people in the West came from propagandistic news media, especially CNN, Baudrillard argues that the 'war' is a simulation rather than a reality. This is not to deny the reality of the deaths or destruction. Rather, the idea that it actually constituted a 'war' should be challenged; instead it should be viewed as a series of atrocities repackaged for the media as an international propagandistic spectacle.

How Did These Ideas Impact on Social Theory?

Post-modernism and post-structuralism revolutionised social theory, bringing about widespread changes in how concepts were developed and deployed. As we discuss below, in keeping with deconstructionist insights, over the past 40 years, social theorists have moved away from concepts predicated on neat oppositional binaries and instead constructed models which embraced fluidity and complexity. Post-structuralist concepts in particular ushered in a new understanding of subjectivity, bringing a new conceptualisation of the social actor which was more complex, fractured, and unstable.

Rejection of Binaries

Up until the late 1950s, sociologists largely understood the social world through clear oppositional categories. For example, there were binary gender identities: 'male' and 'female'; clear 'racial' categories: 'black' or 'white', and clear sexuality classifications: 'gay', 'bisexual', and 'heterosexual'. After the post-structural revolution, many social theorists rejected neat binaries, holding them to be intellectually unsound and politically problematic. This turn away from binary categories doesn't just focus on the labels used to capture identities, but it extends to a cynicism towards binary conceptual pairings such as structure and agency, or sex and gender.

Queer Theory played a large role in deconstructing old binary categories. In place of static, polar identities such as 'male' and 'female', or 'gay' or 'straight', Queer Theorists place identity on a fluid continuum. As such, in Queer Theory, gender and sexuality are both held to exist on a spectrum, with subjects' identities constantly shifting. As discussed in Chapter 8 on Gender, this idea of 'queering' fixed categories is a key feature of third-wave feminism and is crucial to the work of scholars such as Judith Butler. Butler's work destabilises both binary *identity* markers ('male' and 'female') and binary *theoretical* concepts ('gender' and 'sex'). While past feminist thinkers such as Simone de Beauvoir [1908–86] provided a conceptual demarcation between biological 'sex' and socialised 'gender', Queer Theorists reject this conceptual binary.

There is instead held to be a dynamic spectrum of 'gender' expressions. The discourses around 'biological sex' are today seen as having been socially constructed and are no longer held to be anchored to a fixed biological objectivity. Gender identities today are more nuanced than the binary 'male' or 'female', captured by a new conceptual vocabulary introducing terms such as 'cisgender', 'transgender', 'gender non-conforming', 'non-binary', 'genderqueer', 'genderfluid', and 'two-spirit'. These concepts all have different academic, cultural, and political inflections and are preferred by different communities.

While Queer Theory has been brought into dialogue with 'race' by various scholars, it remains primarily focused on gender and sexuality. Critical Race Theorists (CRTs) have drawn upon a variety of traditions, including post-structuralism, when considering the social construction of 'race'. In keeping with gender theorists, Critical Race Theorists argue that 'race' does not reflect biological 'facts' but is instead a discourse in the Foucauldian sense. 'Racial' identities are therefore fundamentally rejected as fixed analytical categories and are shown instead to reflect shifting 'power/knowledge'. Echoing developments in gender theory, it is not merely 'racial identities' that are problematised but also the related conceptual demarcation of 'race' and 'ethnicity'. In place of this neat division, most Critical Race Theorists argue that 'ethnicity' is also a discursively produced charity which can function as a placeholder for 'race'. This is not to say that post-structuralist insights call for 'race' to be ignored and for a 'colour-blind' approach to be taken to politics and social research. Rather, the inequalities caused by the discourses of 'race' must be the focus of research. Indeed, post-structuralists are aware that 'colour-blind' ideologies can serve to obscure inequality and exploitation. The difference is that social research must be done with an awareness of the socially constructed notion of 'race', seeking to explore the conditions of those whose lives are impacted on by the discourse itself, rather than viewing 'race' as capturing some fundamental, pre-discursive, scientific reality.

Clearly, we are living in a more complicated and conceptually rich terrain in the wake of the post-structuralist and post-modernist revolution. Our conceptual vocabulary has exploded, with a mass of new terms in circulation. The social researcher is faced with a substantially more daunting task when investigating identity construction with the nuances of identity requiring a vastly more sophisticated theoretical and empirical observational toolkit. In term, the social theorist is challenged to produce concepts which can account for such plurality, fluidity, and socio-cultural variation.

Subjectivity

By subjectivity, sociologists and philosophers refer to the amalgamation of consciousness, perceptions, experiences, and values which combine in the mind and shape the identity of each social actor. Traditional (typically liberal) notions of subjectivity considered consciousness and perception to be stable and anchored to an individual's fixed identity and relation to self. Post-structuralism brought about a radically different account of subjectivity, focusing on fragmentation, instability, and irrationality, and emphasised the importance of the unconscious mind.

For traditional, liberal scholars, subjectivity is characterised by rationality, coherence, and independence. It is comprehensible and accessible: you can talk to people and see an independent autonomous agent with a rational mind. While social actors are shaped by, and respond to, their social worlds, they remain coherent individuals within it, with a self-identity which is discrete and stable. From such a perspective, what it is to be 'me', the voice that exists in my head, my sense of self, does not constantly bleed into the social world and get reshaped on a second-by-second basis. For liberals, individuals are masters of their own destiny; they are comparatively atomistic, capable of independent calculation about their own social actions. In contrast, following post-structuralism, a new account of subjectivity has emerged, rejecting this liberal account. For post-structuralists, subjectivity is typified by volatility and is fundamentally social. Today, it is harder to 'box' subjects into a neat 'individual' versus 'social' distinction. Subjectivity is held to be fundamentally social and in flux; shaped by swirling and competing discourses, the assault of different signs, and reshaping, surfacing, and sinking patterns of desire and repression.

For Judith Butler in *The Psychic Life of Power* [1997], subjectivity exists both in the conscious and the unconscious mind. This adds yet further complexity to the understanding of social life and poses further challenges to conducting social research. Butler's work shows how we are shaped by changing discourses and desires which we are not fully aware of and which social researchers will struggle to access. Drawing upon Sigmund Freud [1856–1939], Georg W. F. Hegel [1770–1831], and Michel Foucault [1926–84], Butler suggests that subjectivation is always co-eval with power. By this, she means that the process of developing a subjectivity occurs within the power-strewn world of discourse: there is no 'pre-social' subjectivity. Just as discourses are forever changing and in flux, reflecting the undulations of power/knowledge across society, the unconscious mind is also forever unstable. We are left with an understanding of subjectivity which is fluid and intrinsically social, but also anchored within the psychic world of the social actor. This poses fundamental challenges for social researchers, presenting an even more fractured, complex, and inaccessible view of social reality.

The Problems With Using These Concepts Today

While post-structuralism and post-modernism have undeniably transformed the academy, they are both highly controversial. Famously, the acclaimed linguist Noam Chomsky (1928–) took part in a public debate with Michel Foucault in 1971, where he rejected core tenets of both post-modernism and post-structuralism, instead arguing that there really is a 'universal grammar' to human understanding and that a stable human nature is an important idea which should be not be rejected. Chomsky is one of many commentators who have accused this school of French thinkers of writing books which are not merely impenetrably complex but often meaningless. The list of criticisms levelled at post-structuralism and post-modernism is extensive; both have been criticised by liberal scholars, Marxists, radical feminists; the list is seemingly endless. Here, we focus on two of the most common criticisms: that post-modernism and post-structuralism lead to a dangerous moral relativism and enable the elevation of nonsensical obscurantist scholarship.

Relativism

In his book *How Mumbo-Jumbo Conquered the World* [2004], Francis Wheen (1957–) described post-modern and post-structuralist thinkers as the 'demolition merchants of reality'. He warned that their attempts to destabilise 'objective' Enlightenment ideas were leading to a position where there is no longer an anchor in any meaningful conception of truth, ethics, or knowledge. Wheen argues that such a position threatens the foundations of science and politics; we are left adrift without a link to ideas of right or wrong and we are increasingly unable to distinguish between fact and fiction. If everything is simply 'discourse', how do we determine meaning or social purpose? For many critics of post-modernism and post-structuralism, both perspectives lead to an inevitable extreme moral and political relativism. As a result, to their critics, the embrace of complexity and fluidity and the demolition of Enlightenment certainties has not aided social or academic progress. Instead, without any foundations in certain knowledge or ethics we are more vulnerable to irrationality and more susceptible to the interests of the powerful.

For Noam Chomsky, the extreme relativism pushed by post-structuralism and post-modernism makes it harder to challenge social injustices and serves the interests of capitalist actors. This is because the category of 'injustice' itself has become destabilised. In a world of such moral–ethical relativism there is a normative crisis; we are no longer able to justify our claims to 'right' and 'wrong'. But this has not changed the reality that the world remains spectacularly unequal, irrational, and unjust. Post-modernism and post-structuralism haven't made the world suddenly 'fair'; yet they have challenged the basis upon which such claims to 'fairness' can be made. Chomsky is particularly concerned that not merely are 'equity' and 'justice' destabilised, so too are notions of objective 'truth'. Indeed, the past few years have shown how we live in a 'post-truth' world. This is typified by Donald Trump's supporters' claims to have not just different opinions on key issues but 'alternative facts', challenging what is empirically observable and self-evident. In short, there is a space in the world to say things which are objectively untrue and claim them to hold the status of 'alternative facts'. For critics of the relativistic tendencies of both post-modernism and post-structuralism, the post-truth world of 'alternative facts' is not a surprise. Neither would it be surprising that such 'post-truth' rhetoric serves the interests of the already rich and powerful. For Wheen and Chomsky, the destruction of Enlightenment certainties was always going to make it harder to challenge injustices and to call power to account.

Recently, there has been a challenge to the work of Michel Foucault in particular, on the basis this his work served to support reactionary and 'ugly' forms of thought and behaviour. Critical scholars have focused on both the political-economic implications of his work, as well as linking disturbing claims about his personal conduct to his broader system of thought. In *The Last Man Takes LSD: Foucault and the end of Revolution* [2021], Mitchell Dean and Daniel Zamora argue that Foucault's work served to nurture the neoliberal revolution across economy and across society. Foucault's contempt for the state is shown to have bled into an appreciation for the economic autonomy promised by neoliberal thinkers. The claim is that Foucault's desire to reduce biopolitical surveillance and governmentality ultimately led him to see emancipatory potential in a market order, free from state control. This puts him substantially at odds with most progressive-left theorists, who see neoliberalism as furthering the worst excesses of capitalism. Simultaneously, Foucault has recently been revealed to have sexually abused young boys in Tunisia. This is a case of a comparatively rich and powerful, highly educated French citizen, abusing 8- and 9-year-old African children. When one considers that Foucault's work is often criticised for leading to a moral relativism, it is relevant that his personal life was filled with what one witness called 'extreme moral ugliness'. The connection between a world of irreducible, unanchored discourses, and the ability to morally justify such behaviours, must be a cause for concern and discussion amongst post-structural scholars.

Obscurantism and Nonsense

A repeated criticism levelled at these French theorists (and those who were inspired by them) is that their work is made deliberately complicated. Foucault famously told his friend, the philosopher John Searle (1932–), that he deliberately made his work harder to read because the French academic audience expects philosophy to be 10 per cent incomprehensible. When he was told this story, Pierre Bourdieu commented that the percentage was much higher: way more than just 10 per cent! Such charges of unnecessary complexity of language and style were not merely levelled at the founding thinkers of post-modernism and post-structuralism. For example, the American philosopher, Martha Nussbaum (1947–), launched into a brutal critique of Judith Butler's writing style, suggesting that Butler deliberately makes it hard to see what her ideas are, presenting an 'extremely high ratio of names to explanations'. For Nussbaum, Butler's aim is to dazzle her reader with abstract, impenetrate prose, inspiring people with her brilliance. Nussbaum argues that this complex assault of names and terms is designed to prevent the reader from actually trying to identify a clear thread to her writing: they are meant to just go 'wow, you are so clever' and not actually think about what argument is being presented. In contrast, Nussbaum wants clear statements, clear definitions, clear arguments. Instead, in keeping with post-modernism and post-structuralism, in Butler's work, meaning is alluded to, definitions are unstable, and interpretations are plural. For Nussbaum this is 'teasing' and 'exasperating' rather than clearly presented and impressive argumentation.

The criticism above is that post-structuralist work is typically 'obscurantist', deliberately made hard to follow. Yet, an even more serious problem has emerged, namely that work inspired by this movement in French social theory can slip into simple meaninglessness. Two scandals rocked academia where this came to a head. On both occasions, work which was post-structuralist and post-modern in style was published in leading journals, and later it emerged that it was a hoax and was in fact total rubbish. The first such scandal is the Sokal Affair (1996). Alan Sokal (1955–) is a physicist and he was frustrated with how post-modernism was misusing scientific terms. He wrote a deliberately meaningless paper using lots of post-structuralist and post-modernist buzzwords: 'Transgressing the Boundaries: Toward a Transformative Hermeneutics of Quantum Gravity'. The paper was accepted for publication in the academic journal *Social Text*. A few weeks after it was published Sokal admitted that the paper was a hoax designed to show the lack of intellectual rigour within the humanities and social sciences in light of the post-modernist and post-structuralist revolutions. Clearly, on the basis of this scandal, it seems that post-modernism and post-structuralism do risk straying into inanity: where totally nonsensical papers were indistinguishable from world-leading scholarship.

The most recent scandal is the so-called 'Grievance studies' hoax which occurred between 2017 and 2018. Here, three authors, Peter Boghossian, James A. Lindsay, and Helen Pluckrose, sought to show that post-modernism and post-structuralism had combined with identity politics to promote a form of academically weak scholarship which 'put social grievances ahead of objective truth'. Focusing on gender, fat, race, queer, and cultural studies, the trio published papers making unsupported arguments on topical themes, such as men could reduce potential transphobia by anally penetrating themselves with sex-toys, or that dogs engage in forms of rape culture. Helen Pluckrose argued that postcolonial theory, gender studies, and critical race theory are particularly susceptible to such unsubstantiated, poor-quality scholarship because of the combination of the primacy of Foucauldian ideas in these fields and the political commitments of each subject. As such, what matters most, for Pluckrose, is the affirmation of the grievance in question, rather than the academic quality or integrity of the research. For Pluckrose, 'identity politics' and post-modernism had combined in a way which 'corrupted scholarship' and that the rejection of modernist values of reason, objective truth, and science were harming the academy. Pluckrose and Lindsay later summarised their position in the book *Cynical Theories: How Activist Scholarship Made Everything About Race, Gender, and Identity – and Why This Harms Everybody* [2020].

How Post-modernism and Post-structuralism Impact on Social Research Today

Clearly, both post-modernism and post-structuralism are controversial. Yet, this has not restricted their reach or hold over the humanities and social sciences. Criminology, gender studies, critical race theory, postcolonial theory, sociology, international relations, and even history are deeply impacted by both schools of thought, despite the Sokal Affair and the 'Grievance studies' hoax. Both served to further a schism within the academy, with some commentators seeing Pluckrose, Lindsay, and Boghossian as being intellectually dishonest and opposed to progressive values. Today, post-structuralist and post-modernist ideas remain as influential as ever.

Critical Discourse Analysis

Critical Discourse Analysis (CDA) emerged in the 1990s as a qualitative method for conducting interdisciplinary social research. The approach was developed by two prominent linguists, Norman Fairclough (1941–) and Ruth Wodak (1950–); however, CDA is deployed far beyond linguistics. Today, CDA is one of the primary tools used by social researchers across disciplines. CDA has clear links with post-structuralism and the work of Michel Foucault through its association with 'discourse' and 'power/knowledge'. Critical discourse analysis is 'critical' insofar as its proponents seek to expose power relations and ideology embedded within discourse(s), identifying how particular subject positions and relationships are socially mediated. An important example of CDA in action is in the field of migration. Through critical discourse analysis, interdisciplinary social researchers seek to disclose how the very terms used in public conversation and in policy documents reinforce binaries and marginalise subjects.

In the field of migration studies, CDA is used to analyse policy discourses and to reveal how the language used in official documents serves to reinforce particular constructions of migrants: 'asylum seekers', 'economic migrants', 'illegal immigrants', 'refugees', etc. Drawing upon Foucault and post-structuralism, CDA scholars are mindful that such categories are discursively constructed and need to be carefully interrogated to explore social power latent within seemingly 'apolitical' technocratic processes. Following Foucault, migration scholars are mindful that it is through the tedious, everyday discourses that power flows, and through which subjects are made susceptible to violence and to the effects of power. There is also a more obvious focus on analysing the language used within political discourses, where CDA has been deployed to see how politicians and civil society groups shape the debate. Discourse does not merely focus on language but on the assemblage of ideas, images, symbols, and norms which are communicated and reinforced through social practices. As such, the idea of a 'swarm' of migrants, or the discussion of an 'invasion', serve to reinforce particular conceptions. An important discursive artefact shaping the perception of migrants in the UK were the infamous 'Go Home' vans which were used by the British Home Office during 2013, advising illegal immigrants to 'go home or face arrest'. This served to reinforce the idea of certain migrants as 'criminals' who do not belong. These were the focus of substantial comparative analysis by migration theorists, with CDA showing how different countries respond very differently to the question of illegal migration. For example, the discourses surrounding asylum seekers were shown to be very different between England and Norway during the same period.

A CDA approach can also lead to various ethical considerations emerging, suggesting that particular terms should be avoided as they risk reproducing particular discourses. For example, the phrase 'swarm' or 'invasion' can be connected with the demonisation and 'Othering' of migrants. In contrast, other terms can be identified which better support mutual self-understanding and which enable productive dialogue. As such, CDA can make interventions at both a macro and micro level, demonstrating how generations of international policy shape subject positions discursively, while also attending to the minutiae of language in particular documents, speeches, and artefacts.

Conclusion

The radical French theories emerging from the 1960s revolutionised social research and transformed the humanities and social sciences. While both post-modernism and post-structuralism had roots within the Marxian tradition, they led to a split in critical social research between 'post-structuralist' and 'Marxist' schools. Post-structuralists are by far the more numerous today and their research has largely been more impactful both inside and outside the academy over the past few decades, shaping policies on a range of topics from immigration to gender identity. Previously, there was something of a cultural war between Marxists and post-structuralists. While this is now largely over, there are still particular journals and institutions which are famous for preferring one branch of critical scholarship over the other.

As with all the traditions we have discussed, there are overlaps and cross-fertilisations of ideas. This can be seen in efforts to bridge post-structuralism and Marxism. A key figure here is Wendy Brown (1955–). In *Undoing the Demos: Neoliberalism's Stealth Revolution* [2015], Brown combines a Marxian class analysis and Marxian categories with a Foucauldian approach to subjectivity, governmentality, and power. Similarly, Frederic Jameson (1934–) is associated with a form of 'post-modern Marxism' where insights from both schools have been combined. In *Postmodernism, or, the Cultural Logic of Late Capitalism* [1991], Jameson argued that post-modernism is a key ideological characteristic of late capitalism. He uses the post-modern description of the present distaste for grand narratives to capture a tendency of capitalism itself, a sentiment which he demonstrates serves to perpetuate capitalism.

Yet, the greatest impact of post-structuralism and post-modernism has not been through its fusion with other traditions but rather through a subtler acceptance of the need to reframe social research in line with their core tenets. There has been a *de facto* acceptance of the rejection of grand narratives, objective knowledge, and universalising theories. The move to micro-sociology is particularly pronounced. This has served to fundamentally recalibrate social research. What is considered a meaningful and prudent topic for social research was undoubtedly changed by the post-structural and post-modern revolution.

Discussion Questions

1 Is everything 'discourse' for post-structuralists?

2 In what ways might global warming pose a challenge to post-structural theorising? Equally, in what ways does post-structuralism help us understand it?

3 What is the relationship between post-structuralism and Marxism?

4 What do post-modernism and post-structuralism share with Frankfurt School Critical Theory and how do they differ?

5 Does post-structuralism's opposition to governmentality reproduce neoliberal values?

Further Reading

Primary Texts

Roland Barthes, *The Death of the Author* [1967]

Historically, the dominant approach to understanding texts was to assume that there had been a singular set meaning intended by the author. The primary task of the reader was implicitly to work hard to grasp this intended meaning. Barthes' book challenged this, instead suggesting that the interpretation of readers is what matters, emphasising instability and ambiguity of meaning.

Jean Baudrillard, *Simulacra and Simulation* [1981]

Baudrillard argues that it is increasingly difficult to distinguish 'reality' from what he calls 'hyperreality', typified by simulations and virtual realities. The mass media, for example, provide a representation of the world which displaces our authentic experiences of it; we live through our phones and television sets. As such, we increasingly live in a world of 'signs' and copies.

Jean Baudrillard, *The Gulf War Did Not Take Place* [1991]

Baudrillard deploys the concepts of reality and hyperreality to show how the Gulf War was a media spectacle rather than a conventional war. The public experienced a media-mediated hyperreality, focusing on 'smart' weapon systems while shielded from the tragic material costs of the bloodshed and the oil fires. Narratives were manipulated and the geopolitical complexity oversimplified.

Judith Butler, *The Psychic Life of Power* [1997]

This builds on Foucault's ideas to create a theory of the psyche in which the very process of becoming a subject is a power-strewn, volatile process. For Butler, it is not merely the case that power acts upon subjects but the very process of becoming a subject, of developing a psyche, is shaped and impacted by the vortices of social power.

Gilles Deleuze and Félix Guattari, *Capitalism and Schizophrenia* [1972/1980]

This is a two-volume work consisting of *Anti-Oedipus* [1972] and *A Thousand Plateaus* [1980]. It is a famously difficult text to read and will challenge even postgraduate students. Throughout the text the authors use 'schizophrenia' as a metaphor for processes they see as being driven by capitalism, leading to the breakdown of clear, rooted structures (deterritorialisation) and their re-establishment in different forms (reterritorialisation).

Jacques Derrida, Of Grammatology [1967]

In this book, Derrida outlines 'deconstructionism', which challenges the ideas of fixed meanings and hierarchies existing in language and in thought. He describes how 'speech' had been problematically seen as being superior to 'writing' throughout history, suggesting that this has served to obscure the ambiguity and elusiveness of meaning which is more pronounced in written texts.

Michel Foucault, *Discipline and Punish: The Birth of the Prison* [1975]

Foucault outlines the rise of disciplinary biopower and self-surveillance. The text starts with a grizzly depiction of the public execution in the past and moves to explore the ways in which people are today disciplined to behave in particular ways while remaining alive, rather than simply put to death. This is shown to reflect a broader change from sovereign power over life and death to disciplinary power which flows through institutions.

Michel Foucault, *Madness and Civilisation* [1961]

Through a focus on the changing societal treatment of the mentally ill, Foucault demonstrates the interconnection between power, knowledge, and social control. The idea of an 'objective' medical science is challenged and what may seem apolitical categories and labels are shown to be deeply connected to social norms.

Michel Foucault, *History of Sexuality: Vols 1–4* [1976/1984/1984/2018]

In similar vein to *Madness and Civilisation*, Foucault investigates discourses surrounding sexuality, demonstrating how social power shapes and regulates how sex is understood and how desire is permitted to manifest.

Jean-François Lyotard, *The Postmodern Condition* [1979]

This book presents Lyotard's famous critique of 'grand narratives' and the quest for singular, universal truths. Instead, he outlines the post-modern tendency to explore located, fragmented, and interconnected narratives.

Secondary Texts

Catherine Belsey, *Post structuralism: A Very short Introduction* [2002]

A very accessible introduction to post-structuralism.

Wendy Brown, *Undoing the Demos: Neoliberalism's Stealth Revolution* [2015]

An excellent example of a text which seeks to unite Marxist and post-structuralist themes to advance social critique. Brown is particularly proficient at engaging with Foucault's work and bringing it into dialogue with Marxist themes.

Lilie Chouliaraki and Norman Fairclough, *Discourse in Late Modernity: Rethinking Critical Discourse Analysis* [1999]

This text shows how critical discourse analysis can enable critical social research, supporting both empirical studies and theory building.

Simon Glendinning, *Derrida: A Very Short Introduction* [2011]

A very accessible introduction to Derrida.

Gary Gutting, *Foucault: A Very Short Introduction* [2019]

A very accessible introduction to Foucault.

Stuart Jeffries, *Everything, All the Time, Everywhere: How We Became Postmodern* [2021]

A very engaging text linking theory, history, culture, and politics. Jeffries is ultimately critical of post-modernism which he argues is a cover for a greedy and dangerous form of capitalism.

Helen Pluckrose and James Lindsay, *Cynical Theories: How Activist Scholarship Made Everything About Race, Gender, and Identity – and Why This Harms Everybody* [2020]

This book came out of the 'Grievance studies' hoax, warning progressive scholars not to be driven by political sentiment at the expense of intellectual rigour.

Jack Reynolds and Jon Roffe, Eds, *Understanding Derrida* [2004]

This edited volume contains 17 introductory essays on Derrida's work. The essays focus either on a particular concept or seek to bring Derrida's ideas into conversation with those of another thinker.

Daniel Zamora and Michael C. Behrent, *Foucault and Neoliberalism* [2016]

The co-authors make a powerful argument that Foucault's relationship with neoliberalism is more complicated and ambivalent than one might intuitively think. An important intervention on a leading figure associated with progressive scholarship.

chapter 10

Decolonial Social Theory: Confronting Coloniality

Contents

DOI: 10.4324/9781003359555-10

Today's world is largely comprised of self-governing nation-states. As such, the increasing focus on 'postcolonialism' and 'decolonisation' may seem rather odd. How can it be a major theme for contemporary social theory all of a sudden? Surely independence has been won and colonialism is over. Decolonial theorists take a very different view. They argue that *coloniality* remains, and that we are only now, slowly, beginning to recognise its complexity and pervasiveness. For Anibal Quijano (1928–2018), Walter Mignolo (1941–), and Maria Lugones (1944–2020), colonial power relations continue to structure the social world *today*. Their works show how coloniality is embedded in trading relationships, cultural norms, even the dominant forms of thought. Decolonial thinkers show how this has been obscured by 'Eurocentric' ways of thinking so that we do not realise the prevalence of the colonial legacy. Through our use of European categories, such as 'modernity' and 'progress', social researchers have been blind to their own imbrication within a colonial matrix of power. This has led to the erasure of indigenous knowledges and the failure of researchers to properly understand non-European experiences. As a result, for decolonial scholars, European social theory is politically problematic and academically weak, ill-equipped to explore non-European societies and unable to grasp the continuing legacies of colonialism.

Decolonial theorists are typically critical as scholars and political activists. Their aims range from the academic (such as promoting epistemic diversity) to the explicitly political (such as resisting neocolonial resource extraction). As such, there is a critical edge to all decolonial scholarship, seeking not merely to understand the world but also to change it. Achille Mbembe (1957–), a leading postcolonial scholar, argued that postcolonial thought is 'characterized by its heterogeneity' and 'cannot be summed up easily in a few words'. It is academic and political, cultural and philosophical, activist and artistic.

While this chapter focuses primarily on decolonial theory, key terms from postcolonial theory are also discussed. This is because decolonial theorists have built upon much postcolonial theory. While the two schools of thought have much in common, they emerged in different contexts and have subtly different foci. Postcolonial thought is typically more cultural/literary in orientation and focuses more on the nineteenth and twentieth centuries. In contrast, decolonial thought is more politically activist and turns the clock back to the original colonisation of the Americas in the 1500s, reconceptualising ideas such as modernity and progress. It is worth having a brief overview of both traditions before we dive in further.

Postcolonial thought emerged in the 1960s with the work of Frantz Fanon (1925–61), Aimé Césaire (1913–2008), and Edward Said (1935–2003). These thinkers focused largely on the literary and cultural aftershocks in the period immediately following the withdrawal of the colonial powers. Fanon's work was particularly groundbreaking. Drawing upon his experiences from the Algerian War of Independence, he offered a psychological analysis of the colonial subject, showing how their relation to self was shaped by the experience of colonial domination. A second wave of postcolonial thought emerged in the late 1980s with a new focus on globalisation and hybridity. Key figures here are Gayatri Chakravorty Spivak (1942–) and Homi K. Bhabha (1949–). In the early 2000s a third wave emerged, drawing upon additional insights from gender studies and critical race theory. Key figures here are Achille Mbembe, Dipesh Chakrabarty (1948–, and Chandra Talpade Mohanty (1955–). Decolonial theorists have always been in dialogue with postcolonial studies. The first wave of decolonial scholarship emerged in the late 1990s, anchored in the work of Anibal Quijano and Walter Mignolo. A second wave of decolonial theory emerged in the early 2000s, with theorists such as Maria Lugones and Ramón Grosfoguel (1956–) adding valuable insights from gender, political economy, and geopolitics.

Decolonial theorists are reshaping social theory today. This is an ongoing process and its ultimate impact is hard to say. As such, this chapter takes a different structure to those preceding it. As this discussion speaks about live, emerging debates within social theory there is no demarcation between how this perspective reshaped social theory and its contemporary application. Rather, we discuss ways in which social theory is currently being challenged as part of its ongoing discussion with decolonial thought.

Key Concepts

Many of the concepts in decolonial and postcolonial theory link colonial domination, power, and knowledge. In this regard there are clear overlaps with the Frankfurt School and post-structuralism, with all three traditions seeing 'power' and knowledge' as fundamentally connected.

Historically there has been more engagement with post-structuralism by decolonial and postcolonial thinkers. While there is common ground in terms of a rejection of universalism and the deconstruction of fixed binary categories, decolonial scholars, such as Walter Mignolo, have argued that even post-structuralism remains too Eurocentric. For Mignolo, while there may be some post-structuralist concepts which can be developed to provide a voice for non-Western peoples, a more explicitly decolonial perspective is required, calling for a return to first principles. As such, while there are shared insights between decolonial/postcolonial theory and Critical Theory and post-structuralism, these are distinct perspectives and should not be conflated.

Coloniality of Power

The coloniality of power is the master concept of decolonial theory. Originating in the work of the Peruvian sociologist Anibal Quijano, the core insight of decolonial theory is to view coloniality not as a time-delimited historical period of colonial occupation but as an enduring condition linked to embedded power structures, which encroach upon knowledge and culture, and which leave enduring hierarchies. Colonialism is understood as creating a system of power ('coloniality') through which hierarchies are instigated and entrenched. These hierarchies can be seen internationally through a world-systems approach (core/semi-periphery/periphery) and within societies (through the imposition of patriarchal and capitalist logics and categorisations). What is essential to Quijano's work is that these dynamics are not natural and inevitable but are outcomes of the imposition of a colonial modernity which continues to impact on societies today. The idea of coloniality can be captured by the phrase 'independence does not mean decoloniality': colonial mentalities, networks, and values remain deeply embedded in the postcolonial world order.

For Quijano, coloniality has racial, epistemic, and socio-cultural manifestations. These three are deeply interconnected. Quijano foregrounds 'race' as a central concern, arguing that it continues to structure society. Racial inferiority/superiority was ascribed on the basis of skin colour, which the Spanish colonisers believed reflected innate essential differences. Their alleged racial superiority was utilised to justify Spanish domination of indigenous communities. Later decolonial theorists, such as Maria Lugones, developed this idea by bringing it into dialogue with gender studies, leading to the concept of 'the coloniality of gender'. For Lugones, the colonisers displaced indigenous fluid categories with hierarchical European male/female bifurcations. This hierarchy continues to be reflected in contemporary post-colonies and its lingering impacts are visible under sociological investigation. While explicit nominal beliefs in 'racial' or gender hierarchy may have substantially receded, social-structuring logics and resource allocations continue to echo along 'racial' and gender divides.

At an epistemic level, coloniality serves to prescribe particular ways of knowing and structuring the world. This is referred to by Quijano as 'the coloniality of knowledge'. Only the European coloniser was seen as having valid 'knowledge'. Local indigenous ways of understanding their societies and their places in the universe, what we call native cosmologies and epistemologies, were considered 'savage' and were dismissed as tribal superstitions. They were rejected as not being real knowledge, not worthy of the 'civilised' Western academy. As such, colonial societies were understood through, and structured via, Western categorisations: gender, 'race', sexuality. This erasure of indigenous forms of knowledge was itself a reflection of the imposed racial hierarchy: only the white race was seen as having meaningful 'knowledge'. The outcome was a denial of knowledge production to the colonised and a devaluation and erasure of their knowledge systems.

The idea of coloniality is multifaceted, but at its core it speaks to the continuing presence of colonial power in formal post-colonies. For Quijano and Mignolo, there exists a colonial matrix of power, through which norms, values, culture, language, and social practices remain tied to a racialised Eurocentric understanding of modernity, progress, and civilisation. As Frantz Fanon's work showed as early as the 1960s, the colonial subject comes to view themselves as legitimate only through their association with the colonist's culture. Coloniality taps into the self-image of (post-)colonial subjects, trapping them within their racialised bodies, forcing them to adopt a 'white mask' to function in the public sphere. Quijano's concept of the coloniality of power, as developed by Mignolo, Lugones, and others, serves to reinforce and develop this fundamental insight. The hierarchical position of 'whiteness' is reinforced long after the former colonial power has retreated.

Eurocentrism

A key objective of postcolonial and decolonial theory is to challenge Eurocentrism: the privileging and centring of European culture, values, and forms of knowledge. Eurocentrism is not (usually) a conscious practice. Academics today are rarely deliberately going around thinking that only European perspectives matter or that other cultures and their values can be ignored and replaced by 'better' European ideas. Eurocentrism is best thought of as being a deeply ingrained bias, something which lurks within philosophies, concepts, disciplines. It suggests an implicit belief that Europe is the centre of world history and the driving force of global change. For decolonial theorists, this is something that needs to be exposed and challenged through careful, meticulous research. The demand from decolonial activist groups is to 'decolonise our minds!'. This process often brings resistance from established traditions, which see it as an assault on their way of knowing the world. Yet for decolonial theorists this is a battle worth fighting; Eurocentrism is held to be integral to the coloniality of power. For decolonial theorists, it is through Eurocentric discourses and practices that inequality, neo-coloniality, and cultural erasures are normalised and sustained. As a result, challenging coloniality requires exposing and pushing back against Eurocentrism.

This is not just a case of an imposition of European languages or ways of thinking in postcolonial states. While scholars such as Walter Mignolo have shown that this is a significant problem, Eurocentrism speaks to bigger stories and deeper ideological values. Decolonial theorists suggest that the Western social sciences and humanities are based around a fundamental notion of history in which European actions have been a driving force for progress and modernisation. There is a narrative of modernity starting in Europe, linking to democracy and rationality: with the industrial revolution, 'rights', and democracy all being presented as European inventions. As such, there is an unwritten rule holding European history as the story of world progress, of liberation and emancipation of all humanity. Decolonial scholars serve to destabilise this, pointing to the centrality of slavery, plunder, and of oppression within European history. The justification for such 'progress' narratives is based on a deeply racialised notion of 'civilising' the colonial Other. As such, challenging Eurocentrism requires challenging both the specifics of language use and conceptual deployment, but also the meta-narratives of 'progress' and 'development' upon which many thought systems depend. Decolonial theorists seek to show that many European grand narratives are immanently contradictory and reflect a self-aggrandising Eurocentrism.

A further feature of Eurocentrism is the global hegemony of the European canon. Whether you are attending a prestigious university in Lagos, Lahore, or Lima, if you are studying the social sciences, you will be expected to engage with Marx, Kant, Plato, Hegel. These are thinkers who have had a profound effect on the European imagination and on European and global history. Yet, their presence reflects a startling asymmetry. There is no expectation for courses on sociology in the Global North to reflect on the epistemologies which are dominant in the Global South. Routinely, philosophy and sociology undergraduates will pass through entire years without reading a single text written by an African social scientist. This is deeply Eurocentric. This is underscored when one considers that the geographical centres of learning on many Global South concerns are located in the former colonial powers. For example, the London School of Hygiene and Tropical Medicine is officially ranked first in the world for the study of tropical medicine. That it is the 'London' School is worthy of comment: London is not in the tropics. The world-leading status of the London-based institute can be understood as a further living legacy of colonial rule.

Epistemicide and Decolonising Knowledge

In *Epistemologies of the South* [2014], Boaventura de Sousa Santos [1940–] refers to 'epistemicide' as the destruction and displacement of indigenous forms of knowing and understanding. It is a broad concept and has been used by various scholars to refer to lost languages, philosophies, approaches to science, to medicine, and to cosmology. It speaks to the process of cultures being stripped of their distinctive characteristics as a result of colonial rule. As with Eurocentrism, epistemicide is not something which is deliberately enacted. Few people consciously decide to take part in the destruction and marginalisation of non-European cultures. Rather, it is a result of the colonial matrix of power which exists long after the formal end of colonialism. To thrive in the neocolonial capitalist world people have to engage with particular concepts, speak in particular languages, know about particular debates, attend particular institutions. These are usually Euro-American. The colonial matrix reproduces knowledge hierarchies which systematically privilege the epistemologies of the old colonial powers. If you want your child to have the best chance in life you teach them English and want them to go to Oxford or to Harvard. This is even the case with students who come from post-colonies and who want to learn *about* post-colonies. For example, Indian students may come to study at the London-based School of Oriental and African Studies on the basis of its prestige, even when they want to conduct research about India. While in the UK, they will likely be taught in the English language about European thinkers, ideas they will then take back and apply to the postcolonial context. When non-European scholars are discussed, it will typically be their take on the European tradition which is focused on. Coloniality curls the tongues of the citizens of post-colonies to speak in the languages and the concepts of the former coloniser. This is a process which occurs even within the field of decolonial theory itself. The leading institutes remain in the Global North and the leading scholars publish in American-English.

One response to this is to demand intellectual liberation: to return to indigenous languages, to retrieve displaced concepts, and to challenge the colonial symbols which infect the education system. This, however, is a difficult struggle. It requires decolonial scholars to run against the systemic logics of the academy: the journals which universities subscribe to, the texts which are in their libraries, the reading lists which are normalised, the languages which lecturers can speak; these all reflect the epistemic hierarchy of Eurocentric knowledge. Even where faculties are supportive of campaigns to diversify the curriculum they are trapped within a political economy of knowledge production and exchange. The most famous example of students seeking to decolonise the university was the 'Rhodes Must Fall' campaign which started in 2015 in South Africa. Cecil Rhodes was a prominent British colonialist whose legacy is deeply associated with white supremacy. The campaign originally sought the removal of a controversial statue of Cecil Rhodes but expanded to include a desire to decolonise the curriculum and to reposition how the legacy of empire was taught. The 'Rhodes Must Fall' movement spread across the world, with campaigns at Oriel College, Oxford, as well as at the Harvard Law School.

A different response to epistemicide is to embrace what Homi K. Bhabha calls 'hybridity'. This refers to the blending of different identities and knowledges which occurs in the colonial and postcolonial context. Hybridity reflects that there are no pure cultural identities, that fixed universal understandings about the world are non-existent, with epistemologies as well as languages always in flux. Rather, in the postcolonial world, we exist in a state of 'in-betweenness'. We live between cultures, merging languages, borrowing traditions. Diaspora communities who merge languages reflect such hybridity with 'Hinglish' reflecting a commonly spoken fusion of 'Hindi' and 'English'. Hybridity reflects both the imposition of colonial epistemes and norms upon the colonised but also the inevitable embrace of certain values, norms, and traditions from the colonised. For example, the English language is full of words from Hindi, such as 'bungalow', 'shampoo', 'khaki', 'pyjamas'. As such, some scholars have argued that embracing hybridity enables marginalised communities to assert their identities and adapt and transform to new contexts, while retaining their heritage in compromises which balance their desire for inclusion with the maintenance of their cultural heritage. Yet, some commentators are critical of the embrace of hybridity, arguing that without attending to the fundamental power dynamics which lead to and which structure cultural encounters, hybridity may itself become a foil for furthering coloniality.

Subalternity

While the term 'subaltern' comes from the writings of the Marxist Antonio Gramsci [1891–1937], it is today primarily associated with the postcolonial theorist Gayatri Chakravorty Spivak [1942–] and her essay *Can the Subaltern Speak?* (1988). Drawing upon Marxist and deconstructionist approaches, Spivak argued that colonialisation led to a particular 'worlding of the world'. By this she means that our understanding of the world is not neutral and objective, but structured according to global power asymmetries which shape whose voice is given credence. The 'subaltern' are people who are structurally marginalised by this 'worlding', such that they are systematically excluded from hegemonic discourses and unable to participate in the cultural world of the imperial power. Subaltern subjects are therefore not merely those who are marginalised or exploited but are structurally excluded from the public sphere on account of their subject position. As Joanne Sharp argues in *Geographies of Post Colonialism* [2008], the only way for postcolonial subjects to be heard, to challenge their subaltern status, is to speak in the language of the imperial power. Without mimicking the colonial occupier their interests go unvoiced. As such, Spivak writes, in subaltern studies the term 'subaltern' is not merely 'a classy word for "Oppressed"'. Rather, it refers to those who are structurally excluded from having a voice and from exerting agency.

One response to subaltern status is for subaltern groups to adopt what Spivak terms 'strategic essentialism'. In the interests of achieving meaningful socio-political change subaltern groups can strategically display a more simplistic collective identity. Through a self-conscious self-essentialising, it can be easier to gain recognition and drive social transformation. For example, despite the plurality and heterogeneity of the Black American experience, Civil Rights leaders spoke of a common 'Soul Force' which was rooted in a shared African-American identity. While a form of strategic essentialism served to support the political cause of African-Americans, the approach is not without its critics. Spivak has rejected the term in her later work, conscious that it has been used to further non-strategic forms of essentialism, for example, within nationalist political movements.

Modernity/Coloniality

The classical understanding of modernity is deeply Eurocentric. In the writings of Marx, Durkheim, and to some extent Weber, there is an assumption that developments in Europe drive world history forward. The implicit (and sometimes explicit) belief is that the 'modern' institutions which emerged in Europe, be they nation-states or capitalism, would spread across the world, driving progress. The programme of modernity, of liberal democracy, sovereign states, and market systems would sweep away traditional, feudal, 'tribal' systems, and provide a more rational, more efficient, more civilised form of life. Decolonial theorists have served to destabilise this narrative, demonstrating the blinkered Eurocentrism of this perspective. This concern with modernity is a distinguishing feature of decolonial theory and is a crucial extension of earlier postcolonial scholarship.

In particular, Anibal Quijano has presented an alternative understanding of modernity which he argued is fundamentally connected to coloniality. His work provides a concept which ties the two together: 'modernity/coloniality'. Quijano presents modernity/coloniality as a particular way of knowing the world, as a Eurocentric epistemology, which is fundamentally connected to European imperial expansion. For Quijano, modernity begins with, and is inseparable from, the colonisation of the Americas in the 1500s. He contends that this period of colonial expansion marked 'the constitution of a new world order'. It was through the process of colonising and controlling the 'Other' in these spaces that Europeans began to identify themselves and came to comprehend 'modernity'. Europe and modernity emerged as ideas through the process of coloniality. This process was exceptionally one-sided and deeply negative for the colonised. Modernity should therefore be recast as a destructive force tied to coloniality (modernity/coloniality), which tore through the non-Western world. The imposition of new categories of social existence (the market, the nation-state, etc.) is not a sign of progress and development, but of coloniality and domination. Walter Mignolo expanded upon Quijano's ideas in his book, *The Darker Side of Western Modernity: Global Futures, Decolonial Options* [2011]. In this work Mignolo shows how the narrative of modernity has been utilised to legitimate colonial exploitation and to normalise continuing forms of neo-colonialism. As such, for Mignolo, what is needed is a systematic 'de-linking' of the colonial experience from European narratives of modernity. If modernity reflects a deeply problematic Eurocentric way of knowing the world, alternative forms of knowledge are urgently required.

One key feature of modernity/coloniality which reshaped the global order was the idea of the nation-state. This European invention was forced upon colonial subjects, with lines being drawn on maps by colonial powers in their attempt to carve up the globe in line with their 'modern' epistemology. This led to the creation of what Quijano calls 'impossible nations' – where there are attempts to corral a plural-national population into a singular national identity. This is made worse by the systematic exclusion of civil society groups in the formation and running of these new states, leading to what the Bolivian sociologist René Zavaleta Mercado (1937–84) called a structural 'disjointedness'.

One response to the destabilisation of Eurocentric modernisation narratives has been to suggest the existence of multiple modernities. Such an idea is associated principally with Shmuel N. Eisenstadt (1923–2010). He argues that there are different ways in which peoples can progress to modernity. Accordingly, there can be different features to each particularly modernity, reflecting socio-cultural variation. As such, there can be non-Western modernities, an idea which fundamentally destabilises the Eurocentric modernisation narrative. The Turkish sociologist Nilüfer Göle has written about these ideas in *The Forbidden Modern* [1996], arguing that there are forms of religious modernity which need to be recognised and engaged with. That university-educated young women in Turkey adopt seemingly 'backward' Islamic practices such as veiling is not a rejection of 'modernity'; rather, it points to a new Muslim identity in the modern world. For Göle, there is a 'historical specificity' to the 'mode of modernisation'. What may seem 'backward' to the Eurocentric scholar therefore needs to be contextualised within the particular articulation of modernity in the Turkish context; modernities are plural and have varied manifestations.

As you can see, decolonial and postcolonial theory developed a rich array of concepts which substantially interlink. These concepts are increasingly being centred in critical social theory, which we turn to next.

How is Decolonial Theory Shaping Social Research Today?

As the Australian sociologist Raewyn Connell (1944–) wrote, decolonial thinking represents a 'revolution' within social theory. It is a revolution which is very much ongoing. Precisely what social theory will look like in its aftermath is hard to say. That said, two clear developments can be drawn out. We can see a tendency towards more epistemic diversity. There has been an internationalisation of the conceptual arsenal deployed by social scientists. Scholars are increasingly turning to traditions beyond Europe to enrich their methodologies and theoretical foundations. In summary, we can see a change in the lens through which social research is conducted. But equally, we can see a shift in the direction in which that lens is pointed: to a focus on the marginalised and subaltern. Where social research once focused overwhelmingly on European-American experiences with 'fringe' 'Oriental studies' focusing on other cultures, we see a thoroughgoing normalisation of the study of the postcolonial experience. These changes in perspective and research focus are likely be permanent legacies of the decolonial revolution.

Epistemic Diversity

In *Decolonising the Mind* [1986], the Kenyan academic and novelist Ngũgĩ wa Thiong'o (1938–) lamented the destruction of native cultures and the suppression of indigenous languages during colonial rule. He argued that this legacy lives on, perpetuating a sense of alienation within indigenous communities because of the assumed subordination of their cultural practices. Ngũgĩ wa Thiong'o is one of various decolonial and postcolonial scholars who argue for a politics of cultural reclamation: writers should write in their traditional languages and should draw upon the concepts and ideas of their heritage. By way of example, Ngũgĩ wa Thiong'o is himself the founder and editor of a Gikuyu-language journal. This embrace of non-European concepts is increasingly commonplace and is seen by some decolonial theorists as a crucial counterweight to epistemicide. Demands for epistemic diversity connect with broader campaigns to 'decolonise the curriculum' across schools and universities.

One way we can see the rise of epistemic diversity is in the increasing interest in what Sumi Madhok has referred to as *Vernacular Rights Cultures* [2021]. The idea of 'human rights' is a powerful one and is associated with modernity, progress, and justice. Yet, as Ratna Kapoor argues in *Gender, Alterity, and Human Rights* [2018], human rights are often delivered as part of the broader unidirectional modernisation narrative, laced with Eurocentric biases. Rights are presented as being 'universal' yet are taught and brought to the world by the West, through Western languages and categories, which can bind the very subjects they seek to emancipate. In contrast to liberal universalisations, Madhok, Kapoor, and others have turned to the rights cultures which exist beyond the West, exploring alternative traditions. Madhok is particularly interested in the vernacular concept of rights referred to as '*haq*'. Through the turn to *haq*, Madhok presents an alternative register linked to entitlements, which is not European in origin and which captures both individual and collective rights. Crucially, *haq* also incorporates socio-economic claims, which are excluded by the legal-political focus of Western rights discourses. This turn to studying vernacular rights discourses shows one way in which epistemic diversity is embraced to challenge Eurocentric universalisms and to recentre indigenous knowledges.

A further challenge to Eurocentric paradigms is the increased turn to Ubuntu philosophy. Ubuntu is a Nguni Bantu term which encapsulates a sense of reciprocal humanity, or a humanity defined by its extension towards others. There are various nuances in what Ubuntu means for different communities, yet they all share this sense that humanity is fundamentally communal and social. The Ubuntu framework has been turned to by various thinkers to challenge Western individualism. Important thinkers here are Thaddeus Metz and Michael Onyebuchi Eze, both of whom have juxtaposed Western atomism with the communal and social interconnectedness presupposed by Ubuntu.

Ubuntu has also been utilised to provide a foundation for a non-Eurocentric ecological ethics, with Archbishop Desmond Tutu writing of eco-Ubuntu as an important foundation for a more stable relationship between people and planet. For Tutu, the argument for eco-Ubuntu flows from the reciprocity of all relationships: 'I am because you are' sweeps into 'We are because the planet is'. For the Nigerian-Canadian Philosopher Edwin Etieyibo, Ubuntu can therefore 'foster a better attitude towards the environment and protect it more robustly' than the '"Western" individualistic system of capitalism'.

Epistemic diversity has undeniably grown in concert with the rise of decolonial thinking. Whatever comes of the broader campaign to 'decolonise' established curricula and to reformat colonial power matrixes, the epistemic wealth of non-Western philosophies will certainly continue to be drawn upon by a range of critical scholars.

Normalising Global Social Research

One of the founding texts of postcolonial theory was Edward Said's pioneering study of the treatment of Asian, North African, and Middle Eastern cultures, *Orientalism* [1978]. He argued that the representation of an 'exotic' 'Other' served to reinforce stereotypes and perpetuate power imbalances. For Said, the problem is not simply a case of saying explicitly that 'black' or 'middle Eastern' people are inferior or less 'civilised'. Rather, Said focused on the additional, less obvious problem of the 'exoticisation' and 'fetishisation' of these subjects, a process he referred to as 'Orientalism'. This speaks to the portrayal of these communities as 'mystical', 'exotic', 'erotic', 'otherworldly'. It often served to produce a simplified, essentialised, reductive image of these communities. 'Orientalising' subtly reinforces narratives of backwardness and irrationality. This served to delegitimate non-European actors as meaningful subjects for sociological research. Historically, this Orientalised subject was not primarily engaged with by sociologists, but within Oriental Studies and within anthropology. As Talal Asad has shown, this was particularly problematic as colonial interests and scholarly research were often explicitly connected: there was a political logic for painting indigenous cultures as 'simple', 'backward', and in need of 'civilising'.

While Orientalising tendencies continue and while academic Euro-centrism certainly remains, there are definite movements towards an embrace of global social research through a shared disciplinary horizon. This can be seen as a clear victory for postcolonial and decolonial theory. Increasingly, 'formal' sociology focuses on non-European actors, not merely as an 'Orientalised' exoticism but as a meaningful area of study within the same register as mainstream social research. For example, we see the highest-ranked sociology journals publishing work on the experiences of different communities beyond Europe, whether it is articles on motherhood in Palestine or the use of Tinder in India. There is also an increased emphasis on diasporic and hybrid identities across mainstream social research. For example, the BSA Philip Abrams Memorial Prize was awarded in 2022 to Natasha Carver for *Marriage, Gender, and Refugee Migration*. This book focused on the lives of Somali Muslims in the UK. The year before, the prize was awarded to Luke De Noronha for his *Deporting Black Britons: Portraits of Deportation to Jamaica*. There is clearly increasing recognition and normalisation of scholarship decentring the white European experience within the official channels of social research.

We can see this as part of a broader transformation in the attitudes adopted towards European research traditions. What is deemed worth exploring is changing in the world of social theory too. In some critical, left-leaning faculties, engaging with classical 'white' 'European' theorists, such as the Frankfurt School, as a primary point of reference, is seen to be *dépassé*. It is not considered fashionable; it is out of keeping with the zeitgeist. In contrast, working with a more diverse palate of thinkers concerned with epistemic diversity and the non-white experience is the new 'fashionable' way to operate. Social theory and social research are changing. There are new perspectives, new theories, and greater diversity.

Problems of Using Decolonial Theory Today

Decolonial and postcolonial theory are clearly in vogue and social theory and social research have changed as a result. There is increased epistemic diversity and the focus of theorists and researchers is moving beyond the European horizon. Few would deny these are positive developments leading to a richer, more inclusive academy. Yet the operationalisation of decolonial theory has been criticised by various thinkers and activists. This is more a case of there being serious problems with how decolonial theory manifests in the academy, rather than there being contradictions in the books or theories of its proponents. First, we discuss the tendency for decoloniality to manifest solely in symbolic gestures, decentring material change; a result of its co-optation by the neoliberal colonial matrix to which it is principally opposed. As such, ironically, decolonial theory risks becoming a product sold by, and which stabilises, the very extractive and exploitative systems decolonial scholars seek to transform. Second, we discuss the problem of the fetishisation of non-European experiences, communities, and knowledges. There is a definite danger in romanticising, tokenising, and essentialising non-European cultures and epistemes as 'pure' and untouched by the 'evil' of coloniality. This obscures the reality that many post-colonies are themselves simultaneously post-colony and present coloniser.

Mute Symbolism and Co-optation

In an influential paper, Eve Tuck and K. Wayne Yang argued that the various decolonising discourses risked turning into an impotent metaphor. Today there are calls to 'decolonise our minds', 'decolonise our schools', 'decolonise our curriculum'. These have gained traction internationally and have served to introduce new ideas challenging Eurocentrism. Yet, these campaigns have fundamentally failed to meet the requirement of *actual* decolonisation, what Tuck and Yang capture as 'the repatriation of indigenous land and life'. That is what decolonisation should actually be about at the end of the day: the transfer and return of lands and resources. This remains a pipedream in a world where decolonial politics focuses on epistemology and diversification rather than on materiality and remuneration. As such, for Tuck and Yang, decoloniality risks turning into a 'set of evasions' to prevent real material change. It can even serve to help settler-colonists feel better about their histories, as 'settler moves to innocence', rather than enabling transformative change.

What is required for true decoloniality is not a decolonial symbolic/epistemic/diversity politics but a politics of material change. As Glenn Sean Coulthard (1974–) argues in *Red Skin, White Masks* [2014], the colonial politics of 'recognition' does not serve to provide the changes indigenous people need; rather, it serves to impose liberal universal abstractions that routinely deliver nothing substantive. As Silvia Rivera Cusicanqui (1949–) argues, decolonial theory requires a decolonial politics; settler colonialism and the neo-colonial matrices of power leave real lives on the line. As such, decoloniality must move away from symbolic conjectures and highfalutin ideals of epistemic diversity or intersubjective recognition of rights. Instead, what matters is access to indigenous lands, waterways, and resources. Decolonial theory thus far seems to have achieved very little substantively while offering a fig leaf for settler guilt and creating a new topic for privileged academics to write about. When one asks how much actual land has been returned to displaced communities, we find that very little, if anything, has actually changed.

This argument can be taken further to show how decolonial demands have not merely been domesticated by established hierarchies but have been co-opted to reinforce the very hierarchies which decolonial scholars seek to challenge. For example, elite universities in the UK are increasingly advertising how their courses offer decolonial content, selling their discussions of indigenous cultures and epistemes as a strength of their offering. This leads to a world where the richest, most privileged students, from the postcolonial setting, fly to the old colonial power to learn about the epistemologies of their own heritage. European institutions, with colonial legacies, thereby retain their cultural hegemony and protect the matrix of colonial power by embracing symbolic decolonial insights, while at the same time using them as a selling point to further expand their reach into the postcolonial recruitment market. The very fact that students can come to Europe to learn about the coloniality of power becomes a mechanism for the stabilisation of the coloniality of power itself.

What occurs is a process where those who are already privileged in the post-colony are fed abstracted essentialisations of 'native cosmologies', typically delivered by an academic with little knowledge of the cultures in question. Most often in the English medium of instruction, elite European institutions teach the richest Asian, South American, and African students a weak caricature of their cultural heritage. Ultimately, these are institutions which reproduce extractivist political economies; places that are charging obscene fees to students from the Global South and that are complicit in hostile immigration environments. The students' classrooms are kept 'secure' by disproportionately immigrant-dependent outsourced casualised labour. To celebrate decolonial theory in such an environment seems extremely premature.

It is worth stressing that these criticisms are not targeted at inconsistencies in the arguments of the founding decolonial thinkers. It is not Quijano's fault that this is happening; it is not down to some error in his social theory. Rather, the co-optation of decolonial theory speaks to how decolonial ideas travel in the matrix of coloniality which he powerfully described. One solution to prevent abstraction and domestication of the decolonial political objectives is to anchor decolonial demands in a more explicitly materialist politics. To some commentators, this speaks to the need for a decolonial Marxism, which centres the material exploitation of the (post-/neo-) colony. This links to key earlier ideas by the Guyanese historian, Walter Rodney (1942–1980), and his famous text *How Europe Underdeveloped Africa* [1972]. The work of Marxist anti-colonial thinkers, such as Samir Amin (1931–2018), also points in this direction.

Neo-nativism and Fetishised Indigeneities

Another problem with decolonial theory is that it risks romanticising the pre-colonial social world and fetishising non-European epistemologies. This is not to deny that the realities of colonialism and neocolonialism are brutal. The scale of the extraction, the brutality of slavery, and the psychic and cultural harms; these cannot be understated. Yet, the increased awareness of coloniality risks slipping into a romanticisation of what came before. This is very problematic, as all societies, including pre- and post-colonies, are laced with structural problems. All ways of thinking have their flaws. There is no pristine pre-colonial world to try and return to, yet there is an increasing romanticisation and politicisation of such hypostatised pre-colonial purity. This idea has been at the core of electorally successful neo-fascist movements, for example, Hindutva in India. Hindutva philosophy appeals to an idea of a pure Indian simple life, anchored in ancient traditions and knowledges of the Hindu nation. Yet, this fetishised past erases the brutality and complexity of the pre-colonial society. The world was one of bride-price and slavery, of internecine conflicts, starvation and exploitation. It was also always a world of hybridity and syncretism; of merged languages, cultures, traditions.

The narratives of a pure Hindu pre-colonial village life have fed into what Achin Vanaik describes as an ascendant 'Hindu authoritarianism'. There is a history of mob attacks on Muslims in India. Racist speeches contrasting 'pure ancient ways' and 'dirty Muslims' inflame tensions and gift key election victories to neo-fascist politicians. This is not merely a case of dog-whistle politics but also of foundational changes in constitutional law. For example, President Modi introduced a controversial Citizenship Amendment Act in 2019, which for the first time placed religion as a criterion for Indian citizenship in a manner which serve to exclude many Muslims. Racism in the post-colony is not solely drawn upon religions lines. There are tragic cases of racist violence directed towards to BAME communities. A widely publicised mob lynching of a Tanzanian student in Bangalore in 2016 received international condemnation.

The idea that there is a purity to non-Eurocentric forms of knowledge is therefore highly problematic. As an example, the foundations of caste society lie in pre-colonial texts, the Vedas and the *Manusmriti*. While it is true that colonial rulers served to codify many of these divisions for their own purposes, the indigenous cosmology was predicated on stark ontological divisions which placed social actors within a clear hierarchy of being. Gandhi, revered today in the West, was deeply invested in the caste system, and his work served to reinscribe the structural exclusions of *dalit*, 'tribal', and OBC groups. Embracing non-Eurocentric epistemologies can serve to foster nationalist essentialisations and reinscribe irrational and unjust native hierarchies, for example, along caste lines.

There is also a risk that decolonial scholarship itself can serve to reinforce native hierarchies. This argument has been put forward powerfully by Silvia Rivera Cusicanqui (1949–), who warns that decolonial and postcolonial theory has created 'empires within empires' where already privileged academic elites appropriate subaltern ideas for their own career advancement. Cusicanqui comments on the dominance of Bengali Brahmins and Hindi-speaking scholars in postcolonial studies, noting that their work ironically serves to reinforce the linguistic and cultural hierarchies in place. With regard to decolonial scholarship, Cusicanqui explicitly targets Walter Mignolo as indicative of a breed of scholar who steals the contributions from indigenous groups and uses them for their own academic career building. Cusicanqui argues that Mignolo merely creates a jargon, a conceptual apparatus, which advances his already privileged position, while remaining forever isolated by his privilege from the material realities of coloniality.

A further problem of romanticising the epistemologies and cosmologies of pre-colonial and postcolonial experience is that it paints a false binary between 'coloniser' and 'colonised'. As Hafsa Kanjwal argues in *Colonizing Kashmir: State-building Under Indian Occupation* [2023], the binary fails to reflect the complexity of geopolitics, and many postcolonial states are involved in spectacularly brutal and expensive occupations of racialised communities. Indeed, the very process of 'decolonising' India, when the British formally granted independence in 1947, was structurally connected to the legacy of internal occupation of Jammu and Kashmir. The very documents which enabled the Independence of India entrenched and normalised the internal colonisation of Kashmir. The example of Kashmir is not merely incidental, an obscure point-making example to show the limits of the 'colonised' and 'coloniser' binary. Rather, Kashmir is recognised internationally as being the most militarised area on the planet and the largest region under occupation by security forces. As Kanjwal argues, the 'colonised'–'coloniser' binary clearly needs to be challenged.

Conclusion

At their best, decolonial and postcolonial theories offer new ways of viewing the world, attuned to the realities of coloniality. When a decolonial perspective to social research is adopted by a skilled exponent it can disclose the limits of Eurocentric imaginations, point beyond tired binaries, and show how racist narratives perpetuate structural inequalities. These are powerful insights and they have been reshaping social research and social theory. Connell is therefore entirely right to consider decolonial theory as a 'revolution'. Over the past decade we have seen an embrace of non-Eurocentric concepts and a recognition of the merits of studying cultures and societies beyond the West. There are definite reasons for decolonial scholars to feel pleased with their accomplishments in reshaping social research.

Yet, it is too soon to celebrate. Decolonial theory is not simply practised by nuanced, critical scholars, mindful of the matrix of neocolonial power, epistemology, and the political economy of knowledge production. Rather, decolonial theory has become increasingly mainstreamed and has been embraced by the very institutions its originators sought to destabilise. We have seen an undeniable domestication of decolonial theory, with Tuck and Yang rightly warning of the displacement of material concerns for the repatriation of land and resources with symbolic 'evasions'. At its worst, decolonial theory can ironically serve to stabilise patterns of exploitation, functioning as a symbolic performance from the powerful: we are 'decolonising our curriculum' while continuing to invest in extractive neocolonial industries. In place of material transformations, decolonial theory risks drifting towards sanctimony and symbolism, co-opted, sold, and repackaged to sustain the logics it was written to critique. We should be mindful of a world where the most privileged non-European students travel to European institutions, paying huge sums of money, to be taught their own 'indigenous epistemologies', before a migrant precarious worker, in a hostile immigration regime, cleans their classroom for the minimum wage. This would not be a victory for decoloniality.

Yet this is perhaps also too one-sided. Decolonial theory is very much of the hour and its legacy will need to be seen from the perspective of history. As the German philosopher Hegel wrote, 'the owl of Minerva only flies at dusk'. It is only with the benefit of hindsight that we will be able to determine the extent to which decolonial demands have served to truly transform social theory. Perhaps, at one level, decolonial theory will have achieved a symbolic victory when textbooks like this one do not end a chapter on decolonial theory by turning naturally to Hegel, but to scholars from the Global South.

Discussion Questions

1   Is decolonial theory actually challenging coloniality?
2   How can decolonial theorists prevent their ideas from being co-opted?
3   What is wrong with Eurocentrism?
4   Should decolonial scholars embrace hybridity?
5. Why do some decolonial scholars reject human rights?

Further Reading

Primary Texts

Homi K. Bhabha, *The Commitment to Theory* [1994]

A crucial text of postcolonial theory that points to the significance of theory for analysing the postcolonial experience. A useful text for understanding his framings of 'hybridity', 'mimicry', and 'ambivalence'.

Aime Césaire, *Discourse on Colonialism* [1950]

A crucial text of postcolonial theory that helped cultivate the Négritude movement. Césaire argues that despite their discourses of 'civilising' and 'progress', the colonial occupiers themselves acted like savages, by killing, raping, and extracting resources solely for their economic enrichment.

Frantz Fanon, *The Wretched of the Earth* [1961]

A wide-ranging book which is arguably the founding text of both postcolonial and decolonial theory. Fanon brings psychoanalysis to explore the colonial experience, showing how coloniality is not just socio-economic but deeply ingrained with psychology and culture. The work includes a discussion on the justification for armed, violent decolonisation. There is also a warning of the dangers of colonial logics continuing after independence, foreshadowing much of the literature on 'coloniality'.

Maria Lugones, *Pilgrimages/Peregrinajes: Theorizing Coalition Against Multiple Oppressions* [2003]

Drawing upon her own experiences, Lugones emphasises the need for an intersectional analysis. This book is a collection of her essays which show the interconnections between class, race, and gender. A very rich book which is worth returning to repeatedly.

Walter Mignolo, *The Darker Side of Western Modernity: Global Futures, Decolonial Options* [2011]

Provides both an analysis of the imbrication of coloniality and modernity, but also points to two ways the Western colonial matrix is being challenged today, through 'de-westernisation' and 'decoloniality'. An important text to understand Mignolo's work and his notion of 'delinking'.

Chandra Talpade Mohanty, 'Under Western Eyes: Feminist Scholarship and Colonial Discourses' [1984]

This is a crucial essay for postcolonial feminist theory which was first published as a journal article. In the essay Mohanty criticised how the West has represented non-Western women as a homogeneous group in need of rescuing. Instead of this problematic misrepresentation, she argues that women from non-Western contexts needs to be able to represent themselves, and thus show their agency and activism.

Anibal Quijano, 'Coloniality of Power, Eurocentrism, and Latin America' [2000]

This is arguably the most famous text in decolonial studies. Quijano introduces many of the themes with which his work is associated: Eurocentrism, coloniality/modernity, racialisation, and the coloniality of power.

Edward Said, *Orientalism* [1978]

A groundbreaking work of postcolonial theory. Said critiques the Western study of Asia and North Africa, suggesting that 'Orientalist' scholarship serves to perpetuate essentialising stereotypes and reinforce colonial power hierarchies.

Boaventura de Sousa Santos, *Epistemologies of the South: Justice Against Epistemicide* [2014]

A key text of decolonial theory which challenges the dominant position of Western ways of knowing the world. The text shows how the erasure of indigenous epistemologies reinforces colonial logics. A decolonial politics therefore needs to give space to non-Western ways of knowing the world.

Gayatri Spivak, *Can the Subaltern Speak?* [1985]

A classic text of postcolonial theory. Spivak argues that Western thinkers often unintentionally fail to ascribe agency to non-Western thinkers. She shows how those who do not adopt the languages and concepts of the West are structurally denied a voice.

Secondary Texts

Gurminder K. Bhambra, 'Postcolonial and Decolonial Dialogues' [2014]

An accessible short article published in *Postcolonial Studies* which introduces both the postcolonial and the decolonial tradition.

Vivek Chibber, *Postcolonial Theory and the Specter of Capital* [2013]

Provides a Marxist critique of postcolonial theory, arguing that fundamental politico-economic concerns can be displaced by the more culturalist and identity-based inflections of postcolonial theory. In essence, Chibber calls for a more Marxist, more class- and capitalism-centric analysis of the postcolonial situation.

George Ciccariello-Maher, *Decolonizing Dialectics* [2017]

Shows how the dialectical method can be used to support decolonial struggles. This is done through an engagement with Fanon, Dussel, and Sorel. This book is an important contribution to decolonial theory, as dialectics has been controversial for decolonial scholars on account of its perceived Eurocentrism and implicit teleology.

Jan C. Jansen and Jürgen Osterhammel, *Decolonization: A Short History* [2017]

This book is less focused on decolonial theory and instead offers a brief overview of the historical movements for decolonisation. A useful contextual primer for the topic.

Christine Keating, *Decolonizing Democracy: Transforming the Social Contract in India* [2011]

This book gives an example of how decolonial ideas can be applied to particular contexts and as part of broader analyses. This text is also important because it avoids the neo-nativist tendency to present an image of a pure pre-colonial nation. Rather, this text acknowledges both the complications of native caste hierarchies as well as the lingering problems caused by colonial legacies.

Dane Kennedy, *Decolonization: A Short Introduction* [2016]

A short, accessible, and synoptic overview. Like Jansen and Osterhammel, the focus is not exclusively on decolonial theory, but on decolonisation more broadly.

Clare Land, *Decolonizing Solidarity: Dilemmas and Directions for Supporters of Indigenous Struggles* [2015]

Focuses on the challenge faced by supporters of indigenous rights who come from colonial backgrounds. This book is both theoretical and practical.

Achille Mbembe, 'What is Postcolonial Thinking? An Interview was Achille Mbembe' [2008]

An accessible and extensive interview was Mbembe for *Eurozine* which also introduces the ideas of many of the other key thinkers in the field. Available at https://www.eurozine.com/what-is-postcolonial-thinking/.

Jeanne Morefield, *Unsettling the World: Edward Said and Political Theory* [2022]

A wide-ranging engagement with Said's political thought, including but extending beyond 'Orientalism'. Includes important discussions on 'contrapuntal' criticism and the experience of exile.

Stephen Morton, *Gayatri Chakravorty Spivak* [2002]

An accessible introduction to Spivak's work. Includes a guide on how to read Spivak's texts.

Eve Tuck and K. Wayne Yang, 'Decolonization Is Not a Metaphor' [2012]

Addresses the problem of 'decolonisation' becoming about immaterial goals which do not unsettle the dominant power structures. Tuck and Yang call these 'settler moves to innocence' which serve to displace the real point of a decolonial politics: the 'repatriation of indigenous land and life'.

Robert C. Young, *Postcolonialism: A Very Short Introduction* [2003]

A short, accessible introduction. Includes a discussion of cultural, ecological, and feminist postcolonial movements.

chapter 11

Conclusion: Key Questions

So that's it. You have come to the end of this critical introduction to social theory. Time now to reflect on some of the key questions from the preceding chapters. Here are ten questions for you to think about to help you refine your own critical perspective. As ever, there are no 'right' or 'wrong' answers here. Helping you to develop your own arguments is the skill that matters most.

1 What is the relationship between power and knowledge?
2 Is modernity the history of empire and colonial dispossession?
3 Has feminism failed?
4 Why are we stuck in an economic system which is destroying the planet?
5 What should our response be to past theorists who are racist and/or patriarchal?
6 Are the 'founding fathers' of sociology still relevant today? Why?
7 What is the relationship between class and culture?
8 Are we living in an 'Iron Cage' today, as Weber suggested?
9 What is the relationship between religion and social theory?
10 Should we 'cancel' Foucault?

These questions are all huge with no short, simple answers available. They are also all very varied, reflecting political, economic, religious studies, epistemological, intellectual historical, and philosophy of social science considerations. But then again, so does all of social theory. As we

DOI: 10.4324/9781003359555-11

have seen in the preceding chapters, social theory is always interconnecting with other subjects, constantly changing, and forever offering more questions than answers.

There has never been a more important time to develop a critical perspective on society. The challenges we face are enormous, ranging from potential extinction due to anthropogenic climate change, to the rise of sophisticated artificial general intelligence threatening to enslave humanity. What is equally remarkable is that there has never been a time where social theory has been more attacked. Consider the 'employability' agenda, the prioritisation of 'STEM' subjects, the assault on freedom of speech by successive governments around the world, the constant demands for quantifiable 'impact' from research, and the explicit defunding of the social sciences and humanities. This leads us to the most important question to ponder:

Why are those in power so scared of social theory?

Index